GW01606657

THE GOLDEN BOOK OF FAIRY TALES

The Golden Book of Fairy Tales

Illustrated by Felicitas Kuhn

Collins
LONDON AND GLASGOW

ISBN 0 00 138131 8

ENGLISH LANGUAGE EDITION

PRINTED AND MADE IN GREAT BRITAIN BY
WM. COLLINS SONS AND CO. LTD.
LONDON AND GLASGOW

CONTENTS

STORIES BY THE BROTHERS GRIMM

Puss in Boots *page* 9
The Seven Crows 16
The Frog Prince 18
The Little Brother and Sister 23
The Musicians of Bremen 30
Old Mother Frost 34
Rumpelstiltskin 38
The Table, The Ass, and The Stick 42
King Thrush-Beard 53
Briar Rose 58
Hansel and Grethel 62
The Wolf and the Seven Little Goats 70
Snow-White and Rose-Red 73
Fortune from the Stars 80
Cinderella 81
Little Snow-White 90
Rapunzel 101
Little Red-Cap 105

STORIES BY HANS ANDERSEN

The Real Princess 111
Thumbelina 112

The Little Match-Girl *page* 124
The Snow Queen 128
The Emperor's New Clothes 161
The Ugly Duckling 166
The Constant Tin Soldier 177

FROM *The Arabian Nights*

Aladdin and his Wonderful Lamp 185

STORY BY LUDWIG BECHSTEIN

The Brave Little Tailor 272

FROM *The Arabian Nights*

Ali Baba and the Forty Thieves 280

Stories by

THE BROTHERS GRIMM

PUSS IN BOOTS

THERE was once a miller who had a windmill, three sons, a donkey and a Tom cat. From childhood the three sons had ground the meal, while the donkey worked the mill and the cat caught mice.

When the miller died, the three sons divided the goods among themselves. To the oldest went the windmill, to the second went the donkey and to the third, the cat, as there was nothing else left. Whereupon the youngest son was very unhappy and grumbled to himself:

"I have come off worst of all. My oldest brother can grind grain, my second brother can ride on the donkey, but what can I do with a Tom cat? If I were to make a pair of gauntlets from his skin then that would be all I possessed!"

"Listen to me," began the cat in a whisper, "you do not need to kill me. You would only have a pair of bad gloves from my skin. But make me a fine pair of top boots that I may go out and show myself off to people; then I shall be able to help you."

The miller's son was amazed that the cat could speak so plainly. But as there was a cobbler's shop nearby, he called the cat to him and asked the cobbler to make a fine pair of boots for him. They didn't take long to make. When they were ready, the cat pulled them on, slung a sack over his shoulder after filling it with grain and, walking on two legs like a man, set out for the fields.

In this country at that time reigned a King whose favourite dish was partridge. Although many ran along the furrows, these birds were so timid that sportsmen found great difficulty in snaring them. This the cat knew and had considered well how he could best set about this task.

When he came to the edge of the wood the cat opened his sack, strewed the grain about, leaving the cord which had secured the sack in the grass. The other end of the cord he held in his paw and crouching behind a hedge, he lay in wait for his prey.

The partridges soon came running out from the field, found the grain and in their eagneress to get at it jumped straight into the sack, one after the other. When a goodly number were in the sack, the cat tied it with the string, and slinging his heavy load over his shoulder, ran to the King's castle.

Before the gate of the splendid royal seat the sentry called out: " Halt, where are you going ? "

" To the King," answered the cat brusquely.

" Are you crazy ?" cried the sentry. " A cat speak to the King ? "

" Let him enter," said another guard. " A King is often bored. Perhaps this cat will entertain him."

Stepping before the King, the cat made a deep bow and began to speak in a loud voice. " Sire, my master the Count," (and he named a great name), " begs leave through me to present these partridges to his King and master."

The King was overjoyed at the sight of the plump partridges and ordered that the cat should have as much money out of his treasury as would go into the sack and as he could carry away.

" Take this to your master and give him my thanks," said the King.

The poor miller's son, meantime, sat at home by his window, leaning his head on his hand, regretting that he had spent all that he had on boots for his cat. What good could the cat possibly bring him ?

At this very moment the door creaked and in walked the cat. He threw down the sack at his master's feet. Purring, he spread the gold before the poor miller's son and said:

" All this I have brought to you in return for my top boots. And the King sends greetings and many thanks to you."

The miller's son was overjoyed at the sight of the treasure, although he did not at all understand how his good fortune had come about.

But while the cat took off his fine boots he recounted everything to his young master, saying finally:

" You have now received much wealth, but it will not last for ever! To-morrow I shall again don my boots."

Early next morning the cat, once more booted, set off to hunt. Again he brought a fine catch to the King. So he went forth several days, each time bringing home rich treasure and always returning the following day to the castle. Soon the cat was so well known and beloved in the royal castle that he could go in and out as he pleased.

One day the cat was warming himself before a glowing fire in the King's kitchen, when suddenly the old coachman entered, cursing mightily.

" To the devil with the King and the Princess! Just when I wanted to go off to the inn for a drink and a game of cards, the King sends for me to take him and his daughter for a ride round the lake."

When the cat heard these words he quietly stole out of the kitchen and hastened home to his master, crying long before he reached him: " If you want to become a count, come with me quickly to the lake for a bathe." The young man, quite at a loss as to what to say to this, nevertheless followed the cat to the lake-side, undressed and jumped into the water. Immediately the cat snatched up his master's clothes and hid them.

Scarcely had he done this than the King's coach rolled up. The cat stopped it in its path, crying mournfully: " Most gracious Sire! My master who is bathing here in the lake left his clothes by the shore, and a thief came and stole them away. Now he cannot come out of the water and if he stays there much longer he will certainly die of cold."

When the King heard this he immediately sent a servant running to fetch some of his own clothes from the castle. Very soon the young miller was clad in royal clothes and, looking at him, the King believed him to be indeed a count. He thanked him graciously for his many gifts of game, and bade him take a seat in his coach. The Princess, who was riding with her father, was pleased at this, for the miller's son was young and in his borrowed clothes looked very handsome.

Meanwhile the cat hastened ahead of the coach. Coming to a broad meadow where many workers were busy bringing in the hay, he cried:

" To whom does this meadow belong?"

" The wicked magician owns this land," the haymakers told him.

" Listen, my friends," the cat continued, " in a few minutes your King will come along. When he asks who your master is you must say to him, ' The Count owns these fields!' If you do not answer thus, great misfortune will befall you."

Then the cat ran on until he reached a large cornfield.

" To whom does this field belong?" asked the cat of the many people who worked there.

" This land belongs to the wicked magician," they replied. Again the cat ordered the workers to tell the King that the land belonged to the Count.

Still farther on the cat came to a wood of tall oak trees where many woodmen were busy felling the fine trees.

"Who owns this wood?" the cat asked of the woodmen.

" It belongs to the wicked magician," was the answer.

And a third time the cat told the workers that they must tell the King that the Count owned the wood. On again went the cat: Everyone gazed at him in wonder as he passed; he looked so elegant in his fine boots, and besides, he walked on two legs like a man.

At last the cat reached the magician's castle. Boldly he marched through the great gate and found himself in the entrance hall. When he came face to face with the master of the castle, the cat greeted him with his deepest bow, saying:

" Great magician and artist, it is said that you can turn yourself into any animal at will—except an elephant!"

" What! " cried the magician, and immediately became an elephant.

" Marvellous! " said the cat, " but what about a lion? "

" Easily," said the magician, and at once a lion appeared before the cat. The cat stood fearlessly in front of the lion and said with only a slight quiver in his voice: " Wonderful! But it would be still more wonderful if you could turn yourself into a very small animal—a mouse for example. That would indeed be the cleverest trick in the world! "

The magician was flattered at the cat's words and said:

" Dear cat, this too I can do quite easily! " And immediately a little mouse was running round the great room. The cat chased the mouse, caught it with one bound and ate it with relish.

The King meantime, with the Princess and the Count, had arrived at the broad meadow.

" To whom does this meadow belong? " asked the King of the workers who were gathering in the hay.

" To the Count," they all cried, just as the cat had told them.

" You have a fine piece of land here, Count," said the King.

Then they came to the cornfield.

" To whom does this field belong? " asked the King.

" To the Count," answered the people who were cutting the corn.

" Ah, my dear Count, you have a splendid piece of land here," cried the King.

And when they reached the wood he asked: " To whom does this wood belong?"

" To the Count! " cried the woodmen who were felling trees.

The King was astonished and turning to the Count said, " You must be a rich man indeed, dear Count. I myself do not possess such a splendid wood."

At last the coach arrived at the castle which had belonged to the magician. The cat stood waiting on the steps. When the royal coach drove up the cat sprang to meet it and, opening the carriage door, he made a deep bow, greeting the King with these words: "Sire, you are welcome at the castle of my master, the rich and powerful Count, who considers it a great honour to receive you here."

The King stepped down from the coach and, looking round, was even more amazed than before. This castle it seemed to him was larger and more splendid than his own. The Count meantime offered his arm to the Princess and led her up the steps to the reception hall which glittered with gold and precious stones.

Great were the festivities which followed. All at once the poor miller's son had become a rich man and a Count besides.

The Princess became engaged to the Count and soon the marriage was celebrated with great splendour and rejoicing. When the couple stepped out of the church the faithful cat went before them strewing flowers in their path.

After a year, when the old King sickened and died, the Count succeeded him as King. And the new King did not forget his booted friend. As a reward for all his services to his master, the cat was appointed Master of the Household.

THE SEVEN CROWS

THERE was once a man who had seven sons, but never a daughter, although he wished very much for one. At last a daughter was born, but the child was so weak and small that the parents decided to baptise her immediately.

Hastily the father sent one of his sons to a spring to fetch some water. The other six ran off with him, and as each strove to be first to fill the pitcher, between them all it fell into the water. They did not know what to do and none of them dared to go home. At first the father was impatient, then he became anxious lest the child should die unbaptised. "I wish my sons were all changed into crows!" he exclaimed. Scarcely were the words out of his mouth when he heard a whirring overhead, and, looking up, he saw seven coal-black crows flying over the house.

The parents could not take back the curse and grieved for their lost sons; but they comforted themselves a little with their dear daughter who soon grew strong and became each day more beautiful. For a long time she did not know she had any brothers, but one day she overheard some people talking about her, and saying, "Certainly she is very beautiful; but the guilt of her seven brothers rests on her head."

This made her very sad, and she went to her parents and asked about her brothers. The old people no longer dared keep their secret, and told her the unhappy story. The maiden then was determined to find her brothers. One day she set out secretly into the wide world to seek and to free them wherever they were. She took with her only a ring belonging to her parents as a remembrance, a loaf of bread, a bottle of water and a little stool.

On and on went the maiden right to the world's end. She came to the Sun, but it was too hot and frightening, and burned up little children. So hastily she ran away to the Moon; but it was too cold and wicked-looking, and said " I smell—I smell man's flesh! " So she ran quickly away and went to the Stars, who were friendly and kind to her. The Morning-star gave her a crooked bone, saying, " This bone will unlock the glass castle where your brothers are."

The maiden wrapped the bone in a handkerchief and on she went again till she came at last to the glass castle. The door was closed and she looked for the little bone. But when she unwrapped her handkerchief it was empty—she had lost it. What was she to do now to save her brothers?

So the good little sister bent her little finger and put it into the keyhole. Luckily it unlocked the door. As soon as she entered, a little dwarf came towards her, saying " My child, what do you seek? "

" I seek my brothers, the Seven Crows," she replied.

The dwarf answered, " My lord crows are not at home, but you may come in and await their return."

Thereupon the little dwarf carried in the food of the Seven Crows upon seven dishes and in seven cups. The maiden ate a little piece from each dish and drank a little out of every cup. In the last cup she dropped the ring which she had brought with her.

All at once she heard a whirring and cawing in the air, and the dwarf said, " My crows are flying home."

Presently they came in and prepared to eat and drink. Then one said to the other, " Who has been eating off my dish? Who has been drinking from my cup? There has been a human mouth here! "

When the seventh came to the bottom of his cup, the little ring rolled out. He looked at it and recognised it as a ring belonging to his parents, and said, " God grant that our sister be here! Then are we saved! "

When the maiden, who had hidden behind the door, heard these words, she came forward. Immediately the crows returned again to their human forms and embraced their sister. Then joyfully they all went home together.

THE FROG PRINCE

IN olden times when to wish was to have, there lived a King whose daughters were all beautiful. But the youngest was so fair that the Sun himself, although he saw her often, was enchanted every time she came out into the sunshine.

Near the castle of this King was a large and gloomy forest, and in the midst grew an ancient linden tree, beneath whose branches splashed a little fountain. So when the days were very warm, the King's youngest daughter would run off to the wood and sit down by the side of the fountain. When she felt dull, she would often amuse herself by throwing a golden ball up in the air and catching it. This was her favourite game.

Now one day it happened that this golden ball did not drop down into her hand, but on to the grass ; and then it rolled past her into the fountain. The King's daughter followed the ball with her eyes, but it disappeared beneath the water, which was so deep that no one could see to the bottom. Then she began to lament and to cry louder and louder. As she wailed, a voice called out to her, " Why do you weep, O Princess? Your tears would move a stone to pity." She looked round to the spot from which the voice came and saw a Frog stretching his fat ugly head out of the water.

" Ah, you old water-paddler," she said, " was it you who spoke? I am crying for my golden ball which has slipped away into the water."

" Well now, do not cry," answered the Frog; " I can tell you what to do. But first tell me what you will give me if I fetch your plaything up again?"

" What will you have, dear Frog?" said she. " My dresses, my pearls and my jewels, or the golden crown that I wear?"

The Frog answered: " Dresses or golden crowns are not for me; but if you will love me, and let me be your companion and playmate, and sit at your table and eat from your little gold plate, and drink out of your cup, and sleep in your little bed—if you will promise me all these things, then I shall dive down and fetch up your golden ball."

" Oh, I shall promise you all," she said, " if you will only get my ball."

But she thought to herself, " What is this silly Frog croaking about? Let him stay in the water with the other frogs; he cannot be company for any human being."

The Frog, as soon as he had received her promise, drew his head under the water, and dived down. Presently he swam up again with the golden ball in his mouth, and threw it on the grass. The Princess was full of joy when she again saw her beautiful plaything; and, taking it up, she ran off immediately.

" Stop! Stop!" cried the Frog; "take me with you. I cannot run as you can."

But all his croaking was useless; although it was loud enough, she did not hear it, but, hastening home, soon forgot about the poor Frog, who was obliged to leap back into the fountain.

The next day, the Princess was sitting at table with her father and all his courtiers. She was eating from her little gold plate when suddenly something was heard coming up the marble stairs, *splish-splash, splish-splash*. When it arrived at the top it knocked at the door and a voice said, " Open the door, youngest daughter of the King, and let me in! "

So the Princess rose and went to see who it was who called her. But when she opened the door and caught sight of the Frog, she shut it again with great vehemence and sat down at the table, looking very pale. The King saw that she was upset and that her heart was beating violently, and asked her if it was a giant come to fetch her away who stood at the door.

" Oh, no! " answered she; " It is no giant, but an ugly Frog."

" And what does the Frog want with you? " said the King.

" Oh, dear Father, yesterday when I was sitting playing by the fountain, my golden ball fell into the water, and this Frog fetched it up again because I cried so much. But first, I must tell you, he made me promise that he and I should be companions. I never thought that he could come out of the water and follow me here to the castle. But somehow he has jumped out and now he wants to come in here."

Just at that moment there was another knock, and a voice said:

" Youngest Princess,
Open the door.
Have you forgotten
Your promises made,
At the fountain so clear
'Neath the lime-tree's shade?
Youngest Princess,
Open the door."

Then the King said, "What you have promised, that you must do; go and let him in."

So she went and opened the door, and the Frog hopped in after her right up to her chair. As soon as the Princess was seated at the table, the Frog said, "Take me up." She hesitated so long that at last the King had to order his daughter to obey. And as soon as the Frog s on the chair, he jumped up on to the table and said, "Now Princess, push your plate near me, that we may eat together." She did so but as everyone saw, she was very unwilling.

The Frog seemed to enjoy his dinner, but every bit that the King's daughter ate nearly choked her. At last the Frog said, "I am satisfied, but I feel very tired; will you please carry me upstairs now to our room, and make our bed ready that we may sleep?"

At this speech the Princess began to cry, for she was afraid of the cold Frog, and dared not touch him. And besides, he actually wanted to sleep in her beautiful, clean bed!

Her tears only made the King very angry, and he said, "He who helped you in your time of trouble must not now be turned away."

So she took the Frog up with two fingers and put him in a corner of her room. But as she lay in bed, he crept up and said, " Do take me up or I shall tell your father." This speech put her in a passion. Catching up the Frog she threw him violently against the wall. But as he fell, the Frog changed into a handsome Prince. The Prince told her how a wicked witch had turned him into a Frog and that only she had the power to release him.

Then did the King's daughter and the Prince become dear companions and one day as bride and bridegroom they travelled joyfully home to the Prince's own kingdom.

THE LITTLE BROTHER AND SISTER

THERE was once a little Brother who took his Sister by the hand, and said, " Since our own dear mother's death we have not had one happy hour; our stepmother beats us every day, and, if we come near her, kicks us away with her foot. Our food is the hard crusts of bread which are left, and even the dog fares better than we, for he often gets a nice morsel. Come, let us wander forth into the wide world."

So the whole day long they travelled over meadows, fields, and stony roads, and when it rained the Sister said, "It is heaven crying in sympathy."

By evening they came to a large forest, and were so wearied with grief, hunger, and their long walk, that they laid themselves down in a hollow tree and went to sleep. When they awoke the next morning, the sun had already risen high in the heavens, and its beams made the tree so hot that the little boy said to his Sister, "I am so thirsty, if I knew where there was a brook I would go and drink. Ah! I think I hear one running;" and so saying, he got up, and taking his Sister's hand, they went in search of the brook.

The wicked stepmother, however, was a witch, and had seen the two children depart; so, sneaking after them secretly, as is the habit of witches, she had enchanted all the springs in the forest.

Presently they found a brook which ran trippingly over the pebbles, and the Brother would have drunk out of it, but the Sister heard how it said, as it ran along, "Who drinks of me will become a tiger!"

So the Sister exclaimed, "Brother, drink not, or you will become a tiger, and tear me to pieces!" So the Brother did not drink, although his thirst was so great, and he said, "I will wait till the next brook."

As they came to the second, the Sister heard it say, "Who drinks of me becomes a wolf!" The Sister ran up crying, "Brother, do not drink, or you will become a wolf, and eat me up!" Then the brother did not drink, saying, "I will wait until we come to the next spring, but then I must drink. You may say what you will; my thirst is much too great."

Just as they reached the third brook, the Sister heard the voice saying, "Who drinks of me will become a fawn—who drinks of me will become a fawn!" So the Sister said, "Brother! do not drink, or you will be changed to a fawn, and run away from me!" But he had already kneeled down and drunk of the water, and, as the first drops passed his lips, his shape became that of a fawn.

At first the Sister cried over her little changed Brother and he wept too, and kneeled by her very sorrowfully, but at last the maiden said, "Be still, dear little Fawn, and I will never forsake you;" and, undoing her golden garter, she put it round his neck and, weaving rushes, made a white girdle to lead him with. This she tied to him and, taking the

other end in her hand, led him away. And so they travelled deeper and deeper into the forest.

After they had walked a long distance they came to a little hut, and the maiden, peeping in, found it empty, and thought, " Here we can stay."

Then she looked for leaves and moss to make a soft couch for the Fawn; and every morning she went out and collected roots and berries and nuts for herself, and tender grass for the Fawn, which he ate out of her hand, and played happily around her. In the evening, when the Sister was tired, she laid her head upon the back of the Fawn, which served for a pillow, and on which she slept soundly. Had but the Brother regained his own proper form, their life would have been happy indeed.

Thus they dwelt in this wilderness; and some time had elapsed, when it happened that the King of the country held a great hunt in the forest; and through the trees was heard the blowing of horns, the barking of dogs, and the lusty cries of the hunters, so that the little Fawn heard them, and wanted very much to join in.

" Ah! " said he to his Sister, " let me go to the hunt; I cannot restrain myself any longer." And he begged so hard that at last she consented.

" But," said she to him, " return again in the evening, for I shall shut my door against wild huntsmen, and, that I may know you, you must knock and say, ' Sister, let me in,' and if you do not speak I shall not open the door."

As soon as she had said this, the little Fawn sprang off quite glad and merry in the fresh breeze. The King and his huntsmen perceived the beautiful animal, and pursued him; but they could not catch him, and when they thought they had him for certain, he sprang away over the bushes and was soon out of sight.

Just as it was getting dark, he ran up to the hut and, knocking, said, " Sister let me in." She undid the little door and he went in and rested all night long upon his soft couch.

The next morning the hunt started up again, and as soon as the little Fawn heard the horns and the tally-ho of the sportsmen, he could not rest, and said, " Sister dear, open the door; I must be off." The Sister opened it, saying, " Return at evening, and say the words as before."

When the King and his huntsmen again saw the Fawn with the golden necklace, they followed him close, but he was too nimble and quick for them. The whole day long they kept up with him, but towards evening the huntsmen made a circle round him, and one wounded him slightly in one foot, so that he could run only slowly.

Then one of them slipped after him to the little hut, and heard him say, " Sister dear, let me in," and saw that the door was opened and immediately shut behind him. The huntsman, having observed all this, went and told the King what he had seen and heard, and he said, " On the morrow I will once more pursue him."

The Sister, however, was terribly frightened when she saw that her Fawn was wounded, and, washing off the blood, she put herbs upon the foot, and said, " Go and rest upon your bed, dear Fawn, that the wound may heal." It was so slight, that the next morning he felt nothing, and when he heard the hunting cries outside, he exclaimed, " I cannot stay away—I must be there, and none shall catch me so easily again! " The Sister wept bitterly, and told him, " Soon they will kill you, and I shall be here all alone in this forest, forsaken by all the world: I cannot let you go."

" I shall die here in vexation," answered the Fawn, " if you do not; for when I hear the horn I think I shall jump out of my skin."

The Sister opened the door with a heavy heart, and the Fawn jumped out, quite delighted, into the forest. As soon as the King perceived him, he said to his huntsmen, " Follow him all day long till the evening, but let no one do him an injury." When the sun had set, the King asked his huntsmen to show him the hut, and when they came to it he knocked at the door, and said, " Let me in, dear Sister."

The door was opened, and stepping in, the King saw a maiden more beautiful than he had ever before seen. She was frightened when she

saw, not her Fawn, but a man step in who had a golden crown upon his head.

But the King, looking at her with a friendly glance, reached her his hand, saying, "Will you come to my castle, and be my dear wife?"

"Oh, yes," replied the maiden; "but the Fawn must go too: him I will never forsake." The King replied, "He shall remain with you as long as you live." In the meantime the Fawn had come in, and the Sister, binding the girdle to him, led him away with her.

The King took the beautiful maiden upon his horse and rode to his castle, where the wedding was celebrated with great splendour, and she became Queen, and they lived happily together a long time; meanwhile the Fawn was taken care of, and lived well.

The wicked stepmother, however, heard how happy the little Brother and Sister had become, and envy and jealousy were roused in her heart and gave her no peace.

Her own daughter, who was as ugly as night, and had but one eye, said, "The luck of being a queen has never yet happened to me."

"Be quiet," said the old woman, "and be content: when the time comes I shall be at hand." As soon, then, as a beautiful little boy was born, which happened when the King was out hunting, the old witch took the form of a chambermaid, and got into the room where the Queen was lying, and said to her, "The bath is ready, which will restore you and give you fresh strength; be quick, before it gets cold." Her daughter being at hand, they carried the weak Queen into the room, and laid her in the bath. Then, shutting the door to, they ran off; but first they had made up an immense fire in the stove, which must soon suffocate the young Queen.

Then the old woman took her daughter and laid her in the bed in the Queen's place. She gave her, too, the appearance of the real Queen: but she could not restore the lost eye, and, so that the King might not notice it, she turned her upon that side where there was no eye.

When he came home at evening and heard that a son was born to him, he was delighted, and prepared to go to his wife's bedside. The old woman called out in a great hurry, "For your life, do not undraw the curtains; the Queen must not yet see the light, and must be kept quiet." So the King went away, and did not discover the false Queen.

At midnight, when everyone was asleep, the nurse, who sat near the cradle in the nursery, saw the door open and the true Queen come in. She took the child in her arms and rocked it, then laid it down again in its cradle. She did not forget the Fawn either, but, going to the corner where he was, stroked his back, and then went silently out of the door.

For many nights afterwards she came constantly, and never spoke a word; and the nurse saw her always, but she dared not tell the King.

Then one night the Queen spoke:

"How fares my child, how fares my fawn?
Twice more will I come, but never again."

The nurse made no reply, but, when she had disappeared, went to the King and told him all. The King exclaimed, "I myself will watch by the child to-morrow."

In the evening he went into the nursery, and about midnight the Queen appeared, and said:

> " How fares my child, how fares my fawn?
> Once more will I come, but never again."

She nursed the child, then disappeared. The King dared not speak; but he watched the following night, and this time she said:

> " How fares my child, how fares my fawn?
> This time have I come, but never again."

At these words the King sprang up, and said, " You can be no other than my dear wife!" Then she answered, " Yes, I am your dear wife," and at that moment her life was restored, and she was again as beautiful as ever. She told the King the fraud which the witch and her daughter had practised upon him, and he had them both tried at once. The daughter was quickly put to death, and the old witch was miserably burned. As soon as she was reduced to ashes the little Fawn was unbewitched, and received again his human form and from that moment the Brother and Sister lived happily to the end of their days.

THE MUSICIANS OF BREMEN

A certain man had a Donkey, which had served him faithfully for many long years, but whose strength was so far gone that at last it was quite unfit to work. His master then began thinking how much he could make out of the skin; but the Donkey, perceiving that no good wind was blowing ran away along the road to Bremen.

"There," thought he, "I can become town musician."

When he had run some way, he found a Hound lying by the roadside, yawning like one who was very tired. "What are you yawning for now, you big fellow?" asked the Ass.

"Ah," replied the Hound, "because every day I grow older and weaker; I cannot go any more to the hunt, and my master has well-nigh beaten me to death, so that I took to flight; and now I do not know how to earn my bread."

"Well, do you know," said the Ass, "I am going to Bremen, to be town-musician there. Suppose you go with me and take a share in the music. I will play on the lute, and you shall beat the kettledrums."

The Dog was delighted, and off they set.

Presently they came to a Cat, sitting in the middle of the path, with a face like three rainy days! "Now then, old shaver, what has crossed you?" asked the Ass.

"How can one be merry when one's neck has been pinched like mine?" answered the Cat. "Because I am growing old and my teeth are worn to stumps, and because I would rather sit by the fire and spin than run after mice, my mistress wanted to drown me; and so I ran away. But now, good advice is dear, and I do not know what to do."

"Go with us to Bremen. You understand nocturnal music, so you can be a town-musician." The Cat agreed, and went with them. The three vagabonds soon came near a farmyard, where, upon the barn-door, the Cock was sitting crowing with all his might. "You crow through marrow and bone," said the Ass. "What do you do that for?"

"That is the way I prophesy fine weather," said the Cock; "but, because grand guests are coming for the Sunday, the housewife has no pity, and has told the cook-maid to make me into soup for the morrow; and this evening my head will be cut off. Now I am crowing with a full throat as long as I can."

"Ah, Red-comb," replied the Ass, "would you not rather come away with us. We are going to Bremen, to find there something better than death; you have a good voice, and if we make music together, it should sound very well."

The Cock consented to this plan, and so all four travelled on together. They could not, however, reach Bremen in one day, and at evening they came into a forest, where they meant to pass the night. The Ass and the Dog laid themselves down under a large tree; the Cat and the Cock climbed up into the branches, but the latter flew right to the top, where he felt safest.

Before he went to sleep, he looked all round the four quarters, and soon thought he saw a little spark in the distance; so, calling his companions, he said they were not far from a house, for he saw a light.

The Ass said, " If it is so, we had better get up and go farther, for the pasturage here is very bad;" and the Dog continued, " Yes indeed! a couple of bones with some meat on would also be very acceptable! "

So they made haste towards the spot where the light was, and which shone now brighter and brighter, until they came to a well-lighted robber's cottage.

The Ass, as the biggest, went to the window and peeped in. " What do you see, Grey-horse?" asked the Cock.

" What do I see? " replied the Ass; " a table laid out with savoury meats and drinks, with robbers sitting round enjoying themselves."

" That were the right sort of thing for us," said the Cock.

" Yes, yes, I wish we were there," replied the Ass. Then these animals took counsel together how they should contrive to drive away the robbers, and at last they thought of a way. The Ass placed his forefeet upon the window-ledge; the Hound got on his back; the Cat climbed up upon the Dog; and, lastly, the Cock flew up and perched upon the head of the Cat.

When this was accomplished, at a given signal they began together to perform their music: the Ass brayed, the Dog barked, the Cat mewed, and the Cock crew; and they made such a tremendous noise, and so loud, that the panes of the window were shivered. Terrified at these unearthly sounds, the robbers leapt up, thinking nothing less than that some spirits had come, and fled off into the forest. The four companions immediately sat down at the table, and quickly ate up all that was left, as if they had been fasting for six weeks.

As soon as the four players had finished, they extinguished the light, and each sought for himself a sleeping-place, according to his nature and custom. The Ass laid himself down upon some straw, the Hound behind the door, the Cat upon the hearth near the warm ashes, and the Cock flew up upon the beam which ran across the room. Weary with their long walk, they soon went to sleep.

At midnight, the robbers perceived from their retreat that no light was burning in their house, and all appeared quiet; so the captain said, " We need not have been frightened into fits;" and, calling one of the band, he sent him forward to spy out the land. The messenger, finding all still, went into the kitchen to strike a light, and, taking the glistening fiery eyes of the Cat for live coals, he held a lucifer-match to them, expecting it to take fire.

But the Cat, not understanding the joke, flew in his face, spitting and scratching, which dreadfully frightened him, so that he made for the back door; but the Dog, who lay there, sprang up and bit his leg; and as he limped upon the straw where the Ass was stretched out, it gave him a powerful kick with its hind foot. This was not all, for the Cock, awaking at the noise, clapped his wings and cried from the beam, "Cock-a-doodle-doo! cock-a-doodle-doo!"

Then the robber ran back as well as he could to his captain, and said, "Ah, my master, there dwells a horrible witch in the house, who spat on me and scratched my face with her long nails; and then before the door stands a man with a knife, who chopped at my leg; and in the yard there lies a black monster, who beat me with a great wooden club; and besides all, upon the roof sits a judge, who called out, 'Bring the knave up, do!' so I ran away as fast as I could."

After this the robbers dared not again go near their house; but everything prospered so well with the four town-musicians of Bremen, that they did not forsake their situation. And there they are to this day for anything I know.

OLD MOTHER FROST

THERE was once a widow who had two daughters, one of whom was beautiful and industrious, and the other ugly and lazy. She behaved most kindly, however, to the ugly one, because she was her own daughter; and made the other do all the hard work, and live like a kitchen-maid. The poor maiden was forced out daily on the high-road, and had to sit by a well and spin so much that the blood ran from her fingers.

Once it happened that her spindle became quite covered with blood, so, kneeling down by the well, she tried to wash it off, but unhappily, it fell out of her hands into the water. She ran crying to her stepmother and told her misfortune; but she scolded her terribly, and behaved very cruelly, and at last said, " Since you have let your spindle fall in, you must fetch it out again! "

Then the maiden went back to the well not knowing what to do, and, in her distress of mind, she jumped into the well to fetch the spindle out. As she fell she lost all consciousness, and when she came to herself again she found herself in a beautiful meadow, where the sun was shining, and many thousands of flowers bloomed around her.

She got up and walked along till she came to a baker's where the oven was full of bread, which cried out, " Draw me out, draw me out, or I shall be burned. I have been baked long enough." So she went up, and taking the bread-peel drew out one loaf after the other.

Then she walked on farther and came to an apple-tree whose fruit hung very thick and which exclaimed " Shake me; my apples are all ripe! " So she shook the tree till the apples fell down like rain and when none were left on the tree she gathered them all together in a heap and went on.

At last she came to a cottage, out of which peeped an old woman who had such very large teeth that the maiden was frightened and started to run away. The old woman, however, called her back, saying, " What are you afraid of, my child? Stay with me: if you will put all things in

order in my house, then shall all go well with you; only you must take care that you make my bed well and shake it thoroughly so that the feathers fly; then it snows upon the earth. I am ' Old Mother Frost '."

As the old woman spoke so kindly, the maiden took courage, and consented to serve her. Now everything went well and she always shook the bed so industriously that the feathers flew down like flakes of snow.

For some time she was happy; but all at once she became homesick, and she said to her mistress, " I wish to go home now; although I have been happy here, I can not stay." The mistress replied, " I knew that you wanted to go home, and, since you have served me so truly, I will fetch you up again myself."

So saying, she led her to a great door, which she undid. When the maiden was just beneath it a great shower of gold fell, and much of it stuck to her, so that she was covered with gold. "That you must have for your industry," said the old woman, giving her the spindle which had fallen into the well.

Thereupon the door was closed, and the maiden found herself upon the earth not far from her mother's house; and as she came into the courtyard the cock called:

"Cock-a-doodle-doo!
Our golden maid's come home again."

The maiden related all that had happened; and, when the mother heard how she had come by these great riches, she wished her ugly, lazy daughter to try her luck. So she was forced to sit by the well and spin; and to make her spindle bloody, she pricked her finger with a thorn. Then throwing the spindle into the well, she jumped in after it.

Then like her sister she came to the beautiful meadow, and took the same path. When she arrived at the baker's the bread called out, "Draw me out, draw me out, or I shall be burned. I have been baked long enough." But she answered, "I have no wish to make myself dirty," and went on. Soon she came to the apple-tree, which called

out, “ Shake me, shake me; my apples are all ripe.” But she refused, saying, “ Perhaps one will fall on my head!” and so she went on. When she came to “ Old Mother Frost’s ” house she was not afraid of the teeth, for she had been warned. And so she engaged herself to her.

The first day she set to work in earnest, was very industrious, and obeyed her mistress in all she said to her, for she thought about the gold which she would present to her. On the second day, however, she began to idle; on the third, still more so. She did not make the beds as she ought, and the feathers did not fly. So the old woman dismissed her from her service, which pleased the lazy one very well; for she thought, “ Now the gold shower will come.”

Her mistress led her to the door, but when she was beneath it, instead of gold a tubful of pitch poured down upon her. “ That is your reward,” said “ Old Mother Frost,” and shut the door. Then came Lazybones home quite covered with pitch; and the cock cried:

“ Cock-a-doodle-doo!
Our dirty maid’s come home again.”

The pitch stuck to her, and, as long as she lived, would never come off again.

RUMPELSTILTSKIN

THERE was once a miller who was very poor, but he had one beautiful daughter. Now it so happened that one day he had business at court and in order to impress the King he boasted:

"I have a daughter who is so clever that she can spin straw into gold."

The King said to the miller, "That is difficult to believe, but if your daughter is as gifted as you say, bring her tomorrow to my castle and I shall put her to the test."

When the maiden presented herself to the King, he led her to a room which was filled with straw. Giving her a wheel and a spindle he said, "Now set to work, and if by morning you have not spun this

straw into gold you shall die." Whereupon the King shut the door and the poor girl was left alone.

There she sat miserably, and for her life she could not think how to begin; she grew more and more worried until at last she burst into tears. Suddenly the door opened and in stepped a dwarf who said, " Good evening my child, why do you weep ? "

" Ah," answered the maiden, " I must spin all this straw into gold, and if I cannot do it then I shall die." The little man said, " What will you give me if I spin it for you ?"

" I shall give you my scarf, " said the maiden.

The dwarf took the scarf and, sitting down before the spinning wheel, he spun it round three times until the spindle was full. Then he spun again three times and the second spindle was full. And so he went on until morning when all the straw had been spun and all the spindles were full of gold.

At sunrise the King appeared, and when he saw the gold he was both astonished and overjoyed. But his heart was now greedy for gold, and he led the miller's daughter to another and larger room full of straw. Again he ordered her to spin the straw into gold during the night. If she failed to do so, she was to lose her life.

The maiden did not know what to do and started to weep. Again the door opened and the little man appeared and asked, " What will you give me if I spin this straw into gold ?"

" I shall give you the ring from my finger," answered the maiden. The dwarf took the ring, and again began to turn the wheel, and by morning had spun all the straw into gleaming gold.

The King was overjoyed at the sight, but was greedy for still more gold. So he led the miller's daughter to a still larger room filled with straw, and said, " This you must spin into gold during the night, and if you succeed you shall become my wife."

" Even though she is a miller's daughter," he thought, " I shall have found the richest wife in the world."

When the maiden was alone, the dwarf appeared for a third time and again asked, " What will you give me if once more I spin this straw into gold ? "

" I have nothing left to give you," answered the maiden sorrowfully.

" Well, promise me that if you become Queen you will give me your first child," said the little man.

" Who knows what might happen by then," thought the miller's daughter, and as there was no other way out she had to agree to his request. She therefore promised the little man to do what he asked, and immediately he began again to spin the straw into gold.

Next morning when the King arrived and found everything as he had wished, the marriage was announced and the miller's beautiful daughter became Queen.

One year later a beautiful child was born, but the maiden had forgotten all about her promise to the dwarf. Suddenly one day he appeared in her room, saying, " Now give me what you promised." The Queen was horror-stricken. She offered the little man all the riches of the kingdom if he would only allow her to keep her child. But the dwarf answered, " No! A living thing is dearer far to me than all the wealth in the world."

Then the Queen began to weep, so that the little man felt some sympathy for her. " I shall give you three days," he said, " to discover my name; if in that time you have guessed correctly you shall keep your child."

All through the night the Queen lay awake thinking of a likely name. Meanwhile she sent out all over the country messengers to enquire for rare names. When, next day, the little man appeared, she began with names like Kaspar, Melchior, Balthasar, and continued with a list of all the names that she had ever heard. But at each the dwarf shook his head and said, " That is not my name."

On the second day she made enquiries in her own neighbourhood. All over the countryside she went, asking for unusual names. To the little man on his return, she said, " Are you perhaps called Gooseneck or Spindleshanks or Spiderlegs? " But always he answered " That is not my name."

On the third day one messenger returned and said: " I can find no new names, but last night as I came to a little wood on a high hill, where the fox and hare say good night, I saw a little house and before it burned a fire. Round the fire jumped a ridiculous little man; he was hopping on one leg and crying:

"To-day I bake, to-morrow I brew,
On the next day I bring the Queen's child here,
Oh how lucky that no one knows
That my name is Rumpelstiltskin."

Now you can imagine how glad the Queen was when she heard this name!

As soon as the dwarf stepped before her that evening and asked, "Now, oh Queen, what is my name?" she asked him, "Are you called Kunz?"

"No!" he cried. "Are you called Hinz?"—"No!" he shouted. "Are you called Rumpelstiltskin?"

"The devil has told you, the devil has told you," shouted the little man in a rage, and stamped his right foot so hard that it went right through the floor. In his fury, he grasped his left foot with both hands and tore himself in two. And that was the end of Rumpelstiltskin.

THE TABLE, THE ASS, AND THE STICK

A long time ago there lived a tailor who had three sons, but only a single goat, which, as it had to furnish milk for all, was obliged to have good fodder every day, and to be led into the meadow for it. This the sons had to do by turns.

One morning the eldest took the goat into the churchyard, where grew the finest herbs, which he let it eat. It frisked about undisturbed till the evening, when it was time to return. Then the boy asked, " Goat, are you satisfied ? " The goat replied:

"I am satisfied, quite;
No more can I bite."

" Then come home," said the youth, and, catching hold of the rope, he led it to the stall and made it fast.

" Now," said the old tailor to his son, " has the goat had its proper food ? "

" Yes," replied the son, " it has eaten all it can." The father, however, had to see for himself; and so going into the stall, he stroked the goat, and asked it whether it was satisfied. The goat replied;

"Why should I be satisfied ?
I only jumped about the graves,
And found not a single leaf."

"What do I hear ? " exclaimed the tailor; and ran up to his son, and said, " Oh, you wicked boy, you said the goat was satisfied, and then brought it away hungry ! " and, taking the yard-measure down from the wall, he hunted his son out of the house in a rage.

The following morning was the second son's turn, and he picked out a place in the garden hedge where some fine herbs grew, which the goat ate up entirely. When, in the evening, he wanted to return, he asked the goat whether it were satisfied, and it replied as before:

"I am satisfied, quite;
No more can I bite."

"Then come home," said the youth and drove it to its stall, and tied it fast.

Soon after the old tailor asked his second son, " Has the goat had its usual food? "

" Oh, yes! " answered his son; " it ate up all the leaves."

But the tailor had to see for himself; and so he went into the stall, and asked the goat whether it had had enough.

"Why should I be satisfied?
I only jumped about the hedge,
And found not a single leaf,"

replied the animal.

" The wicked scamp! " exclaimed the tailor, " to let such a capital animal starve! " and, running indoors, he drove his second son out of the house with his yard-measure.

It was now the third son's turn, and he, willing to make a good beginning sought some bushes full of beautiful tender leaves, of which he let the goat have his fill; and at evening time, when he wished to go home, he asked the goat the same question as the others had done.

" Goat, are you satisfied? " and he too received the same answer as his brothers.

"I am satisfied, quite;
No more can I bite."

So then he led it home, and tied it up in its stall; and presently the old man came and asked whether the goat had had its regular food, and the youth replied, " Yes."

But the father had to go and see for himself. Then the wicked beast told him as it had done before:

"Why should I be satisfied?
I only jumped about the bush,
And found not a single leaf."

" Oh, the scoundrel! " exclaimed the tailor in a rage; " he is just as careless and forgetful as the others; he shall no longer eat my bread;" and rushing into the house, he dealt his youngest son such tremendous blows with the yard-measure that the boy ran away.

The old tailor was now left alone with his goat, and the following morning he went to the stall, and fondled the animal, saying, " Come, my dear little creature, I will lead you myself into the meadow; " and, taking the rope, he brought it to some green lettuces, and let it feed to its heart's content. When evening arrived he asked it, as his sons had done before, whether it were satisfied, and it replied:

"I am satisfied, quite;
No more can I bite."

So he led it home, and tied it up in its stall; but before he left it, he turned round and asked once more, " Are you quite satisfied? " The malicious brute immediately answered in the same manner as before:

"Why should I be satisfied?
I only jumped about the green,
And found not a single leaf."

As soon as the tailor heard this he was thunder-struck, and perceived directly that he had driven away his three sons entirely without cause.

" Stop a bit, you ungrateful beast! " he exclaimed. " To drive you away would be too little punishment; I will mark you so that you shall no more dare to show yourself among honourable tailors."

So saying, he sprang up with great speed, and fetching a razor, shaved the goat's head as bare as the palm of his hand; and because the yard-measure was too honourable for such service, he laid hold of a whip, and gave the animal such hearty cuts with it that it ran off as fast as possible.

When the old man sat down again in his house he was overcome by grief and would have been only too happy to have had his three sons back; but no one knew whither they had wandered.

The eldest, however, had become an apprentice to a joiner, with whom he worked industriously and cheerfully; and when his time was out his master presented him with a table. This table was certainly very ordinary in appearance, and was made of common wood; but it had one excellent quality. If its owner placed it before him, and said, "Table, cover thyself," the good table was at once covered with a fine cloth; and plates, and knives and forks, and dishes of roast and baked meat took their places on it, and a great glass filled with red wine, which gladdened one's heart.

Our young fellow thought to himself, "Now you have enough for your lifetime," and went, full of glee, about the world, never troubling himself whether the inn were good or bad, or whether it contained anything or nothing. Whenever he pleased he went to no inn at all, but into field or wood, or any meadow; in fact, just wherever he liked to take the table off his back. He would set it before him, saying, "Table, cover thyself," and immediately he had all he could desire to eat and drink.

At last it came into his head that he would return to his father, whose anger, he thought, would be abated by time, and with whom he might live very comfortably with his excellent table. It fell out that, on his journey home, he one evening arrived at an inn which was full of people, who made him welcome, and invited him to come in and eat with them, or he would get nothing at all.

But our joiner replied, "No; I will not take a couple of bites with you; you must rather be my guests." At this the others laughed, and thought he was making fun of them; but he placed his wooden table in the middle of the room, and said, "Table, cover thyself;" and in the twinkling of an eye it was set out with meats as good as any that the host could have furnished, and the smell of which mounted very savoury into the noses of the guests.

"Be welcome, good friends," said the joiner; and the guests, when they saw he was in earnest, waited not to be asked twice, but, quickly seating themselves, set to enthusiastically with their knives.

What made them most wonder, however, was that when any dish became empty, another full one instantly took its place; and the landlord, who stood in a corner looking on, thought to himself, "You could make good use of such a cook as that in your trade." But he said nothing aloud.

The joiner and his companions sat making merry till late at night; but at last they went to bed, and the joiner too, who placed his wishing table against the wall before going to sleep. The landlord, however, could not get to sleep, for his thoughts troubled him, and, suddenly remembering that there stood in his lumber-room an old table which was useless, he went and fetched it, and put it in the place of the wishing-table. The next morning the joiner counted out his lodging money, and placed the table on his back, ignorant that it had been changed, and went his way. At noon-day he reached his father's house and was received with great joy.

"Now, my dear son," said the old man, "what have you learned?"

"I have become a joiner, father."

"A capital trade, too. But what have you brought home with you from your travels?"

"The best thing I have brought," said the youth, "is this table."

The father looked at it on every side, and said, "You have made a very bad bargain; it is an old, worthless table."

"But," interrupted the son, "it is one which covers itself; and when

I place it before me and say, ' Table, cover thyself,' it is instantly filled with the most savoury meats and wine, which will make your heart sing. Just invite your friends and acquaintances, and you shall soon see how they will be refreshed and revived."

As soon, then, as the company was arrived, he placed his table in the middle of the room and called out to it to cover itself. But the table did not stir, and remained as any other table which does not understand spoken words. The poor joiner at once realised that the table was changed, and he was ashamed to appear thus like an imposter before the guests, who laughed at him, and were obliged to go home without eating or drinking. So the father had to take up his mending again, and stitched away as fast as ever, while the son was obliged to go and work for a master carpenter.

Meanwhile the second son had been living with a miller and learning his trade. As soon as his time was up his master said to him, " Because you have served me so well, I present you with this ass, which has a wonderful gift, although it can neither draw a wagon nor carry a sack."

" For what, then, is it useful?" asked the youth.

" It speaks gold," replied the miller, " if you tie a pocket under his chin, and cry ' Bricklebrit,' then the good beast will pour out gold coin like hail."

" That is a very fine thing," thought the youth; and, thanking his master, he went off upon his journey.

Now, whenever he needed money, he had only to say to his ass, " Bricklebrit," and it rained down gold pieces, so that he had no other trouble than to pick them up again from the ground. Wherever he went the best only was good enough for him, and the dearer it was the better, for he had always a full purse.

After he had wandered about the world for some time, he thought he would go and visit his father, whose anger he supposed must have lessened by this time. Moreover, since he brought with him an ass of gold, he would no doubt receive him gladly. It so happened that he came to the very same inn where his brother's table had been changed. As he came up, leading his ass by the hand, the landlord stepped forward to take and tie it up. But our young master said to him, "You need not trouble yourself; I will lead my grey beast myself into the stable and tie him up, for I must know where he stands."

The landlord wondered at this, and he thought that one who looked after his own beast would not spend much; but presently our friend, dipping into his pocket and taking out two pieces of gold, gave them to him, and bade him fetch the best he could. This made the landlord open his eyes, and he ran and fetched, in a great hurry, the best he could get. When he had finished his meal, the youth asked if he owed anything further. The landlord, hearing this and wishing to take advantage of his guest, said that a couple of gold pieces more was due. The youth felt in his pocket, but his money was just at an end; so he exclaimed, "Wait a bit, my landlord; I will go and fetch some gold," and, taking the tablecloth with him, he went out.

The landlord knew not what to think, but, being curious as well as greedy, he slunk out after him. The youth bolted the stable-door behind him but the landlord knew of a hole in the wall through which he could peep. The youth spread the cloth beneath the ass, and then called out, " Bricklebrit," and in a moment the beast began to speak out gold, as if rain were falling.

" By the powers! " exclaimed the landlord, " that is a very splendid sort of purse to have!"

The youth now paid his bill and lay down to sleep. But in the middle of the night the landlord slipped into the stable and led away the ass, and tied up a different one in its place.

In the morning early the youth drove away with the ass, thinking it was his own. At noon-day he arrived at his father's house who was very glad to see him return, and received him kindly.

" What trade have you followed? " asked the father.

" A miller's," was the reply.

" And what have you brought home with you? "

" Nothing but an ass."

" Oh, there are plenty of that sort here now; it had far better to have been a goat," said the old man.

" Yes," replied the son, " but this is no common animal, but one which, when I say ' Bricklebrit,' speaks gold right and left. Just call your friends here, and I will make them all rich in a twinkling."

"Well," exclaimed the tailor, "that would please me very well, and so I need not use my needle any more;" and running out, he called together all his acquaintances.

As soon as they were assembled, the young miller bade them make a circle, and, spreading out a cloth, he brought the ass into the middle of the room.

"Now, pay attention," said he to them, and called out "Bricklebrit!" but not a single gold piece fell, and it soon appeared that the ass did not at all understand what he was expected to do.

The poor young man began to make a long face when he saw that he had been deceived; and he was obliged to beg pardon of the guests, who were forced to return as poor as they came. So it happened that the old man had to take to his needle again, and the youth to bind himself to another master.

Meanwhile the third brother had gone to a turner to learn his trade; but he got on very slowly, as it was a very difficult art to acquire. And while he was there his brothers sent him word how badly things had gone with them, and how the landlord had robbed them of their wishing-gifts on their return home. When the time came round that he had learned everything, and wished to leave, his master presented him with a sack, saying, "In it there lies a stick."

"I will take the sack readily, for it may do me good service," replied the youth. " But what is the stick for? It only makes the sack heavier to carry."

" That I will tell you. If any one does you an injury, you have only to say, ' Stick, out of the sack! ' and instantly the stick will spring out, and dance about on the people's backs in such style that they will not be able to stir a finger for a week afterwards; and, moreover, it will not leave off till you say, ' Stick, get back into the sack '."

The youth thanked him, and hung the sack over his shoulders; and when any one came too near, and wished to meddle with him, he said, ' Stick, come out of the sack,' and immediately it sprang out and began laying about it; and when he called it back, it disappeared so quickly that no one could tell where it came from.

One evening he arrived at the inn where his brothers had been basely robbed, and, laying his knapsack on the table, he began to talk of all the wonderful things he had seen in the world. " Yes," said he, " one may find, indeed, a table which supplies itself, and a golden ass, and such-like things—all very good in their place, and I do not despise them; but they shrink into nothing beside the treasure which I carry with me in this sack."

The landlord pricked up his ears, saying, " What on earth can it be?" but he thought to himself, " The sack is certainly full of precious stones, and I must manage to get hold of them; for all good things come in threes."

As soon as it was bedtime our youth stretched himself upon a bench, and laid his sack down for a pillow; and when he appeared to be in a deep sleep, the landlord crept softly to him and began to pull very gently and cautiously at the sack, to see if he could manage to draw it away, and put another in its place. The young turner, however, had been waiting for him to do this, and just as the man gave a good pull, he exclaimed, " Stick, out of the sack with you! " Immediately out it jumped, and thumped about on the landlord's ribs with a good will.

The landlord began to cry for mercy; but the louder he cried the more forcibly did the stick beat time on his back, until at last he fell exhausted to the ground.

Then the turner said, " If you do not give up the table which feeds itself, and the golden ass, the stick dance shall begin again."

"No, no!" cried the landlord, in a weak voice; "I will give them up with pleasure, but just let your horrible stick get back into its sack."

"I will give you pardon if you do right; but take care what you are about," replied the turner; and he let him rest, and bade the stick return.

On the following morning the turner accordingly went away with the table and the ass on his road home to his father, who, as soon as he saw him, felt very glad, and asked what he had learned in foreign parts.

"Dear father," replied he, "I have become a turner."

"A difficult business that; but what have you brought with you from your travels?"

"A precious stick," replied the son.

"A stick! Well, that is not worth the trouble! Why, you can cut one from every tree!"

"But not such a stick as this; for if I say, 'Stick, out of the sack,' it instantly jumps out and executes such a dance upon the back of any one who would injure me, that at last he is beaten to the ground, crying for mercy. Do you see? With this stick I have got back again the wonderful table and the golden ass of which the thievish landlord robbed my brothers. Now, let them both be summoned home, and invite all your acquaintances, and I will not only give them plenty to eat and drink, but pockets full of money."

The old tailor would scarcely believe him; but nevertheless, he called in his friends. Then the young turner placed a table-cloth in the middle of the room, and led in the ass, saying to his brother, "Now speak to him."

The miller called out, "Bricklebrit!" and in a moment the gold pieces dropped down on the floor in a pelting shower; and so it continued, until they had all so much that they could carry no more.

After this the table was fetched in, and the joiner said, "Table, cover thyself;" and it was at once filled with the choicest dishes. Then they began such a meal as the tailor had never had before in his house; and the whole company remained till late at night merry and jovial.

The next day the tailor forsook needle and thread, and put them all away, with his measures and iron, in a cupboard, and for ever after lived happily and contentedly with his three sons.

KING THRUSH-BEARD

A certain King had a daughter who was very beautiful but also so proud and haughty that no suitor was good enough for her, and sne not only refused every one but also made fun of them all.

Once the King proclaimed a great festival, and invited from far and near all the marriageable young men. When they arrived they were all set in a row, and the King's daughter was led down the row. But she found something to make fun of in all. She nicknamed every one of the suitors, and she made particularly merry with a good young King whose chin had grown rather crooked. "Ha, ha!" laughed she, "he has a chin like a thrush's beak;" and after that day he went by the name of Thrush-Beard.

The old King, however, when he saw that his daughter did nothing

but mock at and make sport of all the suitors who were collected, became angry, and swore that she should take for a husband the first decent beggar who came to the gate.

A couple of days after this a player came beneath the windows to sing and earn some bounty if he could. As soon as the King saw him he ordered him to be called up, and presently he came into the room in all his dirty ragged clothes, and sang before the King and Princess. When he had finished he begged for a slight reward.

The King said, " Thy song has pleased me so much that I will give thee my daughter for a wife."

The Princess was terribly frightened; but the King said, " I have taken an oath, and mean to perform it, that I would give you to the first beggar." All her pleadings were in vain; the priest was called, and the Princess was married to the player. When the ceremony was performed, the King said, " Now, it is impossible for you to stay here with your husband in my house; no! you must travel about the country with him."

So the beggar-man led her away with him, and she was forced to trudge along with him on foot. As they came to a large forest, she said:

" To whom does this beautiful wood belong? "

The echo replied:

" King Thrush-Beard the good!
Had you taken him, so was it thine."

" Ah, silly," said she, " What a lot had been mine, had I happily married King Thrush-Beard! "

Next they came to a meadow, and she said, " To whom does this meadow so green belong? "

" To King Thrush-Beard," called the echo.

" Ah, what a simpleton was I that I did not marry him when I had the chance! " exclaimed the poor Princess.

" Come," broke in the player, " it does not please me I can tell you, that you are always wishing for another husband. Am I not good enough for you? "

By and by they came to a very small hut, and she said, " Dear me, to whom can this miserable, wretched hovel belong? "

The player replied, " That is my house, where we shall live together."

The Princess was obliged to stoop to get in at the door, and when she was inside, she asked, "Where are the servants? "

" What servants? " exclaimed her husband. " You must yourself do all that you want done. Now make a fire and put on some water, that you may cook my dinner, for I am quite tired."

The Princess, however, understood nothing about making fires or cooking, and the beggar had to set to work himself, and as soon as they had finished their scanty meal they went to bed.

In the morning the husband woke up his wife very early, that she might set the house to rights, and for a couple of days they lived on in this way. Then the husband said, " Wife, we must not go on this way any longer, stopping here doing nothing: you must weave some baskets."

So he went out and cut some osiers and brought them home, but when his wife attempted to bend them, the hard twigs wounded her hands and made them bleed.

" I see that won't suit," said her husband. " You had better spin; perhaps that you will do better."

So she sat down to spin, but the harsh thread cut her tender fingers very badly, so that the blood flowed freely.

" Do you see," said her husband, " how you are spoiling your work? I made a bad bargain in taking you! Now I must try and make a business in pots and earthern vessels; you shall sit in the market selling pots."

" Oh, if anybody out of my father's dominions should come and see me in the market selling pots," thought the Princess to herself, " how they will laugh at me!"

However, all her excuses were in vain: she must either do that or die of hunger.

The first time all went well, for the people bought from the Princess because she was so pretty, and not only gave her what she asked, but some even laid down their money and left the pots behind. On her earnings this day they lived for some time, as long as they lasted;

and then the husband purchased a fresh stock of pots. With these the Princess placed her stall at a corner of the market, offering them for sale.

All at once a drunken hussar came plunging down the street on his horse, and rode right into the midst of her earthenware shattering it into a thousand pieces. The accident, as well it might, set her a-weeping, and in her trouble, not knowing what to do, she ran home crying.

" Ah, what will become of me? What will my husband say? "

When she had told him, he cried out, " Whoever would have thought of sitting at the corner of the market to sell earthenware? But well I see you are not accustomed to any ordinary work. There, leave off crying; I have been to the King's palace to ask if they needed a kitchen-maid. They have promised to take you, and there you will live free of cost."

Now the Princess became a kitchen-maid, and was obliged to do as the cook bade her, and wash up the dirty things. Then she would put a jar into each of her pockets, and in them she took home what was left of the good things from the King's table. Of these she and her husband made their meals.

Not many days afterwards it happened that the wedding of the King's eldest son was to be celebrated, and the poor wife placed herself near the door of the salon to look on. As the lamps were lit, and guests more and more beautiful entered the room, and all dressed most sumptuously, she reflected on her fate with a saddened heart, and repented of the pride and haughtiness which had so humiliated and impoverished her. From the costly dishes which were carried to and fro, the fragrant smell of which increased her regrets, the servants now and then threw her a few morsels, and these she put in her pocket to carry home.

Presently the King's son entered, clothed in silk and velvet, and having a golden chain round his neck. As soon as he saw the beautiful maiden standing at the door, he seized her by the hand and asked her to dance; but she, terribly frightened, refused, for she saw it was King Thrush-Beard, who had wooed her, and whom she had laughed at. Her struggles were of no avail. He drew her into the ball-

room, and there tore off the band to which the pockets under her dress were secured; the jars rolled out and the soup ran over the floor, while the pieces of meat and game skipped about in all directions.

When the guests saw the sight they burst into one universal shout of laughter and derision, and the poor girl was so ashamed that she wished herself a thousand fathoms below the earth. She ran out at the door and would have escaped; but on the steps she met a man who took her back, and when she looked at him, lo! it was King Thrush-Beard again.

He spoke to her kindly, and said, " Be not afraid; I and the musician who dwelt with you in the wretched hut, are one; for love of you I have acted thus; and the hussar who rode in among the pots was also myself. All this has taken place in order to humble your haughty disposition, and to punish you for your pride, which led you to mock me."

At these words she wept bitterly, and said, " I am not worthy to be your wife; I have done you so great a wrong." But he replied, " Those evil days are past; we will now celebrate our marriage."

Immediately after came the bridesmaids and dressed her in the most magnificent clothes; and then her father and the whole court arrived and wished her happiness on her wedding-day. Now began her true joy as Queen of the country of King Thrush-Beard.

BRIAR ROSE

IN olden times there lived a King and Queen who lamented day by day that they had no children. One day, as the Queen was bathing and thinking of her great wish a Frog skipped out of the water, and said to her. " Your wish shall be fulfilled—before a year passes you shall have a daughter."

As the Frog had said, so it happened, and a little girl was born who was so beautiful that the King almost lost his senses; but he ordered a great feast to be held, and invited to it not only his relatives, friends, and acquaintances, but also all the wise women who are kind and affectionate to children. There happened to be thirteen in his dominions, but, since he had only twelve golden plates out of which they could eat, one had to stay at home.

The fête was celebrated with all the magnificence possible, and, as soon as it was over, the wise women presented the infant with their wonderful gifts: one with virtue, another with beauty, a third with riches, and so on, so that the child had everything that is to be desired in the world.

Eleven wise women had given their presents when suddenly the thirteenth old lady stepped in. She was in a tremendous passion because she had not been invited, and, without greeting or looking at anyone, she exclaimed loudly, " The Princess shall prick herself with a spindle on her fifteenth birthday and shall die! " and without a further word she turned her back and left the hall.

All were terrified, but just then the twelfth wise woman who had not yet given her wish, stepped up; and because she could not take away the evil wish, but only soften it, she said, " She shall not die, but shall fall into a sleep of a hundred years' duration."

The King, who naturally wished to protect his child from this misfortune, issued a decree commanding that every spindle in the kingdom should be burned. Meanwhile all the gifts of the wise women were fulfilled, and the maiden became so beautiful, gentle, virtuous, and clever, that every one who saw her fell in love with her.

It so happened on the day when she was just fifteen years old that the Queen and the King were not at home, and she was left alone in the castle. The maiden wandered about as she pleased, going through all the rooms and chambers in the castle, until she came at last to an old tower. Up the narrow winding staircase she tripped until she arrived at a door, in the lock of which was a rusty key. This she turned. The door sprang open, and there in the little room sat an old woman with a spindle, spinning flax. "Good-day, my good old lady," said the Princess. "What are you doing here?"

"I am spinning," said the old woman, nodding her head.

"What thing is that which twists round so merrily?" inquired the maiden, and she took the spindle to try her hand at spinning. Scarcely had she done so when the prophecy was fulfilled. She pricked her finger; and at the very same moment she fell back upon a bed into a deep sleep.

This sleep extended over the whole palace. The King and Queen, who had just come in, fell asleep in the hall, and all their courtiers with them—the horses in the stables, the doves upon the eaves, the flies upon the walls, and even the fire upon the hearth, all ceased to stir—the meat which was cooking ceased to sizzle, and the cook at the instant of pulling the hair of the kitchen-boy lost his hold and began to snore too. The wind also fell entirely, and not a leaf rustled on the trees round the castle.

Now, around the palace a thick hedge of briars began to grow, which every year grew higher and higher, till the castle was quite hidden from view, so that one could not even see the flag upon the tower. Then there went a legend through the land of the beautiful maiden, Briar Rose, for so was the sleeping Princess named, and from time to time Princes came endeavouring to penetrate through the hedge into the castle; but it was not posssible, for the thorns held them as if by hands, and the youths were unable to free themselves, and therefore perished miserably.

After the lapse of many years there came another King's son into the country, and heard an old man tell the legend of the hedge of briars:

how that behind it stood a castle where slept a wondrously beauteous Princess called Briar Rose, who had slumbered nearly a hundred years, and with her the Queen and King and all their Court. The old man further related what he had heard from his grandfather, that many Princes had come and tried to penetrate the hedge, and died a miserable death.

But the youth was not to be daunted, and, however much the old man tried to dissuade him, he would not listen, but cried out, "I fear not; I must see this hedge of briars!"

Just at that time came the last day of the hundred years, when Briar Rose was to awake again. As the young Prince approached the hedge, the thorns turned to fine large flowers, which of their own accord made a way for him to pass through and again closed up behind him. In the courtyard he saw the horses and dogs lying fast asleep, and on the eaves were the doves with their heads beneath their wings. As soon as he went into the house there were the flies asleep upon the wall, the cook still stood with his hand on the hair of the kitchen-boy, and a maid stood at the table with an unplucked fowl in her hand. He went on, and in the hall he found the courtiers lying asleep, and beyond, by the throne, were the King and Queen. He went on farther and all was so quiet that he could hear himself breathe. At last he came to the

tower and opened the door of the little room where slept Briar Rose.

There she lay, looking so beautiful that he could not turn his eyes from her, and he bent over and kissed her. Just as he did so she opened her eyes, awoke and greeted him with smiles. They went down the staircase together, and immediately the King and Queen awoke, then the whole Court, and all stared at each other in wonderment. Now the horses in the stables got up and shook themselves; the dogs wagged their tails; the doves upon the eaves drew their heads from under their wings, looked around, and flew away; the flies upon the walls began to crawl; the fire began to burn brightly and to cook the meat—the meat began to sizzle; the cook gave his lad a box upon the ear, which made him call out; and the maid began to pluck the fowl furiously. The whole palace was once more in motion as if nothing had occurred, for the hundred years' sleep had made no change in any one.

By and by the wedding of the Prince with Briar Rose was celebrated with great splendour, and to the end of their lives they lived happy and contented.

HANSEL AND GRETHEL

ONCE upon a time there dwelt near a large wood a poor woodcutter, with his wife, and two children by his former marriage—a little boy called Hansel, and a girl named Grethel. He was very poor; and once, when there was a great famine in the land, he could not buy even his daily bread. As he lay thinking in bed one evening, restless and troubled, he said to his wife, " What will become of us? How can we feed our children when we have no more than we can eat ourselves?"

"My husband," answered she, " we will lead them away early in the morning into the thickest part of the wood, there make them a fire, and give them each a little piece of bread. Then we will leave them alone and they will not find the way home again."

" No, wife," replied he, " that I can never do. I could not leave my children all alone in the wood: The wild beasts would soon come and tear them to pieces."

" Oh, you simpleton!" said she, " then we must all four die of hunger." She left him no peace till he consented, saying, " Ah, but I shall regret the poor children."

The two hungry children, however, had not gone to sleep, and they, overheard what the stepmother said to their father. Grethel wept bitterly, and said to Hansel, " What will become of us?"

" Do not cry, Grethel," said he. " I will help you." And as soon as their parents had fallen asleep, he got up, and, unbarring the back door slipped out.

The moon shone brightly, and the white pebbles which lay before the door seemed like silver pieces, they glittered so brightly. Hansel stooped down and put as many into his pocket as it would hold; and then going back, he said to Grethel, " Be comforted, dear sister, and sleep in peace; all will be well" And so saying, he crept into bed again.

Early next morning, the wife awoke the two children. " Get up, you lazy things; we are going into the forest to chop wood." Then she gave them each a piece of bread, saying, " There is something for your dinner; do not eat it before then for you will get nothing else."

Grethel took the bread in her apron, for Hansel's pocket was full of pebbles. And so they all set out. When they had gone a little distance, Hansel stood still, and peeped back at the house. This he did several times, till his father said, " Hansel, what are you peeping at, and why do you lag behind? "

" Ah! father," said Hansel, " I am looking back at my white cat sitting upon the roof of the house, and trying to say good-bye."

" You simpleton! " said the wife, " that is not a cat; it is only the sun shining on the white chimney." But Hansel was not really looking at a cat. Every time he stopped he dropped a pebble out of his pocket upon the path.

When they came to the middle of the wood, the father told his children to collect some sticks and he would make a fire. Hansel and Grethel gathered quite a little mountain of twigs. Then they set fire to them, and as the flame burned up high, the wife said, " Now, you children, lie down near the fire and rest whilst we go into the forest and chop wood. When we are ready, I will call you."

Hansel and Grethel sat down by the fire, and when it was noon, each ate the piece of bread; and because they could hear the blows of an axe, they thought their father was near; but it was not an axe, but a branch which he had bound to a withered tree, so as to be blown to and fro by the wind. They waited so long that at last their eyes closed from weariness, and they fell fast asleep.

When they awoke it was quite dark, and Grethel began to cry, "Oh, Hansel, how shall we ever find our way out of the wood at night?"

But Hansel tried to comfort her by saying, "Wait a little while till the moon rises, and then I promise you we will quickly find the way."

The moon soon shone forth, and Hansel taking his sister's hand, followed the pebbles, which glittered like new-coined silver pieces, and showed them the path. All night long they walked on, and as day broke they came to their father's house. They knocked at the door, and when their stepmother opened it and saw Hansel and Grethel standing there, she exclaimed, "You wicked children! Why did you sleep so long in the wood? We thought you were never coming home again."

But their father was very glad, for it had grieved his heart to leave them all alone.

Not long afterwards there was again great scarcity in every corner of the land; and one night the children overheard their stepmother talking to their father.

"Everything is again consumed," she said. "We have only half a loaf left, and then there will be nothing: the children must be sent away. We will take them deeper into the woods this time, so that they may not find the way out again; it is the only thing to do."

But her husband's heart was heavy.

"It were far better to share the last crust with the children," said he.

His wife, however, would listen to nothing that he said, and scolded and reproached him without end.

The children, however, had heard the conversation as they lay awake, and as soon as the old people went to sleep Hansel got up, intending to pick up some pebbles as before. But the wife had locked the door, so that he could not get out. Nevertheless he comforted Grethel, saying: "Do not cry; sleep in peace; God will surely not forsake us."

Early in the morning the stepmother came and pulled them out of bed, and gave them each a slice of bread, which was still smaller than before. On the way, Hansel broke his in his pocket, and, stopping every now and then, dropped a crumb upon the path.

"Hansel, why do you stop and look about?" said the father; "keep in the path."

"I am looking at my little dove," answered Hansel, "nodding a good-bye to me."

"Simpleton!" said the wife, "that is no dove, but only the sun shining on the chimney." But Hansel still kept dropping crumbs as he went along.

The mother led the children deep into the wood, where they had never been before, and there they built an immense fire.

"Sit down here and rest," she said to them, "and when you feel tired you can sleep for a little while. We are going into the forest to hew wood, and in the evening, when we are ready, we will come and fetch you."

When noon came, Grethel shared her bread with Hansel, who had strewn his on the path. Then they went to sleep; but the evening arrived, and no one came to fetch the poor children. It was dark when they awoke, and Hansel comforted his sister.

"Only wait, Grethel, till the moon comes out," he said, "then we shall see the crumbs of bread which I have dropped, and they will show us the way home."

The moon shone, and they got up, but they could not see any crumbs, for the thousands of birds which had been flying about in the woods and fields had picked them all up.

Hansel kept saying to Grethel, "We will soon find the way." But they did not, and they walked the whole night long and the next day, but still they did not come out of the wood; and they got so hungry for they had nothing to eat but the berries which they found upon the bushes. Soon they were so tired that they could not drag themselves along, and wearily they lay down under a tree and went quickly to sleep.

It was now the third morning since they had left their father's house, and they still walked on; but they only went deeper and deeper into the wood, and Hansel saw that if help did not come very soon they would die of hunger.

As soon as it was noon they saw a beautiful snow-white bird sitting upon a bough, which sang so sweetly that they stood still and listened to it. It soon stopped and, spreading its wings, flew away. They followed it until it arrived at a cottage, upon the roof of which it perched; and when they went close up to it they saw that the cottage was made of bread and cakes, and the window-panes were of clear sugar.

"We will go in there," said Hansel, "and have a glorious feast. I will eat a piece of the roof, and you can eat the window. Will they not be sweet?"

So Hansel reached up and broke a piece off the roof in order to see how it tasted; while Grethel stepped up to the window and began to bite it.

Then a sweet voice called out from inside, "Tip-tap, tip-tap, who raps at my door." And the children answered, "The wind, the wind, the child of heaven;" and they went on eating.

Hansel thought the roof tasted very good, and he tore off a large piece, while Grethel broke a large round pane out of the window and sat down quite happily. Just then the door opened and a very old woman, walking upon crutches, came out. Hansel and Grethel were so frightened that they let fall what they had in their hands; but the old woman, nodding her head, said, "Ah, you dear children, what has brought you here? Come in and stay with me and no harm shall befall you." So saying, she took them both by the hand and led them into her cottage.

A good meal of milk and pancakes with sugar, apples and nuts, was spread on the table. In the back room were two nice little beds, covered in white, where later Hansel and Grethel lay down, and thought themselves in heaven. The old woman behaved very kindly to them; but in reality she was a wicked witch who waylaid children and built the bread-house in order to entice them in. As soon as they were in her power she killed, then cooked and ate them, and made a great festival of the day.

Witches have red eyes, and cannot see very far; but they have a fine sense of smell, like wild beasts, so that they know when children are approaching. When Hansel and Grethel came near the witch's house she laughed wickedly, saying, "Here come two who shall not escape me." And early next morning, before they awoke, she went up to them, and saw how sweetly they lay sleeping, and looking at their chubby red cheeks, she mumbled to herself, "That will be a good bite."

Then she seized Hansel with her rough hand, and shut him up in a little cage with a lattice-door; and although he screamed loudly it was of no use. Next she went to Grethel, and, shaking her till she awoke, said, "Get up, you lazy thing, and fetch some water to cook something good for your brother, who must remain in that stall and get fat. When he is fat enough I shall eat him." Grethel began to cry, but it was all useless, for the old witch made her do as she wished. So a fine meal was cooked for Hansel, but Grethel got nothing but a crab's claw.

Every morning the old witch came to the cage, and said, " Hansel, stretch out your finger that I may feel whether you are getting fat." But Hansel used to stretch out a bone, and the old woman, having very bad sight thought it was his finger, and wondered very much why he did not get fatter.

When four weeks had passed, and Hansel still seemed quite thin she lost all patience.

" Grethel," she called out in a rage, " get some water quickly; be Hansel fat or lean, this morning I will kill and cook him."

Oh! how terrified the poor little sister was; but she was forced to fetch the water, while the tears ran down her cheeks! " Had we only been eaten by the wild beasts in the wood," she exclaimed, " then we should have died together." But the old witch called out, " Stop that noise; it will not help you a bit. First we will bake; I have already heated the oven and kneaded the dough;" and so saying, she pushed poor Grethel up to the oven where the flames were burning fiercely.

" Creep in," said the witch, " and see if it is hot enough, and then we will put in the bread." But she intended when Grethel got in, to shut the oven, and let her bake, so that she might eat her as well as Hansel. Grethel saw what she was thinking, and said, " I do not know how to do it; how shall I get in? "

" You stupid goose," said she, " the opening is big enough. See, I could even get in myself!" And she got up and put her head into the oven. Grethel gave her a push, so that she fell right in, and quickly she pushed the iron door shut.

Grethel ran to Hansel, and, opening his door, called out, " Hansel, we are saved; the old witch is dead! " He sprang out, like a bird out of his cage when the door is opened and joyfully kissed his sister. And now, as there was nothing to fear, they went into the witch's house, where in every corner were caskets full of precious stones.

" These are better than pebbles," said Hansel, putting as many into his pocket as it would hold; while Grethel thought, " I will take some home too," and filled her apron full. " We must be off now," said Hansel, " and get out of this enchanted forest." But when they had walked for two hours they came to a broad stretch of water. " We cannot get over," said Hansel; " I can see no bridge at all."

" And there is no boat either," said Grethel, " but there swims a white duck. I will ask her to help us over; " and she sang:

> " Little Duck, good little Duck,
> Grethel and Hansel, here we stand;
> There is neither stile nor bridge—
> Take us on your back to land. "

The duck came to them, and Hansel sat himself on its back and bade his sister sit behind him. " No," answered Grethel, " that is too much for the Duck; she shall take us over one at a time." This the good little bird did. When they had reached the other side safely, and had gone a little way, they came to a well-known wood, which became more familiar with every step they took. At last they saw their father's house. Then they began to run, and, bursting into the house, they found their father alone—their stepmother was dead. How glad their father was to see them. Grethel shook her apron, Hansel emptied his pockets and the precious stones rolled out upon the floor.

All their sorrows were ended, and they lived ever after in great happiness.

THE WOLF AND THE SEVEN LITTLE GOATS

THERE was once an old goat who had seven little kids which she loved as a mother loves her children. One day she wanted to go into the wood to look for food, so she called her seven kids to her and said: " Dear children, I must go into the wood; be on your guard against the wolf. If he should come in here, he will eat you all up, skin and hair. The wicked creature often disguises himself but by his rough voice and black paws will you recognise him."

The little goats said: " Dear mother, we shall take great care. You can go off without worrying about us."

It was not long before someone knocked at the door and cried, " Open up, dear children, your mother is here."

But the little goats listened to the husky voice and knew it was the wolf's.

" We shall not open up," they called. " You are not our mother; She has a sweet and gentle voice, but your voice is rough."

Then the wolf went off to a shop and bought himself a large piece of chalk which he ate so that his voice would become sweet and gentle. Then he returned, knocked at the door and called, " Open up, dear children, your mother is here."

But the wolf had placed his black paws against the window. The little goats saw them and cried, " We shall not open the door; our mother has not black paws like you. You are the wolf."

Then the wolf ran off to a baker and said, " I have bruised my paws, spread dough on them." And when the baker had done so the wolf ran to the miller and said, " Spread white meal on my paws." The miller thought: He means to cheat someone; and he hesitated. But the wolf cried, " If you will not do it, I shall eat you." Then the miller was frightened and made the wolf's paws white.

For the third time the villain went to the goats' door, knocked and said: " Open up, children, your dear mother is home and has brought each of you something from the wood."

The little goats cried, " Show us first your paws that we shall know that you are indeed our dear mother! "

Then the wolf put his paws against the window and when they saw that they were white, they believed that it was truly their mother and opened the door. But who came in but the wolf!

The little goats were terrified and tried to hide. One jumped under the table, the second into the bed, the third into the oven, the fourth behind the door, the fifth into the cupboard, the sixth under the wash basin, the seventh into the grandfather clock. But the wolf soon found them and made short work of them. One after another he caught and swallowed them up; only the youngest one in the clock was he unable to find. When the wolf had satisfied his hunger, he took himself off, lay down in a green meadow under a tree and fell fast asleep.

Not long afterwards the mother goat came home from the wood. What a sight met her eyes!

The door stood wide open, the table, stool and bench were overturned, the wash basin lay in pieces, and covers and pillows had been pulled from the bed. One after another she called her children by name but no one answered.

At last, when she called the youngest, a small voice answered, " Dear mother, I am hiding in the clock! " She fetched him out and the little goat told her that the wolf had come and that he had eaten up all the others.

Immediately the mother in her grief ran outside and the youngest little goat ran after her. They ran until they had reached the meadow, and there under a tree lay the wolf snoring so loudly that the branches trembled.

The mother goat examined him from all sides and saw that in his full stomach something moved.

Oh, thought she, what if my poor children whom he has gobbled up for supper should be still alive?

Quickly she sent the little goat home to fetch scissors, needle and thread. Then she cut the monster's stomach and scarcely had she made one small slit than a little goat pushed its head out, and as she snipped further, one after another all six little goats sprang out. Not one was harmed at all, for the robber in his greed had simply swallowed them whole.

" Now," said their mother, " go and look for some large stones: with them I will fill this beast's stomach while he is still asleep."

Then quickly the seven little goats brought as many stones as they could carry, stuffed them into the wolf's stomach and their mother sewed it up again with all speed.

At last the wolf awoke and finding that he was very thirsty went down to the well to drink. But when he began to move, the stones in his stomach knocked and rattled against each other. Then the wolf cried. " What is rattling and bouncing in my stomach? I thought it was six little goats but now they seem heavier than boulders."

When he reached the well he bent over to drink; the stones were so heavy that he overbalanced, fell into the deep water and was never seen again.

" The wolf is dead," cried the seven little goats and with their mother they danced for joy round and round the well.

SNOW-WHITE AND ROSE-RED

THERE was once a poor widow who lived alone in a cottage with her two children, who, because they looked like the flowers which bloomed on two rose bushes which grew before the house, were called Snow-White and Rose-Red. They were two as good, industrious, and amiable children as were to be found in the world, only Snow-White was quieter and more gentle than Rose-Red.

For Rose-Red would run and jump about the meadows, seeking flowers and catching butterflies, while Snow-White sat at home helping her mother to keep house, or read to her if there was nothing to do. The two children loved one another dearly, and always took each other's hand when they went out together; and always when they talked of it they agreed that they would never separate from each other, and that whatever one had the other should share.

Often they ran deep into the forest and gathered wild berries; but no beast ever harmed them. For the hare would eat cauliflowers out of their hands, the fawn would graze at their side, the goats would frisk about them in play, and the birds remained perched on the boughs singing as if nobody were near. No accident ever befell them; and if they stayed late in the forest and night came upon them, they used to lie down on the moss and sleep till morning; and because their mother knew they would do this, she felt no anxiety about them.

Once when they had passed the night in the forest, and the dawn light awoke them, they saw a beautiful child dressed in shining white sitting quite near where they lay. She got up and looked at them kindly, but, without saying anything, went into the forest; and when the children looked round they saw that the place where they had slept was close to the edge of a pit, into which they would have certainly fallen, had they walked a couple of steps farther in the dark. Their mother told them the figure they had seen was, doubtless, one of the angels who watch over good children.

Snow-White and Rose-Red kept their mother's cottage so clean that it was a pleasure to enter it. Every morning in the summer-time Rose-Red would first put the house in order and then gather a nosegay for her mother, in which she always placed a bud from each rose-tree. Every winter's morning Snow-White would light the fire and put the kettle on to boil, and, although the kettle was made of copper it shone like gold because it was scoured so well. In the evenings, when the snowflakes were falling, their mother would say, "Go, Snow-White, and bolt the door." Then they used to sit down on the hearth, and their mother would put on her spectacles and read out of a great book, while her children sat spinning. By their side, too, lay their pet lamb, and on a perch behind them a little white dove slept with her head under her wing.

One evening, when they were thus sitting comfortably together, there came a knock at the door, as if somebody wished to come in. "Make haste, Rose-Red," cried her mother; "make haste and open the door; perhaps there is some traveller outside who needs shelter." So Rose-Red went and drew the bolt and opened the door, expecting to see some poor man outside; but, instead, a great fat bear poked his black head in. Rose-Red shrieked and ran back, the little lamb bleated, the dove fluttered on her perch, and Snow-White hid herself behind her mother's bed. The bear, however, began to speak, and said, "Be not afraid! I will do you no harm; but I am half frozen, and wish to come in and warm myself. Will you let me shelter with you for a little?"

"Poor bear!" cried the mother; "come in and lie down before the fire, but take care you do not burn your skin." And then she continued, "Come here, Rose-Red and Snow-White; the bear will not harm you." So the children both came back, and by degrees the lamb too and the dove overcame their fears and welcomed the rough visitor.

"You children!" said the bear, before he entered, "come and knock the snow off my coat." And they fetched their brooms and swept him clean. Then he stretched himself before the fire and grumbled out his satisfaction, and in a little while the children became familiar enough to play tricks with the unwieldly animal. They pulled his long shaggy coat, set their feet upon his back and rolled

to and fro, and even ventured to tickle him with a hazel-stick, laughing when he grumbled. The bear bore all their tricks good-naturedly and indeed seemed to enjoy them, but if they tickled too hard he cried out:

" Leave me my life, you children,
Snow-White and Rose-Red,
Or you'll never wed."

When bedtime came and the others were gone, the mother said to the bear, " You may sleep here on the hearth if you like, and then you will be safe from the cold and the bad weather."

As soon as day broke the two children let the bear out again, and he trotted away over the snow, and ever afterwards he came every evening at a certain hour. He would lie down on the hearth and allow the children to play with him as much as they liked, till by degrees they became so accustomed to him, that the door was left unbolted till their black friend arrived.

But as soon as spring returned, and everything out of doors was green again, the bear one morning told Snow-White that he must leave her, and could not return during the whole summer.

" Where are you going, then, dear Bear? " asked Snow-White.

" I am obliged to go into the forest and guard my treasures from the evil dwarfs," said the bear. " In the winter, when the ground is hard, they have to keep in their holes, and cannot burrow through; but now, since the sun has thawed the earth and warmed it, the dwarfs pierce through and steal all they can find; and what has once passed into their hands, and is concealed by them in their caves, is not easily brought to light."

Snow-White, however, was very sad at the departure of the bear, and opened the door so hesitatingly that when he pressed through it he left behind on the latch a piece of his hairy coat; and through the hole which was made in his coat Snow-White fancied she saw the glittering of gold, but she was not quite certain of it. The bear, however, ran hastily away, and was soon hidden from sight behind the trees.

Some time afterwards, the mother sent the children into the wood to gather sticks, and while doing so they came to a tree which was lying across the path. On the trunk something kept bobbing up and down from the grass, and they could not imagine what it was. When they came nearer they saw a dwarf with an old wrinkled face, and a snow-white beard a yard long. The end of this beard was fixed in a split of the tree, and the little man kept jumping about like a dog tied by a chain, for he did not know how to free himself. He glared at the maidens with his fiery-red eyes, and exclaimed, " Why do you stand there? Are you going to pass without offering me any assistance? I always did think that little girls were selfish and very stupid."

"What have you done, little man?" asked Rose-Red, coming closer.

"You stupid, inquisitive goose!" exclaimed he, "I wanted to split the tree in order to get a little wood for my kitchen; for the little food which we use is soon burned up with great faggots, unlike the food you rough, greedy people devour! I had driven the wedge in properly, and everything was going on well, when the wedge sprang out suddenly, and the tree closed so quickly together that I could not draw my beautiful beard out; and here it sticks, and I cannot get away. There, don't laugh, you silly things! Are you dumb?"

The children took all the pains they could to pull the dwarf's beard out, but without success. "I will run and fetch some help," cried Rose-Red at length.

"Stupid child that you are!" snarled the dwarf. "What are you going to call other people for? You are already two too many for me. Can you think of nothing else?"

"Don't be impatient," replied Snow-White; "I have thought of something;" and, pulling her scissors out of her pocket, she cut off the end of his beard.

As soon as the dwarf found himself at liberty, he snatched up his sack, which lay between the roots of the tree, filled with gold, and, throwing it over his shoulder, marched off, grumbling and groaning and crying, "Stupid people, to cut off a piece of my beautiful beard! Plague take you!" and away he went without once looking at the children.

Some time afterwards Snow-White and Rose-Red went fishing and as they neared the pond they saw something like a great locust hopping about on the bank, as if going to jump into the water. They ran up and recognised the dwarf.

"What are you doing?" asked Rose-Red. "You will fall into the water."

"I am not quite such a simpleton as that," replied the dwarf. "But do you not see this fish will pull me in?" The little man had been sitting there angling, and, unfortunately, the wind had entangled his beard with the fishing line. When a great fish bit at the bait, he was not

strong enough to pull it out. The dwarf held on by the reeds which grew near, but the fish pulled him where it liked. Luckily, just then the two maidens arrived, and tried to release the dwarf's beard from the fishing-line. But both were too closely entangled, so Snow-White pulled out her scissors again and cut off another piece of the beard.

When the dwarf saw this done he was in a great rage, and exclaimed, " Was it not enough to cut my beard once! I dare not show myself now to my own people." So saying, he took up a bag of pearls, which lay among the rushes, and disappeared behind a stone.

A few days later their mother sent the two maidens to the next town to buy thread, needles and pins, laces and ribbons. As they crossed a common, they saw overhead a great bird flying round and round. Every now and then it dropped lower and lower, till at last it flew down behind a rock. Immediately afterwards they heard a piercing shriek, and, running up, they saw that the eagle had caught their old acquaintance the dwarf, and was trying to carry him off. The children quickly seized the little man and held him fast till the bird gave up the struggle and flew off.

As soon as the dwarf had recovered from his fright, he exclaimed, in his squeaking voice, " Could you not hold me more gently? You have torn my fine brown coat! " With these words he shouldered a bag filled with precious stones, and slipped away to his cave among some nearby rocks.

The maidens now accustomed to his ingratitude, walked on to the town. Their shopping done, they returned over the same common, and unawares walked up to a certain spot, on which the dwarf thinking nobody was near, had shaken out his bag of precious stones. The bright stones glittered in the sun and the two maidens stopped to admire them.

" What are you gaping for ? " snarled the dwarf, while his face grew red with rage. But suddenly a loud roaring noise was heard, and a great black bear came rolling out of the forest. The dwarf jumped up terrified, and began to run. But the bear easily overtook him. " Spare me, my dear Lord Bear ! " cried the dwarf, " I will give you all my treasures. Only give me my life. There are two wicked girls. They would make you nice tender morsels."

The bear, however, without speaking, gave the bad-hearted dwarf a single blow with his paw, and he never stirred again.

The maidens were going to run away, but the bear called, " Snow-White and Rose-Red, fear not ! Wait for me ! " They recognised his voice, and stopped. And as they turned the bear's rough coat suddenly fell off, and he stood up, a tall man dressed entirely in gold. " I am a King's son," he said, " and was condemned by the wicked dwarf, who stole all my treasures, to wander about in this forest as a bear till his death released me."

They went home, and Snow-White was soon married to the Prince, and Rose-Red to his brother. The old mother also lived for many years happily with them, and the rose-trees which had stood before the cottage were planted before the palace, and produced every year beautiful red and white blooms.

FORTUNE FROM THE STARS

THERE was once a little girl whose mother and father had both died. She was so poor that she had not even a little room to live in nor a little bed to sleep in. She had nothing in the world but the clothes she wore and a little piece of bread in her hand which some kind person had given her. But she was a good little maiden, and because she was all alone in the world, she put her trust in God and set out to seek her fortune.

Walking through a field she met a poor man who said to her: " Oh, please give me something to eat. I am so hungry." The little girl gave him her piece of bread, saying, " God bless you." She walked on until she met a child who wept: " My head is so cold, please give me something to cover it." And the maiden took off her little cap and gave it to the child.

She had not gone much farther on her way when she met another child who had no clothes at all and was freezing. To this child she said, " Here is my coat." Still farther on another child, a little girl, appeared. " Please give me your little skirt," she said. " I am so cold." And the maiden gladly gave it to her.

It was already dark when at last she reached a wood. Then came still another child to her who asked for her little petticoat, and the good maiden thought. " It is dark; no one will see me. I can easily give away my petticoat." And she took it off and gave it to the child.

As she stood there alone with nothing left at all, stars began to fall from Heaven, and as they fell they turned into shining coins. Although she had given away her little dress, the maiden suddenly found herself wearing a new one and it was made of the finest stuff. Joyfully, she held out the skirt of her dress and gathered the coins into it and so was rich for the rest of her life.

CINDERELLA

ONCE upon a time the wife of a rich man fell very ill, and as she felt her end drawing nigh she called her only daughter to her bedside, and said, "My dear child, be pious and good, and God will always protect you, and I will look down upon you from heaven."

Soon afterwards she closed her eyes and died. Every day the maiden went to her mother's grave and wept over it, and she continued to be good and pious. Then winter came followed by spring and the maiden's father took to himself another wife.

The wife brought home with her two daughters, who were fair of face but wicked at heart. Then an unhappy time began in the poor stepchild's life. " Shall the stupid goose sit in the parlour with us?" said the two daughters. " Into the kitchen with her."

So they took off her fine clothes, and gave her an old grey cloak and wooden shoes. " See how the once proud princess is decked out now," they mocked as they led her into the kitchen.

Then she had to work hard from morning till night, fetching water, making the fire, cooking and scouring. The sisters insulted and ridiculed her, and shook the peas and beans into the ashes, so that she had to pick them out again. At night she had no bed to lie on but the ashes

on the hearth; and because she looked dirty by sleeping there, they named her CINDERELLA.

One day the father wanted to go to the fair; so he asked his two daughters what he should bring them. "Some beautiful dresses," said one. "Pearls," replied the other. "But you, Cinderella," said he, "what will you have?" "The first bough, father, that knocks against your hat on your way homewards, break it off for me," she replied.

So he bought the fine dresses, and the pearls for his stepdaughters; and on his return, as he rode through a thicket, a hazel-bough touched his hat which he broke off and took with him. As soon as he got home he gave his stepdaughters what they had asked for, and to Cinderella he gave the hazel-branch.

She thanked him, and, going to her mother's grave, she planted the branch on it, and wept so long that her tears fell and watered it, so that it grew into a beautiful tree. Thrice a day Cinderella went beneath it to weep and pray; and each time a little white bird flew on to the tree, and if she wished aloud, the little bird threw down to her whatever she wished for.

After a time it happened that the King declared a festival which was to last three days, and to which all the beautiful maidens in the country were invited. From these his son was to choose a bride.

The two stepdaughters were delighted and calling Cinderella, they said, "Comb our hair, brush our shoes. We are going to the festival at the King's palace." Cinderella obeyed, crying, because she too wanted to go to the dance. She asked her stepmother if she might go.

"You, Cinderella!" said she; "you are covered with dirt. You have no clothes or shoes, and how can you dance?" But, as Cinderella pleaded, the mother said at last, "I have thrown into the snow a tubful of beans; if you have picked them out again in two hours, you shall go."

The maiden went into the garden, and called out, "You tame pigeons, and turtle doves, and all birds under heaven, come and help me to gather the beans into the tub."

Down into the garden below flew two white pigeons, and after them the turtle-doves, and soon all the birds under heaven flew down upon the snowy path. They then began to pick, pick, pick, and gathered all the seeds into the tub. Scarcely an hour had passed when all was completed.

Then the maiden took the tub to her stepmother, rejoicing at the thought that she might now go to the festival; but the stepmother said, " No, Cinderella, you have no clothes, and cannot dance; you will only be laughed at."

As she began to cry, the stepmother said, " If you can pick up two tubs of beans which I throw into the garden in one hour, you shall accompany them;" and she thought to herself, " She will never manage it."

As soon as the two tubs had been shot into the snow, Cinderella went out at the back door into the garden, and called out as before, " You tame pigeons, and turtle-doves, and all birds under heaven, please come and help me to gather the good beans into the tubs that I may go to the festival." Presently, down into the garden flew two white pigeons, and soon after them the turtle-doves, and soon all the birds under heaven flew chirping down among the snow. Then they began to pick, pick, pick, and gathered all the seeds into the tubs; and scarcely had half an hour passed before all were picked up, and off they flew again.

The maiden now took the tubs to her stepmother, rejoicing at the thought that she could go to the festival. But the mother, said, "It does not help you a bit; you cannot go with us, for you have no clothes, and cannot dance; we should be ashamed of you." Thereupon she turned her back upon the maiden, and hastened away with her two proud daughters.

As there was no one at home, Cinderella went to her mother's grave under the hazel-tree, and said:

" Rustle and shake yourself, dear tree,
And silver and gold throw down to me."

Then the bird threw down a dress of gold and silver, and silken slippers ornamented with silver. These Cinderella put on in great haste, and then she went to the ball. Her sisters and stepmother did not know her at all, and took her for some foreign princess, as she looked so beautiful in her golden dress; for of Cinderella they did not dream but that she was sitting at home keeping warm among the ashes.

Presently, the Prince came up to her, and, taking her by the hand, led her to the dance. He would not dance with any one else, and would not even let go her hand; so that when she was asked by others to dance, he said, " She is my partner." They danced till evening, when she wished to go home. But the Prince said, " I will go with you, and see you safe," for he wanted to see to whom the maiden belonged. She flew away from him, however, and sprang into the pigeon-house. So the Prince waited till her father came. Then he told him that a strange maiden had run into the pigeon house. The step-mother thought, " Could it be Cinderella ? "

And they brought an axe with which the Prince might cut open the door, but inside there was no one. And when they came into the house, there lay Cinderella in her dirty clothes among the ashes, and an oil-lamp was burning in the chimney. For she had jumped quickly out on the other side of the pigeon house, and had run to the hazel-tree, where she had taken off her fine clothes and laid them on the grave. The bird had taken them again, and afterwards she had put on her little grey cloak and seated herself among the ashes in the kitchen.

The next day, when the festival was renewed, and her stepmother and her sisters had set out again, Cinderella went to the hazel-tree and sang as before:

" Rustle and shake yourself, dear tree,
And silver and gold throw down to me."

Then the bird threw down a much more splendid dress than the former, and when the maiden appeared at the ball, every one was astonished at her beauty.

The Prince, however, who had waited till she came, took her hand, and would dance with no one else; and if others came and asked, he replied as before, " She is my partner." As soon as evening came she wished to depart, and the Prince followed her, wanting to see into whose house she went; but she sprang away from him, and ran into the garden behind the house.

There stood a fine large tree on which in autumn hung the most beautiful pears. Now the boughs creaked as though someone hid there. But the Prince could see nothing. He waited, however, till the father came, and then said, " The strange maiden has escaped from me, and I think she has climbed up into this tree." The father thought to himself, " Can it be Cinderella? " and, taking an axe, he chopped down the tree; but there was no one in it.

When they went into the kitchen, there lay Cinderella among the ashes, as before; for she had sprung down on the other side of the tree, and having taken her beautiful clothes again to the bird upon the hazel-tree, she had put on once more her old grey cloak.

The third day, when her stepmother and her sisters had again set out, Cinderella went once more to her mother's grave, and said:

" Rustle and shake yourself, dear tree,
And silver and gold throw down to me."

Then the bird threw down to her a dress which was more splendid and glittering than she had ever had before, and the slippers were of pure gold.

When she arrived at the ball they knew not what to say for wonderment, and as before the Prince danced with her alone, and replied to everyone who asked her to dance, " She is my partner."

As soon as evening came she wished to go, and, as the Prince followed her, she ran away so quickly that he could not overtake her. But he had thought of a plan, and spread the whole way with pitch, so that it happened as the maiden ran that her left slipper came off.

The Prince took it up, and saw it was small and graceful, and of pure gold; so the following morning he went with it to the father, and

said, " My bride shall be no other than she whose foot this golden slipper fits." The two sisters were glad of this, for they had beautiful feet, and the elder went with it to her chamber to try it on, while her mother stood by. She could not, however, get her great toe into it, and the shoe was much too small. But the mother reaching for a knife, said, " Cut off your toe, for if you are queen you need not go any longer on foot."

The maiden cut it off and squeezed her foot into the shoe, and, concealing the pain she felt, went down to the Prince. Then he placed her as his bride upon his horse, and rode off; and as they passed by the grave there sat two little doves upon the hazel tree, singing:

" Backwards peep, backwards peep,
There's blood upon the shoe;
The shoe's too small, and she behind
Is not the bride for you."

Then the Prince looked behind, and saw the blood flowing. So he turned his horse back, and took the false bride home again, saying she was not the right one.

Then the other sister must needs fit on the shoe; so she went to her chamber and got her toes nicely into the shoe, but the heel was too large. The mother, reaching for a knife, said, " Cut a piece off your heel, for when you become queen you need not go any longer on foot."

She cut a piece off her heel, squeezed her foot into the shoe, and, concealing the pain she felt, went down to the Prince. Then he put her upon his horse as his bride, and rode off; and as they passed the hazel-tree there sat two little doves, who sang:

" Backwards peep, backwards peep,
There's blood upon the shoe,
The shoe's too small and she behind
Is not the bride for you."

Then he looked behind, and saw the blood trickling from her shoe, and that the stocking was dyed quite red. So he turned his horse back, and took the false bride home again, saying " Neither is this one the right maiden. Have you no other daughter? "

" No," replied the father, " except little Cinderella, daughter of my first wife, who cannot possibly be the bride." The Prince asked that she might be fetched; but the stepmother said, " Oh no! she is much too dirty; I dare not let her be seen."

But the Prince would have his way. So Cinderella was called, and she, first washing her hands and face, went in and curtseyed to the Prince, who gave her the golden shoe. Cinderella sat down on a stool, and, taking off her heavy wooden shoes, put on the slipper. It fitted her perfectly, and as she stood up, the Prince looked in her face, and recognising the beautiful maiden with whom he had danced, exclaimed, " This is my true bride."

The stepmother and the two sisters were amazed, and white with rage. But the Prince took Cinderella upon his horse, and rode away. And as they came up to the hazel-tree the two little white doves sang:

" Backwards peep, backwards peep,
There's no blood on the shoe;
It fits so well, and she behind
Is the true bride for you."

And, as they finished, they flew down and lighted upon Cinderella's shoulders, and there they remained.

The wedding was celebrated with great festivities, and the two sisters were smitten with blindness as a punishment for their wickedness and Cinderella lived happily ever after with her Prince.

LITTLE SNOW-WHITE

ONCE upon a time in the depth of winter, when the flakes of snow were falling like feathers from the clouds, a Queen sat at her palace window, which had an ebony black frame, stitching her husband's shirts.

While she was sewing and looking out at the flakes, she pricked her finger, and three drops of blood fell upon the snow. And because the red looked so well upon the white, she thought to herself, " Had I now but a child as white as this snow, as red as this blood, and as black as the wood of this frame! "

Soon afterwards a little daughter was born to her, who was as white as snow, and red as blood, and with hair as black as ebony, and so she was named " Snow-White! " But alas when the child was born, the mother died.

About a year afterwards the King married another wife, who was very beautiful, but so proud and haughty that she could not bear any one to be prettier than herself. She possessed a wonderful mirror, and when she stepped before it and said:

" Oh, mirror, mirror on the wall,
Who is the fairest of us all? "

it replied:

"Thou art the fairest, lady Queen."

Then she was pleased, for she knew that the mirror spoke truly.

Little Snow-White, however, grew up and became prettier and prettier, and when she was seven years old she was as beautiful as the noon-day, and fairer far than the Queen herself. When the Queen now asked the mirror:

" Oh, mirror, mirror on the wall,
Who is the fairest of us all? "

It replied:

> "Thou wert the fairest, lady Queen;
> Snow-White is fairest now, I ween."

This answer so frightened the Queen that she became yellow with envy. From that hour, whenever she saw Snow-White, she hated the maiden more.

Her envy and jealousy increased, so that she had no rest day or night, till at length she said to a huntsman, "Take the child away into the forest. You must kill her, and bring me her heart and tongue for a token."

The huntsman listened, and took the maiden away; but when he drew out his knife to kill her, she began to cry, "Ah, dear huntsman,

give me my life! I will run into the wild forest, and never come home again."

This speech softened the huntsman's heart, and her beauty so touched him that he took pity on her, and said, "Well, run away then, poor child." But he thought to himself, " The wild beasts will soon devour you." Still, he felt as if a stone had been taken from his heart, because her death was not by his hand. Just at that moment a young boar came roaring along to the spot, and as soon as he caught sight of it the huntsman pursued it, and, killing it, took its tongue and heart, and carried them to the Queen for a token of his deed.

But now the poor little Snow-White was left motherless and alone, and overcome with grief. She was bewildered at the sight of so many trees, and knew not which way to turn. Presently she set off running, and ran over stones and through thorns; and wild beasts bellowed as she passed them, but they did her no harm. She ran on till her feet refused to go further, and as it was getting dark, and she saw a little house near, she went in to rest.

In this cottage everything was very small, but more neat and elegant than I can tell you. In the middle stood a little table with a white cloth over it, and seven little plates upon it, each plate having a spoon and a knife and a fork, and there were also seven little mugs. Against the wall were seven little beds ranged in a row, each covered with a white counterpane. Little Snow-White, being both hungry and thirsty, ate a morsel of bread and meat from each plate and drank a little out of each mug, for she did not wish to take away the whole share of any one.

After that, because she was so tired, she laid herself down on one bed, but it did not suit; she tried another, but that was too long; a fourth was too short, a fifth too hard, but the seventh was just right, and, tucking herself up in it, she went to sleep.

When it became quite dark the masters of the cottage came home, seven Dwarfs, who dug and delved for ore in the mountains. They first lighted seven little lamps, and noticed at once—for they illuminated the whole apartment—that somebody had been there, for everything was not in the order in which they had left it.

The first Dwarf asked, " Who has been sitting on my chair ? " The second, "Who has been eating off my plate ? " The third, "Who has been nibbling at my bread ? " The fourth, " Who has been at my meat ? " The fifth, "Who has been meddling with my fork ? " The sixth grumbled out, " Who has been cutting with my knife ? " The seventh said, "Who has been drinking out of my mug ? " Then the first, looking round, began again. "Who has been lying in my bed ? " he asked, for he saw that the sheets were tumbled. At these words the others came, and looking at their beds, cried out too, " Someone has been lying in our beds ! "

But the seventh little man, running up to his, saw Snow-White sleeping in it; so he called his companions, who shouted with wonder, and held up their seven lamps, so that the light fell upon the maiden.

" Oh ! oh ! " they exclaimed, " what a beauty she is ! " and they were so much delighted that they would not awaken her, but left her to her repose, and the seventh Dwarf, in whose bed she was, slept with each of his fellows one hour, and so passed the night.

As soon as morning dawned Snow-White awoke, and was quite frightened when she saw the seven little men; but they were very

friendly, and asked her what she was called. " My name is Snow-White," was her reply.

" Why have you entered our cottage? " they asked.

Then she told them how her stepmother would have had her killed but the huntsman had spared her life; and how she had wandered about the whole day until at last she had found their house. When her tale was finished, the Dwarfs said " Will you look after our house—be our cook, make the beds, wash, sew and knit for us, and keep everything in neat order? If so, we will keep you here, and you shall want for nothing."

And Snow-White answered, " Yes, with all my heart I will." And so she remained with them, and kept their house in order. In the mornings the Dwarfs went into the mountains and searched for ore and gold and in the evenings they came home and found their supper ready for them.

During the day the maiden was left alone, and therefore the good Dwarfs warned her and said, " Be careful of your stepmother, who

will soon know of your being here; therefore let nobody enter the cottage."

The Queen, meanwhile, supposing she had eaten the heart and tongue of her stepdaughter, did not think but that she was beyond all comparison the most beautiful of every one around. One day she stepped before her mirror and said:

"Oh, mirror, mirror on the wall,
Who is the fairest of us all?"

and it replied:

"Thou wert the fairest, lady Queen;
Snow-White is fairest now, I ween.
Amid the forest, darkly green,
She lives with Dwarfs—the hills between."

This reply frightened her, for she knew that the mirror spoke the truth, and she realised that the huntsman had deceived her, and that Snow-

White was still alive. Now she thought and thought how she should accomplish her purpose, for so long as she was not the fairest in the whole country, jealousy left her no rest.

At last a thought struck her, and she dyed her face and clothed herself as a pedlar woman, so that no one could recognise her. In this disguise she went over the seven hills to the house of the seven Dwarfs, knocked at the door, and called out, " Fine goods for sale! Beautiful goods for sale!"

Snow-White peeped out of the window, and said, " Good-day, my good woman. What have you to sell? " " Fine goods, beautiful goods! " she replied, " stays of all colours;" and she held up a pair which was made of variegated silks. " I may let in this honest woman," thought Snow-White; and she unbolted the door and bargained for one pair of stays. " You can't think, my dear, how it becomes you! " exclaimed the old woman. " Come, let me lace it up for you."

Snow-White suspected nothing, and let her do as she wished, but the old woman laced her up so quickly and so tightly that all her breath went, and she fell down like one dead. " Now," thought the old woman to herself, hastening away—" now am I once more the most beautiful of all!

Not long after her departure, at eventide, the seven Dwarfs came home, and were much frightened at seeing their dear little maid lying on the ground, and neither moving nor breathing, as if she were dead. They raised her up, and when they saw she was laced too tight they cut the stays in pieces, and presently she began to breathe again, and little by little she revived.

When the Dwarfs now heard what had taken place, they said, " The old pedlar woman was no other than your wicked stepmother: take care of yourself, and let no one enter when we are not with you."

Meanwhile the old Queen had reached home, and, going before her mirror, she repeated her usual words:

" Oh, mirror, mirror on the wall,
Who is the fairest of us all? "

And it replied as before:

> "Thou wert the fairest, lady Queen;
> Snow-White is fairest now, I ween.
> Amid the forest, darkly green,
> She lives with Dwarfs—the hills between."

As soon as it had finished, all her blood rushed to her heart, for she was frightened to hear that Snow-White was yet living. "But now," thought she to herself, "will I contrive something which shall destroy her completely."

Thus saying, she made a poisoned comb by arts which she understood, and then disguising herself, she took the form of an old widow. She went over the seven hills to the house of the seven Dwarfs, and, knocking at the door, called out, "Good wares to sell to-day!" Snow-White peeped out, and said, "You must go away for I dare not let you in."

"But still you may look," said the old woman, drawing out her poisoned comb and holding it up. The sight of this pleased the maiden so much that she allowed herself to be persuaded, and opened the door. As soon as she had bought the comb, the old woman said, "Now, let me for once comb you properly," and Snow-White consented. But scarcely was the comb drawn through the hair when the poison began to work, and the maiden soon fell down senseless. "You pattern of beauty," cried the wicked Queen, "it is now all over with you;" and so saying, she departed.

Fortunately, evening soon came, and the seven Dwarfs returned, and whenever they saw Snow-White lying like dead upon the ground, they suspected the old Queen, and soon discovering the poisoned comb, they immediately drew it out, and the maiden presently revived and related all that had happened. Then they warned her again against the wicked stepmother, and bade her to open the door to nobody.

Meanwhile the Queen, on her arrival home, had again consulted her mirror, and received the same answer as twice before. This made her tremble and foam with rage and jealousy, and she swore Snow-White should die, if it cost her her own life. Thereupon she went into an inner secret chamber where no one could enter, and there made an apple of the most deep and subtle poison. Outwardly it looked nice enough, and had rosy cheeks which would make the mouth of every one who looked at it water; but whoever ate the smallest piece of it would surely die.

As soon as the apple was ready, the old Queen again dyed her face and clothed herself like a peasant's wife, and then over the seven mountains to the seven Dwarfs' house she made her way. She knocked at the door, and Snow-White stretched out her head, and said, " I dare not let anyone enter; the seven Dwarfs have forbidden me."

" That is hard for me," said the old woman, " for I must take back my apples ; but there is one which I will give you."

" No," answered Snow-White; " no, I dare not take it."

" What ! Are you afraid of it ? " cried the old woman. " There, see, I will cut the apple in halves; do you eat the red cheeks, and I will eat the core." (The apple was so artfully made that the red cheeks alone were poisoned). Snow-White very much wished for the beautiful apple, and when she saw the woman eating the core she could no longer resist, but, stretching out her hand, took the poisoned part. Scarcely had she placed a piece in her mouth than she fell down dead upon the ground.

Then the Queen, looking at her with glittering eyes, and laughing bitterly, exclaimed, " White as snow, red as blood, black as ebony! This time the Dwarfs cannot re-waken you."

When she reached home she consulted her mirror:

" Oh, mirror, mirror on the wall,
Who is the fairest of us all ? "

It answered:

"Thou art the fairest, lady Queen."

Then at last her envious heart was at rest.

When the little Dwarfs returned home in the evening they found Snow-White lying lifeless on the ground. They raised her up, and searched if they could find anything poisonous, unlaced her, and even uncombed her hair, and washed her with water and with wine; but nothing availed—the dear child was really and truly dead. Then they laid her upon a bier, and all seven placed themselves around it, and wept for three days without ceasing.

Afterwards they would bury her; but she looked still so fresh and lifelike, and even her red cheeks had not deserted her, so they said to one another, "We cannot bury her in the black ground," and they ordered a case to be made of transparent glass. In this one could view her on all sides, and the Dwarfs wrote her name with golden letters upon the glass, saying that she was a King's daughter. They placed the glass case upon the ledge of a rock, and one of them always remained by it, watching.

For a long time Snow-White lay peacefully in her case, and changed not, but looked as if she were only asleep, for she was still white as snow, red as blood, and black-haired as ebony. By and by it happened that a King's son was travelling in the forest and came to the Dwarfs' house to pass the night. He soon perceived the glass case upon the rock, and the beautiful maiden lying within, and he read also the golden inscription.

When he had examined it, he said to the Dwarfs, " Let me have this case, and I will pay what you like for it."

But the Dwarfs replied, " We will not sell it for all the gold in the world."

" Then give it to me," said the Prince, " for I cannot live without Snow-White. I will honour and protect her so long as I live."

When the Dwarfs saw he was so much in earnest, they pitied him, and at last gave him the case, and the Prince ordered it to be carried away on the shoulders of his attendants. Presently it happened that they stumbled over a rut, and with the shock the piece of poisoned apple which lay in Snow-White's mouth fell out. Very soon she opened her eyes, and, raising the lid of the glass case, she rose up and asked, " Where am I? "

Full of joy, the Prince answered, " You are safe with me," and he related to her what she had suffered, and how he would rather have her than any other for his wife; and he asked her to accompany him home to the castle of the King, his father. Snow-White consented, and when they arrived there the wedding between them was celebrated with great splendour and magnificence.

By chance Snow-White's stepmother was invited to the wedding, and, when she was dressed in all her finery she first stepped in front of her mirror, and asked:

" Oh, mirror, mirror on the wall,
Who is the fairest of us all? "

and it replied:

" Thou wert the fairest, oh lady Queen;
The Prince's bride is more fair, I ween."

At these words the old Queen was in a fury. At first she resolved not to go to the wedding, but she could not resist the wish for a sight of the young Queen. As soon as she entered she recognised Snow-White, and was so terrified with rage and astonishment that she fell down in a fit, from which she was never to recover.

RAPUNZEL

ONCE upon a time there lived a man and his wife who much wished to have a child, but for a long time in vain. These people had a little window in the back part of their house, out of which one could see into a beautiful garden, where grew the finest flowers and vegetables; but it was surrounded by a high wall, and no one dared to go in because it belonged to a Witch, who possessed great power, and who was feared by the whole world.

One day the woman stood at this window looking into the garden, and there she saw a bed which was filled with the most beautiful radishes, and which seemed so fresh and green that the very sight of them made her happy. Then a great desire seized her to eat of them. This wish tormented her daily, and as she knew that she could not have them, she fell ill and looked very pale and miserable. This frightened her husband, who asked her, " What ails you, my dear wife ? "

" Ah ! " she replied, " if I cannot have some of these radishes to eat out of the garden behind the house, I shall die ! "

The husband, loving her very much, thought. " Rather than let my wife die, I must fetch her some radishes, cost what they may."

So, in the gloom of the evening, he climbed the wall of the Witch's garden, and, snatching a handful of radishes in great haste, brought them to his wife, who made herself a salad with them, which she enjoyed extremely. However, they were so good and so well-flavoured that the next day she felt the same desire for the radishes. She could not rest, so that her husband was obliged to promise to fetch her some more.

So, in the evening, he made himself ready, and began clambering up the wall. But oh! how terribly frightened he was, for there he saw the old Witch standing before him. " How dare you," she began, looking at him with a frightful scowl—" how dare you climb over into my garden to take away my radishes like a thief? Evil shall befall you for this."

"Ah!" replied he, "please pardon me. I have done this from great necessity: my wife saw your radishes from her window, and took such a fancy to them that she would have died if she had not eaten of them." Then the Witch in a passion, cried, "If she behaves as you say, I will let you take away all the radishes you please; but I make one condition—when it is born, you must give me your child. All shall go well with it, and I will care for it like a mother."

In his anxiety the man consented, and when a child was born the Witch appeared, gave the child the name "Rapunzel," and took it away.

Rapunzel grew to be the most beautiful child under the sun, and when she was twelve years old the Witch shut her up in a tower which had neither stairs nor door, and only one little window at the top. When the Witch wished to enter, she stood beneath, and called out:

"Rapunzel! Rapunzel!
Let down your hair."

For Rapunzel had long and beautiful golden hair, and, as soon as she heard the Witch's voice, she unbound her tresses, opened the window, and the hair fell down twenty ells, and the Witch mounted up by it.

After a couple of years had passed away, it happened that the King's son was riding through the wood, and came by the tower. There he heard a song so beautiful that he stood still. It was Rapunzel's sweet voice. The King's son wanted to climb to her but he could find no door.

So he rode home, but the song had touched his heart so much that he went every day to the forest and listened. As he stood thus one day behind a tree, he saw the Witch come up, and heard her call out:

"Rapunzel! Rapunzel!
Let down your hair."

Then Rapunzel let down her tresses, and the Witch mounted up. "Is that the ladder by which one must climb? Then I will try my luck too," said the Prince. And the very next day he went to the tower and called:

"Rapunzel! Rapunzel!
Let down your hair."

Then the tresses fell down, and he climbed up.

Rapunzel was frightened at first when a man appeared, but the King's son talked in a loving way to her, and told how his heart had been so moved by her singing that he had no peace until he had seen her.

So Rapunzel lost her terror, and when he asked her if she would have him for a husband, and she saw that he was young and handsome, she thought, "How wonderful it would be to leave forever the old woman;" so saying "Yes," she put her hand within his. "I will willingly go with you, but I know not how I am to descend. When you come, bring with you a skein of silk each time, out of which I will weave a ladder, and when it is ready I will come down by it, and you must take me upon your horse."

Then they agreed that they should never meet till the evening, as the Witch came in the daytime. The old woman found out nothing, until one day Rapunzel innocently said, " Tell me, mother, how it happens you find it more difficult to come up to me than the King's young son, who is with me in a moment! "

" Oh, you wicked child! " exclaimed the Witch; " what did I hear? I thought I had separated you from all the world, and yet you have deceived me." And, seizing Rapunzel's beautiful hair in a fury, she took a pair of scissors in her right hand. Snip, snap, she cut off all her beautiful tresses, and they fell in a golden heap upon the ground.

" Never more will you see a living soul," cried the hard-hearted witch. And taking the poor maiden by the hand she spirited her away to a far distant desert. There she left her in great misery and grief.

But in the evening of the same day on which she had carried off Rapunzel, the old Witch bound fast to the window-latch the maiden's tresses. Presently the King's son came, and called out:

" Rapunzel! Rapunzel!
Let down your hair! "

She let down the tresses and the Prince mounted; but when he got to the top he found, not his dear Rapunzel, but the Witch, who looked at him with furious and wicked eyes.

" Aha! " she exclaimed scornfully, " you have come to fetch your golden maiden; but the beautiful bird sits no longer in her nest, singing; the cat has taken her away, and will now scratch out your eyes. To you Rapunzel is lost. Never again will you see her."

Upon hearing these cruel words, the Prince lost his senses with grief, and in his bewilderment sprang out of the window of the tower. His life he escaped with, but the thorns into which he fell put out his eyes. So he wandered blind, in the forest, eating berries and roots, and doing nothing but weep and lament for the loss of his dear Rapunzel.

He wandered about thus, in great misery, for some few years, and at last arrived at the desert where Rapunzel lived in sorrow. Hearing a voice singing a melancholy tune, he followed its direction. As he approached, Rapunzel recognised her Prince and fell upon his neck and wept. Two of her tears moistened his eyes, and they became clear again, so that he could again see as well as ever.

Together they left that desolate place and after many weeks of wandering, they arrived in the Prince's kingdom, There they were received with great demonstrations of joy and carried off in triumph to the palace where they were to live long, contented and happy.

What became of the old Witch no one ever knew.

LITTLE RED-CAP

ONCE upon a time there lived a sweet little maiden, whose grandmother was so fond of her that she was never able to do enough for her.

One day her grandmother gave the little girl a red velvet cap; and as it fitted so well, she would never wear anything else. And so she was called Little Red-Cap.

One day her mother said to her, " Come, Red-Cap, here is a piece of nice meat, and a bottle of wine; take these to your grandmother; she is ill and weak, and will enjoy them. Go carefully and do not run, lest you should fall and break the bottle."

" I will be very careful," promised Red-Cap.

Her grandmother dwelt far away in the wood, and as Little Red-Cap entered among the trees, she met a wolf. She did not know what a wicked beast it was, and was not at all afraid. " Good-day, Little Red-Cap," he said.

" Good-day, Wolf," said she.

" Where are you going so early, Little Red-Cap ? "

" To my grandmother's," she replied.

" What are you carrying under your apron ? "

" Meat and wine," she answered. " My grandmother is ill and needs strengthening."

" Where does your grandmother live ?" asked the Wolf.

" A good quarter of an hour's walk farther into the forest. The cottage stands under three great oak trees; near it are some nut-bushes, by which you will easily know it."

But the Wolf thought to himself, " She is a nice tender thing, and will taste better than the old woman: I must act craftily, that I may snap them both up."

Presently he came up again to Little Red-Cap, and said, " Just look at the beautiful flowers which grow around you; listen how beautifully the birds sing. You walk on as if you were going to school; see how merry everything is around you in the forest."

So Little Red-Cap opened her eyes; and when she saw how the sunbeams glanced and danced through the trees, and how the flowers were blooming in her path, she thought, " I shall take my grandmother a fresh nosegay; it is early yet and I can still get there in good time." She ran into the forest, going deeper and deeper among the trees in search of more beautiful flowers. The Wolf, meanwhile, ran straight to the house of the old grandmother, and knocked at the door.

" Who's there ? " asked the old lady.

" Only Little Red-Cap, bringing you some meat and wine: please open the door," replied the Wolf.

" Lift up the latch," cried the grandmother; " I am too weak to get up."

So the Wolf lifted the latch, and the door flew open; and, jumping without a word on to the bed, he gobbled up the poor old woman. Then putting on her clothes, the Wolf tied her cap over his head, got into bed and drew the blankets over him.

All this time Red-Cap was gathering flowers; and when she had plucked as many as she could carry, she remembered her grandmother and made haste to the cottage. She wondered very much to see the

door wide open, but she went into the room saying, " Good-morning grandmother! " She received no answer, so she went up to the bed, and drew back the curtains. There lay her grandmother, as she thought, looking very fierce.

" Oh, grandmother, what great ears you have! "

" The better to hear with," was the reply.

" And what great eyes you have! "

" The better to see with."

" And what great hands you have! "

" The better to touch you with."

" But grandmother, what great teeth you have! "

" The better to eat you with; " and scarcely were the words out of his mouth than the Wolf sprang out of bed and swallowed up poor Little Red-Cap.

As soon as the Wolf had satisfied his appetite, he lay down again in the bed, and began to snore very loudly. A huntsman passing by overhead him, and thought, " How loudly the old woman snores! I must see if she wants anything."

So he stepped into the cottage; and when he came to the bed, he saw the Wolf lying in it. " What ! do I find you here, you old sinner! I have long sought you," exclaimed he; and taking aim with his gun, he shot the old Wolf dead.

Some folks say that this story is not the true one, but that one day, when Red-Cap was taking some baked meats to her grandmother, a Wolf met her, and wanted to mislead her. She went straight on, however and told her grandmother that she had met a wicked Wolf, who looked as if he would have liked to eat her.

So her grandmother said, " Let us shut the door fast."

Soon afterwards the Wolf knocked at the door and exclaimed, " I am Red-Cap, grandmother; I bring you some roast meat." But they kept quite still, and did not open the door. The Wolf crept several times round the house and at last jumped on the roof. He meant to wait till Red-Cap went home in the evening, then sneak after her and devour her in the darkness.

The old woman, however, saw what the rascal intended. Before the door stood a great stone trough, and she said to Little Red-Cap, " Take this pail, child: yesterday I boiled some sausages in this water; go pour it into that stone trough." Red-Cap poured until the trough was quite full. The Wolf sniffed the smell of sausages, and smacked his lips, and wished very much to taste. At last he stretched his neck too far over, so that he lost his balance, and slipped off the roof right into the great trough beneath, where he promptly drowned. Little Red-Cap ran home in high glee and no one sorrowed for Mr. Wolf.

Stories by

HANS ANDERSEN

THE REAL PRINCESS

THERE was once a Prince who wished to marry a Princess; but she must be a real Princess. He travelled all over the world hoping to find such a lady; but there was always something wrong. Princesses he found in plenty; but whether they were real Princesses it was impossible for him to decide, for now one thing, now another, seemed to him not quite right. At last he returned to his palace quite cast down, because he wished so much to find a real Princess.

One evening a fearful tempest arose. It thundered and lightened, and the rain poured down from the sky in torrents. All at once there was heard a violent knocking at the door, and the old King, the Prince's father, went out himself to open it.

It was a Princess who was standing outside the door. She was in a sad condition—the water trickled from her hair and her clothes clung to her body. She said she was a real Princess.

"Ah, we shall soon see about that!" thought the old Queen-mother. However, she said not a word of what she was going to do; but went quietly into the bedroom, took all the bedclothes off the bed, and put three little peas on the bedstead. She then laid twenty mattresses one upon another over the three peas, and put twenty feather beds over the mattresses. Upon this bed the Princess was to pass the night.

The next morning she was asked how she had slept. "Oh, very badly indeed!" she replied. "I have scarcely closed my eyes the whole night through. I do not know what was in my bed, but I had something hard under me, and am black and blue all over."

Now it was plain that the lady must be a real Princess, since she had been able to feel the three little peas through the twenty mattresses and twenty feather-beds. None but a real Princess could have had such a delicate sense of feeling.

The Prince accordingly made her his wife, being now convinced that he had found a real Princess. The three peas were, however, put into the cabinet of curiosities, where they are still to be seen, provided they are not lost.

THUMBELINA

THERE was once a woman whose one desire was to have a tiny child, but she did not know where to find one. One day she went to an old witch and said to her:

" With all my heart I should like a little child; will you tell me where I can find one? "

" Oh, that is easy! " said the old witch. " Here is a barley corn which is *very* special—it is not like those which grow in the farmer's field and which he feeds to his hens. Put it in a flower head—then you will see something."

" Oh, thank you! " said the woman and gave the kind witch a piece of silver.

When she arrived home she planted the barley-corn and immediately a large and beautiful flower began to grow from it; it looked rather like a tulip but the petals remained shut just as if it were still a bud.

" That is a charming flower," said the woman and kissed its red and gold petals: she was still caressing the flower when it opened with a loud snap. Before her eyes it had blossomed into a tulip. And right in the heart of the flower where the stalk grew, sat a tiny maiden, fair and lovely to look upon but no bigger than a thumb; and for this reason she was named Thumbelina.

A pretty painted walnut shell served Thumbelina as a cradle, violet petals were her mattress and a rose petal she had for a cover. There she slept at nights; but in the daytime she played on the table. There the woman had placed a plate round which lay a circle of flowers whose stems rested in the water and on a leaf Thumbelina would sit and sail from one side of the plate to the other, using for oars, two white horse hairs.

One night, while Thumbelina lay in her pretty little bed, there came stealing through the open window an old toad.

The toad was ugly, large and wet and she hopped right down on to the table where Thumbelina lay sleeping under her red rose petal.

"Ah, this little one would make a fine wife for my son," said the toad to herself, and seizing the walnut shell in which Thumbelina slept, she hopped off through the window and down into the garden.

There a broad brook flowed between swampy, muddy banks and down in the mud lived the toad with her son. He was also large and ugly—the very picture of his mother. "Koack, Koack," was all he could say when he saw the pretty little maiden in the walnut shell.

"Be quiet!" said the toad, "she will wake up and run away from us! She is as light as a feather, indeed so small and light is she that we shall lay her on a broad water-lily leaf in the middle of the brook—it will be just right for her, like an island. Then she cannot run away but stay there safely while we get ready a guest room deep in the mud where she will live with us."

In the middle of the brook there grew many water lilies with broad green leaves: they looked as if they were swimming on the water. The leaf farthest away from the bank was the biggest of all and to this one the toad swam out and set down the walnut shell containing Thumbelina.

When the poor little maiden woke up early next morning and saw where she was, she began to cry bitterly. Water—there was nothing but water round the great green leaf. She could not possibly reach

land. In the mud below the bank, the old toad was busily decorating the guest room with rushes and golden water-lily buds. She was arranging everything as beautifully as she could for her new daughter-in-law. When she had completed her preparations, the old toad and her ugly son swam out to the lily leaf where they had left Thumbelina. First they wanted to fetch her pretty little bed which they would put in the bridal chamber before she herself arrived.

The old toad curtsied deeply to her, saying, " May I present to you your husband with whom you will dwell most comfortably in the swamp."

" Koack, Koack! " was again all that her son could say. Then they took the little bed and swam off to the bank with it.

All alone again on her lily leaf island, Thumbelina sat weeping. She did not want to live with the ugly toad or marry her ugly son.

But the little fish who swam under the water had seen the old toad and heard all that she had said, and pushing their heads out of the water they looked at the tiny maiden. How pleased they were at the sight of the fair Thumbelina. No, never, they decided should she go down into the swamp to live with the ugly toads. And they gathered round the stem of the water lily below the surface and began to nibble through the stalk which held it up. Suddenly, the leaf, parted from its stem, began to float down the brook with Thumbelina on it—on and on it sailed, and very soon was quite out of reach of the toad and her ugly son.

Thumbelina swept past many towns, both large and small and the birds in the bushes saw her and sang, " What a dear little maiden! " On and on the leaf floated until Thumbelina had reached another country.

A little white butterfly which never tired of flying round her, at last fluttered down on to the leaf beside her, so much did it like the little maiden.

Thumbelina was delighted that the toad could no longer reach her and the journey became ever more beautiful. The sun shone on the water and made it glitter like gold, and Thumbelina, taking off her belt, tied one end round the butterfly and fastened the other end to the leaf; so drawn by the butterfly she glided on even faster.

Suddenly a great cockchafer flew by, and catching sight of Thum-

belina, flew down and in its claws snatched up the slender figure and flew off with her into a tree. The water-lily leaf floated off down the brook still pulled by the butterfly which was quite unable to free itself. It was bad enough for the cockchafer to have carried off Thumbelina but it was all the sadder for the beautiful white butterfly bound fast to the leaf and quite unable to escape. But the cockchafer did not care. It just sat with Thumbelina on a leaf, gave her nectar to sup and told her how beautiful she was. Later, all the other cockchafers who lived in the tree came to visit them. They studied Thumbelina from all sides and the cockchafer wives turned up their feelers and tittered.

" She has only two feet which make her look very funny! " said some. " She has no feelers," said others. " And how slender round the hips she is. She looks like a human being." " How ugly she is," laughed all the cockchafer wives.

But to the cockchafer who had carried her off, she seemed beautiful. Gradually, however, as all the others thought her so ugly he began to agree with them and soon wanted to have nothing more to do with her. Thumbelina could go whenever she wanted. And flying down from the tree with her he put her on a daisy plant among the grass. There Thumbelina wept because she was so ugly that not one of the cockchafers had liked her. She could not know that she was finer and more beautiful than the most splendid rose.

For the whole summer Thumbelina lived all alone in the forest. She wove for herself a little bed out of blades of grass and hung it under a large burdock leaf which at least gave her shelter from the rain. For food, Thumbelina looked for nectar in the flowers and drank

the dew which gathered on the leaves in the morning. So summer and autumn passed and now the long, cold winter was approaching. All the birds which had sung so sweetly flew away, flowers and leaves withered, the large burdock leaf under which her little bed hung, curled up and all that remained was a dry yellow stalk.

Thumbelina was bitterly cold, her clothes were torn and she was so delicate and tiny that she could not help shivering. It began to snow, and as each snowflake fell on the little maiden it was as if someone had thrown a shovelful of snow over her—she was so very tiny. There she crouched under a dry leaf and trembled with cold.

Then Thumbelina began to wander through the bare trees. At last she came to the edge of the wood and there before her lay a broad cornfield. The corn had long before been gathered in and only the bare dry stubble stood up in the frozen earth.

To Thumbelina this stubble was a great thick forest, and still she shivered with cold. At last she came to the house of a field-mouse who had made her little home in a dry hollow among the stubble. Here the field-mouse lived warm and comfortably in one room and a kitchen—her little dining-room she had completely filled with a store of corn. Thumbelina stopped before the door like a poor beggar-maid and asked if she might have a little piece of barley corn as she had eaten nothing for two days.

"You poor child," said the field-mouse, for at heart she was a kind old field-mouse, "come into my warm room and eat with me!" She thought Thumbelina was very pretty and after a little while she said: "If you like, you can stay here in comfort with me for the winter. In return you must keep my house tidy and tell me stories—listening to stories is my greatest joy!"

So Thumbelina stayed and did what the field-mouse asked and everything went splendidly.

One day the field-mouse said to her: " Very soon now we shall be having a visitor. My neighbour visits me every week. He is better off than I am, owns a fine house with large rooms and has a splendid black velvet coat. If you can please this man, then you will be well cared for. Unfortunately, he can see nothing, so you must tell him the most beautiful stories that you know."

Thumbelina was not very happy about this. She did not want to have anything to do with this neighbour, for he was a mole. Next day, however, the mole made a formal call in his black fur coat. He was rich and also learned, according to the field-mouse. Certainly he was rich. His house was twenty times bigger than that of the field-mouse. Learned he may have been, but he knew nothing of the sun and the beautiful flowers and even said that he hated them.

Thumbelina had now, to please the field-mouse, to sing many songs. The mole liked the little maiden very much and enjoyed her singing, but in the meantime he said nothing, for he was a prudent man.

The mole had dug a long passage through the earth from the field-mouse's house to his own. Along this passage the mole said that the field-mouse and Thumbelina could walk as often as they liked. But to-day he would accompany them, and he requested them not to be afraid of the dead bird which lay in their path. It had died of cold, he said, a short time before at the beginning of winter. The mole seized in his mouth a piece of rotten wood which shone dimly in the dark and went ahead of the others to light the way along the long dark passage. When they came to the place where the dead bird lay, the mole pushed the earth up with his snout so that a large hole appeared in the roof of the passage and daylight streamed down.

Now Thumbelina could see lying on the ground the body of a swallow. Its beautiful wings were pressed against its sides and its legs and head were tucked down under its feathers. The poor bird was frozen stiff. Thumbelina felt so sorry for it and she thought of all the little birds who sang and chirped so happily throughout the summer. But the mole pushed the swallow aside impatiently with its short legs and said: " Now it will whistle no more, the silly creature. What good are birds? All they can do is whistle and sing in summer with no thought for the winter. And yet it is pitiful to think that a little bird should be born only to come to such an end! Thank goodness that can never happen to my children."

"Yes, you are a sensible man!" the field-mouse agreed. "What good does a bird do for all his twittering; when winter comes it must starve and freeze."

All this time Thumbelina was silent. But when the other two turned their backs she bent down and parting the feathers on its head, she kissed the bird's closed eyes. Perhaps it was this very swallow which had sung so beautifully to her in the summer, she thought.

The mole now stopped up the hole through which the daylight was shining and accompanied the ladies home. But that night Thumbelina could not sleep. She rose and with straw began to weave a fine cover. This she carried down the long passage and spread it over the dead bird. She also tucked under him some cotton wool which she had found in the field-mouse's room so that he might lie comfortably on the cold earth.

"Farewell, dear bird," she said, "and thank you for your beautiful summer song which you sang when the trees were still green and the sun shone warmly down."

Then Thumbelina laid her little head on the bird's breast. Suddenly she started up, terrified, for it was as if she had heard a loud knocking. It was the bird's heart. The swallow was not dead after all, only numb with cold. Now that it was growing a little warmer, life was gradually returning.

In autumn when all the swallows fly away to warmer lands there are always one or two who are late in starting; these are the ones which become so cold that often they fall to the ground where they appear to be dead. The snow spreads its blanket over them and soon their little hearts stop beating.

Thumbelina shivered. The bird opposite her, since after all she was only the length of a thumb, seemed suddenly as big as a giant. But at last she took courage, packed the cotton wool tighter round the swallow, fetched the leaf which served him as cover and laid it over the bird's head.

The next night she again stole down to the swallow; now it was really living, but so feebly that it could only open its eyes for a brief moment, to look at Thumbelina, who stood there holding a rotten piece of wood in her hand, for she had no other lamp.

"Thank you, dear child," whispered the sick swallow. "I am beautifully warm now. Soon I will have regained my strength and will fly again into the warm sun!"

"It is still very cold outside," said Thumbelina. "It is snowing and freezing hard; stay in bed where it is warm, and I shall take care of you."

Thumbelina brought the swallow water to drink in a flower petal and the swallow told her how it had torn its wing on a thorn bush and therefore could not fly as quickly as the other swallows who had all departed to warmer lands. It had fallen to the ground and could remember nothing else; it did not know at all how it had arrived there.

The whole winter the swallow remained underground and Thumbelina was good to it; but neither the field-mouse nor the mole knew anything about this. That was a good thing for they did not like the poor swallow.

As soon as spring came and the sun again warmed the earth, the swallow prepared to say good-bye. Thumbelina opened the hole in the roof that the mole had made earlier and then stopped up again, and the sun shone in warmly. The swallow asked Thumbelina if she would not like to come too. She could sit on his back, he said, and together they could fly far off into the greenwood.

But Thumbelina knew that it would annoy the old field-mouse if she went away without saying good-bye.

"No, I cannot do that," she said sadly.

"Good-bye," called the swallow, and flew out into the sunshine. Thumbelina looked after him anxiously, with tears in her eyes; she had become very fond of the swallow.

"Kivit," sang the swallow and flew off into the greenwood.

How unhappy Thumbelina was that she too could not fly into the warm sunshine. The corn grew high over the field-mouse's house and the stalks seemed as tall as forest trees to the little Thumbelina.

"Now that summer is come you must sew for your trousseau," said the field-mouse one day to Thumbelina. "Our neighbour has asked for your hand in marriage—a great honour for a poor maiden! You must have plenty of garments of wool and linen."

Thumbelina began to spin—the field-mouse hired four more spindles and Thumbelina had to weave and spin all day and all night. Each morning the mole called upon her and spoke of nothing but the sun which, thank goodness, he said was not shining so brightly. When the summer came to an end, he complained, the earth would be burned as hard as a brick. It was arranged that the marriage would take place at the beginning of autumn.

Thumbelina was not at all happy about this; she had no love for the tiresome mole. Each morning when the sun rose and each evening when it set she would steal out to the door and wait until the wind, rustling through the ears of corn, parted them and she could see a small patch of shining blue sky. Then Thumbelina thought how gay and beautiful it looked out there and how she wished that the dear swallow would come to see her; but he never came; he had flown far away into the greenwood.

When autumn came, Thumbelina had her trousseau all ready.

"In four weeks' time we shall have the wedding!" said the field-mouse. But Thumbelina wept and said, "I do not want to marry the old mole."

"Tut, tut," said the field-mouse. "If you are silly I shall have to nip you with my white teeth. Is he not a handsome fellow in his black velvet coat? Even the queen would not refuse him. And he has a splendid house and cellar. What more could you want?"

The day of the wedding came. The mole had already arrived to fetch Thumbelina. Deep under the earth she would have to live; never more would she see or feel the warmth of the sun. Thumbelina could scarcely bear the thought of it. She must now say farewell forever to the sun which she had at least sometimes been allowed to see from the field-mouse's door.

" Farewell, fair sun! " said the wretched child, and stretching her arms high towards the sky she stepped a little farther from the field-mouse's door, for the corn had already been cut and here stood only the dried stubble. " Farewell," she cried as she embraced a little red flower which bloomed there. " Send greetings from me to the swallow if you should see him."

" Kivit, Kivit," was suddenly heard above Thumbelina's head, and looking up she saw the swallow. As soon as he caught sight of Thumbelina, he was overjoyed and swooped down to her. Thumbelina told him how unwilling she was to become the mole's wife, and how she would have to live forever underground, where the sun never shone; and she wept bitterly.

"Thumbelina," chirped the swallow, " now that the cold winter is coming, I shall fly far away to a warmer land. Will you not come with me? I shall take you on my back; tie your sash round my neck and we shall fly from the hateful mole and his dark room—fly away over the mountains to a land where the sun shines even more brightly than it does here, where it is always summer and always beautiful flowers bloom. Fly with me, dear little Thumbelina, who saved my life when I lay frozen in the dark cellar of the earth."

" How I should love to come with you! " cried Thumbelina, overjoyed, and settling herself at once on the swallow's back with her feet on his outstretched wings, she tied her sash round his strongest feathers. Then the swallow flew high into the air above wood and lake and over high mountains, where the snow never melted. When Thumbelina began to shiver in the cold air she crouched under the bird's warm feathers, stretching out only her little head to see all the wonders which lay below.

At last they came to the warm lands. There the sun shone brighter,

the sky was twice as high and on the trees and hedges grew the most beautiful green and blue grapes. In the woods hung lemons and oranges, there was a scent of myrtle and peppermint and in the village streets children played with large bright butterflies.

But the swallow flew on and the landscape became more and more beautiful. Under the lovely green trees on a blue lake stood an ancient castle of snow-white marble; vines climbed the high pillars and far above many swallows' nests were perched. In one of these lived the little swallow who had brought Thumbelina here.

"This is my home!" said the swallow. "Look for the most beautiful flower which blooms there and I shall put you down in it and you will be happier than you have ever been before!"

"How beautiful!" exclaimed Thumbelina, clapping her hands. Down there lay a great white marble pillar which had fallen to the ground and broken into three pieces. Between the pieces grew the most marvellous white flowers. The swallow flew down and set Thumbelina on one of their broad petals. But how astonished Thumbelina was! In the middle of the flower sat a tiny man as white and transparent as if he were made of glass. He wore a golden crown on his head, wings grew from his shoulders and most wonderful of all he was no larger than Thumbelina.

In each of the flowers lived a little man or a little woman but this one was king of them all.

"How handsome he is," whispered Thumbelina to the swallow. The little prince at first shrank back from the swallow who seemed to him as large as a giant. But when he saw Thumbelina he was very happy—here was the most beautiful maiden that he had ever seen. Taking the gold crown from his head he placed it on Thumbelina's and asked her her name, and begged her to become his wife. Then, he said, she would be queen of all the flowers.

This was indeed quite a different suitor from the hateful frog's son or the boring mole in his black velvet coat. Thumbelina said " yes " to the handsome prince. And from every flower stepped little people so slender and delicate that one could not help admiring them all. Each one of them brought a gift to Thumbelina, their queen. The best present of all was a pair of beautiful wings which were fastened to Thumbelina's shoulders so that she could fly from flower to flower. This was her greatest joy.

The little swallow in his nest above, sang to her as sweetly as he knew how, but in his heart he was very sad. He held Thumbelina very dear and was unhappy at the thought of being separated from her.

" You shall no longer be called Thumbelina," said the flower prince to his delicate little bride. " You are much too beautiful for such an ugly name. We shall call you Queen Maia."

" Farewell, farewell," called the swallow and flew off from the sunny land on his way back to the North. There he had a little nest which he had built just above the window where lived the man who told this story.

" Kivit, Kivit," he sang and it is thanks to the swallow that we know the story of Thumbelina.

THE LITTLE MATCH-GIRL

IT was dreadfully cold; it was snowing fast, and almost dark; the evening—the last evening of the old year—was drawing in. But, cold and dark as it was, a poor little girl, with bare head and feet, was still wandering about the streets.

When she left her home she had slippers on, but they were much too large for her—indeed, they belonged to her mother—and had dropped off her feet while she was running very fast across the road, to get out of the way of two carriages. One of the slippers was not to be found; the other had been snatched up by a little boy, who ran off with it, thinking it might serve him as a doll's cradle.

So the little girl now walked on, her bare feet red and blue with the cold. She carried a small bundle of matches in her hand, and a good many more in her tattered apron. No one had bought any of them the livelong day—no one had given her a single penny. Trembling with cold and hunger she crept on, the picture of sorrow—poor little child!

The snow-flakes fell on her long fair hair, which curled in such pretty ringlets over her shoulders; but she did not think of her own beauty, or of the cold. Lights were glimmering through every window, and the savour of roast goose reached her from several houses; it was New Year's Eve, and it was of this that she thought.

In a corner formed by two houses, one of which projected beyond the other, she sat down, drawing her little feet close under her, but in vain—she could not warm them. She dared not go home; she had sold no matches, earned not a single penny, and her father would be furious with her. Besides, her home was almost as cold as the street, for it was an attic; and although the larger of the many chinks in the roof were stopped up with straw and rags, the wind and snow often penetrated through.

Her hands were nearly dead with cold; one little match from her bundle would warm them, perhaps, if she dared light it. She drew one out, and struck it against the wall. Bravo! it was a bright, warm flame, and she held her hands over it. It was quite an illumination for that poor little girl; nay, call it rather a magic taper, for it seemed to her as if she were sitting before a large iron stove with brass ornaments, so beautifully blazed the fire within! The child stretched out her feet to warm them also. Alas! in an instant the flame had died away; the stove vanished; the little girl sat cold and comfortless, with the burnt match in her hand.

A second match was struck against the wall; it kindled and blazed, and, wherever its light fell, the wall became transparent as a veil; the little girl could see into the room within. She saw the table spread with a snow-like damask cloth, on which were ranged shining china dishes. The roast goose stuffed with apples and dried plums stood at one end, smoking hot, and—which was pleasantest of all to see—the goose, with knife and fork still in her breast, jumped down from the dish, and waddled along the floor right up to the poor child.

The match was burned out, and only the thick, hard wall was beside her.

She kindled a third match. Again up shot the flame; and now she was sitting under a most beautiful Christmas-tree, far larger, and far more prettily decked out than one she had seen last Christmas Eve

through the glass doors of the rich merchant's house. Hundreds of wax tapers lighted up the green branches, and tiny painted figures, such as she had seen in the shop windows, looked down from the tree upon her.

The child stretched out her hands towards them in delight, and in that moment the light of the match was quenched; still, however, the Christmas candles burned higher and higher. She beheld them beaming like stars in heaven; one of them fell, the light streaming behind it like a long, fiery tail.

"Now some one is dying," said the little girl softly; for she had been told by her old grandmother—the only person who had ever been kind to her, and who was now dead—that whenever a star falls an immortal spirit returns to the God who gave it. She struck yet another match against the wall; it flamed up, and, surrounded by its light, that same dear grandmother appeared before her, gentle and loving as always, but bright and happy, as she had never looked during her lifetime.

"Grandmother!" exclaimed the child. "Oh, take me with you; I know thou wilt leave me as soon as the match goes out; thou wilt vanish like the warm fire in the stove, like the splendid New Year's feast, like the beautiful Christmas-tree;" and she hastily lighted all the remaining matches in the bundle lest her grandmother should disappear.

And the matches burned with such a blaze of splendour, that noon-day could scarcely have been brighter. Never had the good old grand-mother looked so tall and stately, so beautiful and kind; she took the little girl in her arms, and they both flew together. Joyfully and gloriously they flew—higher and higher, till they were in that place where neither cold, nor hunger, nor pain is ever known. They were in Paradise.

But in the cold morning hour, crouching in the corner of the wall, the poor little girl was found—her cheeks glowing, her lips smiling—frozen to death on the last night of the Old Year. The New Year's sun shone on the lifeless child; motionless she sat there with the matches in her lap, one bundle of them quite burned out.

"She has been trying to warm herself, poor thing!" the people said; but no one knew of the sweet visions she had beheld, or how gloriously she and her grandmother were celebrating their New Year festival.

THE SNOW QUEEN

I. *Which treats of the Mirror and its Fragments*

LISTEN! We are beginning our story! When we arrive at the end of it we shall, it is to be hoped, know more than we do now. There was once a magician! a wicked magician!! a most wicked magician!!! Great was his delight at having constructed a mirror possessing this peculiarity—that everything good and beautiful, when reflected in it, shrank up almost to nothing, whilst those things that were ugly and useless were magnified, and made to appear ten times worse than before.

The loveliest landscapes reflected in this mirror looked like boiled spinach; and the handsomest persons appeared ugly, or as if standing upon their heads, their features being so distorted that their friends could never have recognised them. Moreover, if one of them had a freckle, he might be sure that it would seem to spread over the nose and the mouth; and if a good or pious thought glanced across his mind a wrinkle was seen in the mirror.

All this the magician thought highly entertaining, and he chuckled with delight at his own clever invention. Those who frequented the school of magic where he taught, spread abroad the fame of this wonderful mirror, and declared that by its means the world and its inhabitants might be seen now for the first time as they really were.

They carried the mirror from place to place, till at last there was no country or person that had not been misrepresented in it. Its admirers now wished to fly up to the sky with it, to see if they could not carry on their sport even there. But the higher they flew the more wrinkled did the mirror become; they could scarcely hold it together. They flew on and on, higher and higher, till at last the mirror trembled so fearfully that it escaped from their hands, and fell to the earth, breaking into millions, billions, and trillions of pieces.

And then it caused far greater unhappiness than before, for fragments of it, scarcely so large as a grain of sand, would be flying about in the air, and sometimes get into people's eyes, causing them to view everything the wrong way, or to have eyes only for what was evil and corrupt; each little fragment having retained the peculiar properties of the entire mirror. Some people were so unfortunate as to receive a little splinter into their hearts—that was terrible! The heart became cold and hard, like a lump of ice. Some pieces were large enough to be used as window-panes, but it was of no use to look at one's friends through such panes as those. Other fragments were made into spectacles, and then what trouble people had with setting and re-setting them!

The wicked magician was greatly amused with all this, and he laughed till his sides ached.

There are still some little splinters of this mischievous mirror flying about in the air. We shall hear more about them very soon.

2. *A Little Boy and a Little Girl*

IN a large town, where there are so many houses and inhabitants that there is not room enough for all the people to have a little garden of their own, and where many are obliged to content themselves with keeping a few plants in pots, there dwelt two poor children, whose garden was somewhat larger than a flower-pot.

They were not brother and sister, but they loved each other as much as if they had been, and their parents lived in two attics exactly opposite. The roof of one neighbour's house nearly joined the other—the gutter ran along between—and there was in each roof a little window, so that you could stride across the gutter from one window to the other.

The parents of each child had a large wooden box in which grew herbs for kitchen use, and they had placed these boxes upon the gutter, so near that they almost touched each other. A beautiful little rose-tree grew in each box, scarlet runners entwined their long shoots over the windows, and, uniting with the branches of the rose-trees, formed a flowery arch across the street. The boxes were very high, and the children knew that they might not climb over them, but they often had permission to sit on their little stools, under the rose-tree, and thus they passed many a delightful hour.

But when winter came there was an end to these pleasures. The windows were often frozen over, and then they heated halfpence on the stove, held the warm copper against the frozen pane, and thus made a little round peep-hole, behind which would sparkle a bright gentle eye—one from each window.

The little boy was called Kay, the little girl's name was Gerda. In summer-time they could get out of a window and jump over to each other; but in winter there were stairs to run down, and stairs to run up, and sometimes the wind roared, and snow fell out of doors.

" Those are the white bees swarming there! " said the old grandmother.

" Have they a Queen bee? " asked the little boy; for he knew that the real bees have one.

" They have," said the grandmother. " She flies yonder where they swarm so thickly; she is the largest of them, and never remains upon the earth, but flies up again into the black cloud. Sometimes on a winter's night she flies through the streets of the town, and breathes with her frosty breath upon the windows, and then they are covered with strange and beautiful forms like trees and flowers."

" Yes. I have seen them! " said both the children—they knew that this was true.

" Can the Snow Queen come in here? " asked the little girl.

" If she does come in," said the boy, " I will put her on the warm stove, and then she will melt."

The grandmother stroked Gerda's hair and told them some stories.

And that same evening, after little Kay had gone home, and was half undressed, he crept upon the chair by the window and peeped through the little round hole. Just then a few snow-flakes fell outside, and one, the largest of them, remained lying on the edge of one of the flower-pots.

The snow-flake appeared to grow larger and larger, and at last took the form of a lady dressed in the finest white crape, that seemed composed of millions of star-like particles. She was exquisitely fair and

delicate, but entirely of ice—glittering, dazzling ice; her eyes gleamed like two bright stars, but there was no rest or repose in them.

She nodded at the window and beckoned with her hand. The little boy was frightened and jumped down from the chair; he then fancied he saw a large bird fly past the window.

There was a clear frost next day, and soon afterwards came spring; the trees and flowers budded, the swallows built their nests, the windows were opened, and the little children sat once more in their little garden upon the gutter that ran along the roofs of the houses.

The roses blossomed beautifully that summer, and the little girl had learned a hymn in which there was something about roses; it reminded her of her own. So she sang it to the little boy, and he sang it with her.

Our roses bloom and fade away,
Our Infant Lord abides alway;
May we be blessed His face to see,
And ever little children be!

And the little ones held each other by the hand, kissed the roses, and looked up into the blue sky, talking away all the time. What glorious summer days were those! How delightful it was to sit under those rose-trees, which seemed as if they never intended to leave off blossoming! One day Kay and Gerda were sitting looking at their picture-book full of birds and animals, when suddenly—the clock on the old church tower was just striking five—Kay exclaimed, " Oh, dear! what was that shooting pain in my heart? and now again, something has certainly got into my eye!"

The little girl turned and looked at him. He winked his eyes; no, there was nothing to be seen.

"I believe it is gone," said he; but gone it was not. It was one of those glass splinters from the Magic Mirror, the wicked glass which made everything great and good reflected in it to appear little and hateful, and which magnified everything ugly and mean. Poor Kay had also received a splinter in his heart; it would now become hard and cold like a lump of ice. He felt the pain no longer, but the splinter was there. "Why do you cry?" asked he; "you look so ugly when you cry! There is nothing the matter with me—Fie!" exclaimed he again, "this rose has an insect in it, and just look at this! After all, they are ugly roses, and it is an ugly box they grow in!" Then he kicked the box, and tore off the roses.

"Oh, Kay, what are you doing?" cried the little girl; but when he saw how it grieved her, he tore off another rose, and jumped down through his own window, away from his once dear little Gerda.

Ever afterwards when she brought forward the picture-book, he called it a baby's book; and when her grandmother told stories he interrupted her with a "but," and sometimes, whenever he could manage it, he would get behind her, put on her spectacles, and speak just as she did; he did this in a very droll manner, and so people laughed at him.

Very soon he could mimic everybody in the street. All that was odd and awkward about them Kay could imitate, and his neighbours said, "What a remarkable head that boy has!" But no, it was the glass splinter which had fallen into his eye and the glass splinter which had pierced his heart—it was these which made him regardless of whose feelings he wounded, and even made him tease the little Gerda who loved him so fondly.

His games were now quite different from what they used to be.

One winter's day when it was snowing, he came out with a large burning-glass in his hand, and, holding up the skirts of his blue coat, let the snow-flakes fall upon them. "Now look through the glass, Gerda!" said he, returning to the house. Every snow-flake seemed much larger, and resembled a splendid flower, or a star with ten points; they were quite beautiful. "See, how curious!" said Kay, "these are far more interesting than real flowers—there is not a single blemish in them; they would be quite perfect if only they did not melt."

Soon after this Kay came in again, with thick gloves on his hands, and his sledge slung across his back. He called out to Gerda, "I have got leave to drive in the great square where the other boys play!" and away he went.

The boldest boys in the square used to fasten their sledges firmly to the wagons of the country people, and thus drive a good way along with them; this they thought particularly pleasant. While they were in the midst of their play, a large sledge painted white passed by; in it sat a person wrapped in a rough white fur, and wearing a rough white cap. When the sledge had driven twice round the square, Kay bound to it his little sledge, and was carried on with it. On they went, faster and faster, into the next street.

The person who drove the large sledge turned round and nodded kindly to Kay, just as if they had been old acquaintances; and every time Kay was going to loose his little sledge, turned and nodded again, as if to signify that he must stay: so Kay sat still, and they passed through the gates of the town.

Then the snow began to fall so thickly that the little boy could not see his own hand, but he was still carried on. He tried hastily to un-

loose the cords and free himself from the large sledge, but it was of no use; his little carriage could not be unfastened, and glided on swift as the wind. Then he cried out as loud as he could, but no one heard him —the snow fell and the sledge flew.

Every now and then it made a spring as if driving over hedges and ditches. He was very much frightened; he would have said a prayer but he could remember nothing but the multiplication table.

The snow-flakes seemed larger and larger, and at last they looked like great white fowls. All at once they fell aside, the large sledge stopped, and the person who drove it rose from the seat. He saw that the cap and coat were entirely of snow; that it was a lady, tall and slender, and dazzlingly white—it was the Snow Queen!

"We have driven fast," said she, "but no one likes to be frozen; creep under my bear-skin;" and she seated him in the sledge by her side, and spread her cloak around him. He felt as if he were sinking into a drift of snow.

"Are you still cold?" asked she; and then she kissed his brow. Oh! her kiss was colder than ice. It went to his heart although that was half frozen already; he thought he should die. It was, however, only for a moment; directly afterwards he was quite well, and no longer felt the intense cold around.

"My sledge! do not forget my sledge!" He thought first of that—it was fastened to one of the white fowls, which flew behind with it on his back. The Snow Queen kissed Kay again, and he entirely forgot little Gerda, her grandmother, and all at home.

"Now you must have no more kisses!" said she, "Else I should kiss thee to death."

Kay looked at her, she was so beautiful; a more intelligent, more lovely countenance he could not imagine. She no longer appeared to him to be ice, cold ice, as at the time when she sat outside the window and beckoned to him. In his eyes she was perfect and he felt no fear. He told her how well he could reckon in his head, even fractions; that he knew the number of square miles of every country, and the number of the inhabitants in different towns.

She smiled, and then it occurred to him that, after all, he did not yet know so very much. He looked up into the wide wide space, and she flew with him high up into the black cloud while the storm was raging; it seemed now to Kay as if it were singing songs of olden times.

They flew over woods and over lakes, over sea and over land; beneath them the cold wind whistled, the wolves howled, the snow glittered, and the black crow flew cawing over the plain; while above them shone the moon, clear and tranquil.

Thus did Kay spend the long, long winter night; all day he slept at the feet of the Snow Queen.

3. *The Enchanted Flower Garden*

BUT how fared it with little Gerda when Kay never returned? Where could he be? No one knew, no one could give any account of him. The boys said that they had seen him fasten his sledge to another larger and very handsome one which had driven into the street, and thence through the gates of the town.

No one knew where he was, and many were the tears that were shed. Little Gerda wept much and long, for the boys said he must be dead—

he must have been drowned in the river that flowed not far from the town. Oh, how long and dismal the winter days were now! At last came the spring with its warm sunshine.

" Alas, Kay is dead and gone," said little Gerda.

" That I do not believe," said the sunshine.

" He is dead and gone," said she to the swallows.

" That we do not believe," returned they; and at last little Gerda herself did not believe it.

" I will put on my new red shoes," said she one morning; " those which Kay has never seen; and then I will go down to the river and ask after him."

It was quite early. She kissed her old grandmother, who was still sleeping, put on her red shoes, and went alone through the gates of the town towards the river.

" Is it true," said she to the river, " that thou hast taken my little play-fellow away? I will give thee my red shoes if thou wilt restore him to me! "

And the wavelets of the river flowed towards her in a manner which she fancied was unusual; she fancied that they intended to accept her offer. So she took off her red shoes—though she prized them more than anything else she possessed—and threw them into the stream; but they fell near the shore, and the little waves bore them back to her, as though they would not take from her what she most prized, seeing they had not got little Kay. However, she thought she had not thrown the shoes far enough; so she stepped into a little boat which lay among the reeds by the shore, and standing at the farthest end of it, threw them thence into the water. The boat was not fastened, and her movements in it caused it to glide away from the shore. She saw this, and hastened to get out; but, by the time she reached the other end of the boat, it was more than a yard distant from the land; she could not escape, and the boat glided on.

Little Gerda was much frightened and began to cry, but no one except the sparrows heard her, and they could not carry her back to the land. However, they flew along the banks, and sang, as if to comfort her, " Here we are, here we are! " The boat followed the stream. Little Gerda sat in it quite still; her red shoes floated behind her, but

they could not overtake the boat, which glided along faster than they did.

Beautiful were the shores of that river; lovely flowers, stately old trees, and bright green hills dotted with sheep and cows, were seen in abundance, but not a single human being.

"Perhaps the river may bear me to my dear Kay," thought Gerda, and then she became more cheerful, and amused herself for hours with looking at the lovely country around her. At last she glided past a large cherry orchard, in which stood a little cottage with thatched roof and curious red and blue windows. Two wooden soldiers stood at the door, who presented arms when they saw the little boat approach.

Gerda called to them, thinking that they were alive; but they, naturally enough, made no answer. She came close up to them, for the stream drifted the boat to the land.

Gerda called still louder, and an old lady came out of the house, leaning on a crutch; she wore a large hat, with beautiful flowers painted on it.

"Poor little child!" said the old woman, "the mighty flowing river has indeed borne thee a long, long way;" and she walked right into the water, seized the boat with her crutch, drew it to land, and took out the little girl.

Gerda was glad to be on dry land again, although she was a little afraid of the strange old lady.

"Come and tell me who thou art, and how thou camest hither," said she.

And Gerda told her all, and the old lady shook her head, and said, "Hem! hem!" And when Gerda asked if she had seen little Kay, the lady said that he had not arrived there yet, but that he would be sure to come soon, and that in the meantime Gerda must not be sad. She might stay with her, might eat her cherries, and look at her flowers which were prettier than any picture book, and could each tell her a story.

She then took Gerda by the hand; they went together into the cottage, and the old lady shut the door.

The windows were very high, and the panes were of different coloured glass—red, blue, and yellow—so that when the bright daylight streamed through them various and beautiful were the hues reflected into the room.

Upon a table in the middle was a plate of fine cherries, and of these Gerda was allowed to eat as many as she liked. And while she was eating them, the old dame combed her hair with a golden comb, and the bright flaxen ringlets fell on each side of her pretty, gentle face, which looked as round and as fresh as a rose.

"I have long wished for such a dear little girl," said the old lady. "We shall see if we cannot live happily together." And as she combed little Gerda's hair, the child thought less and less of her foster-brother Kay, for the old lady was an enchantress. She did not, however, follow magic for the sake of mischief, but merely for her own amusement.

Now she wished very much to keep little Gerda, to live with her; so, fearing that if Gerda saw her roses, she would be reminded of her own flowers and of little Kay, and that then she might run away, she went out into the garden, and held her crutch out over all her rose-bushes. At once, although they were full of leaves and blossoms, they sank into the black earth, and no one would have guessed that such plants had ever grown there.

Then she led Gerda into this flower garden. Oh, how beautiful and how fragrant it was! Flowers of all seasons and all climes grew there in perfection—certainly no picture-book could be compared with it.

Gerda jumped with delight, and played among the flowers till the sun set behind the tall cherry-trees. Then a pretty little bed, with crimson silk cushions, stuffed with blue violet leaves, was prepared for her and here she slept so sweetly, and had such dreams as a queen might have on her marriage eve.

The next day she again played among the flowers in the warm sunshine, and many more days were spent in the same manner. Gerda knew every flower in the garden, but, numerous as they were, it seemed to her that one was wanting—she could not tell which.

She was sitting, one day, looking at her hostess's hat, which had flowers painted on it, and, behold, the loveliest among them was a rose! The old lady had entirely forgotten the painted rose on her hat, when she caused the real roses to disappear from her garden and sink into the ground.

" What! " cried Gerda, " are there no roses in the garden? " And she ran from one bed to another, sought and sought again, but no rose was to be found. She sat down and wept, and it so chanced that her tears fell on a spot where a rose-tree had formerly stood, and as soon as her warm tears had moistened the earth, the bush shot up anew, as fresh and as blooming as it was before it had sunk into the ground. Gerda threw her arms around it, kissed the blossoms, and immediately recalled to memory the beautiful roses at home, and her little playfellow Kay.

" Oh, how could I stay here so long! " exclaimed the little maiden. " I left my home to seek for Kay. Do you know where he is? " she asked of the roses; " think you that he is dead? "

" Dead he is not," said the roses. " We have been down in the earth; the dead are there, but not Kay."

" I thank you," said little Gerda; and she went to the other flowers, bent low over their cups, and asked, " Know you not where little Kay is? "

But every flower stood in the sunshine dreaming its own little tale. They related their stories to Gerda, but none of them knew anything of Kay.

The tiger-lily who dreamt of India said:

" Listen to the drums beating, boom! boom! They have but two notes—always boom! boom! Listen to the dirge the women are singing! Listen to the chorus of priests! Clothed in her long red robes stands a Hindu wife on the funeral pyre of her dead husband. How the flames blaze around them, but the Hindu wife stands quite still awaiting death. She thinks no more of living, now that her husband is dead. Always she thinks of him alone. Her eyes burn brighter than the fire which will soon turn her body to ashes. Then will she be reunited with him—so says her faith—in an eternal after-life."

"I do not understand that at all," said little Gerda.

"That is my tale!" said the tiger-lily.

"What says the convolvulus?"

"Hanging over a narrow mountain causeway, behold an ancient baronial castle. Thick evergreens grow amongst the time-stained walls their leafy branches entwine about the balcony, and there stands a beautiful maiden. She bends over the balustrade and fixes her eyes with eager hopes on the road winding beneath. The rose hangs not fresher and lovelier on its stem than she; the apple-blossom, which the wind threatens every moment to tear from its branch, is not more fragile and trembling. Listen to the rustling of her silken robe! Listen to her half-whispered words, 'He comes not yet!'"

"Is it Kay you mean?" asked little Gerda.

"I do but tell you my tale—my dream," replied the convolvulus.

"What says the little snowdrop?"

"Between two trees hangs a swing. Two pretty little maidens, their dresses as white as snow, and with long green ribbons fluttering from their hats, sit and swing themselves in it. Their brother stands up in the swing; he has thrown his arms round the ropes to keep himself steady, for in one hand he holds a little cup, in the other a pipe made of clay; he is blowing soap bubbles. The swing moves and the bubbles fly upwards with bright, ever-changing colours; the last hovers on the edge of the pipe, and moves with the wind. The swing is still in motion, and the little black dog, almost as light as the soap bubbles, rises on his hind feet, and tries to get into the swing also. Away goes the swing; the dog falls, is out of temper, and barks; he is laughed at, and the bubbles burst. A swinging board, a frothy, fleeting picture is my song."

"What you describe may be all very pretty, but you speak mournfully, and there is nothing about Kay.

"What say the hyacinths?"

"There were three fair sisters; transparent and delicate they were. The dress of the one was red, that of the second blue, of the third pure white. Hand in hand they danced in the moonlight beside the quiet lake; they were not fairies, but daughters of men. Sweet was the fragrance when the maidens vanished into the wood; the fragrance grew stronger. Three biers, on which lay the fair sisters, glided out from the depths of the wood, and floated upon the lake; the glow-worms flew shining around like little hovering lamps. Sleep the dancing maidens, or are they dead? The fragrance from the flowers was so sweet and the evening bells pealed out in the distance."

"You make me quite sad," said little Gerda. "Your fragrance is so strong I cannot help thinking of the dead maidens. Alas! and is little Kay dead? The roses say no!"

"Ding dong! ding dong!" rang the hyacinth bells. "We toll not for little Kay—we know him not! We do but sing our own song!"

And Gerda went to the buttercup, which shone so brightly from among her smooth green leaves.

"Thou art like a little bright sun," said Gerda; "tell me, if thou canst, where I may find my play-fellow."

And the buttercup glittered brightly, and looked at Gerda. What song could the buttercup sing? Neither was hers about Kay.

"One bright spring morning, the sun shone warmly upon a little courtyard, the bright beams streamed down the white walls of a neighbouring house, and close by grew the first yellow flower of spring, glittering like gold in the warm sunshine. An old grandmother sat without in her arm-chair, her granddaughter, a pretty, lowly maiden, had just returned home from a short visit; she kissed her grandmother; there was gold, pure gold, in the loving kiss.

" Gold was the flower!
Gold the fresh, bright, morning hour! "

" That is my little story," said the buttercup.

"My poor old grandmother! " sighed Gerda; " yes, she must be sighing for me, just as she wished for little Kay. But I shall soon go home again and take Kay with me. It is of no use to ask the flowers about him; they know only their own songs."

And she folded her little frock round her, that she might run the faster; but, in jumping over the narcissus, it caught her foot, as if wishing to stop her: so she turned and looked at the tall yellow flower, " Have you any news to give me? " She bent over the narcissus, waiting for an answer.

And what said the narcissus?

" I can look at myself! I can see myself! Oh, how sweet is my fragrance! " Up in the little attic-chamber stands a little dancer. She rests sometimes on one leg, sometimes on two. She has trampled the whole world under her feet; she is nothing but an illusion. She pours water from a teapot under a piece of cloth she holds in her hand—it is her bodice; cleanliness is a fine thing! Her white dress hangs on the hook; that has also been washed by the water from the teapot, and dried on the roof of the house. She puts it on, and wraps a saffron-coloured handkerchief round her neck; it makes the dress look all the whiter. With one leg extended, there she stands, as though on a stalk. " I can look at myself, I see myself! "

" I don't care if you do," said Gerda. " You need not have told me that! " and away she ran to the end of the garden.

The gate was closed, but she pressed upon the rusty lock till it broke. The gate sprang open, and little Gerda, with bare feet, ran out into the wide world. Three times she looked back, but there was no one following her; she ran till she could run no longer, and then sat down

to rest upon a large stone. Casting a glance around, she saw that the summer was past, that it was now late in autumn. Of course, she had not remarked this in the enchanted garden, where there were sunshine and flowers all the year round.

"How long I must have stayed there!" said little Gerda. "So, it is now autumn! Well, then, there is no time to lose!" and she rose to pursue her way.

Oh, how sore and weary were her little feet! and all around looked cold and barren. The long willow-leaves had already turned yellow, and the dew trickled down from them like water. The leaves fell off the trees, one by one; the sloe alone bore fruit, and its berries were sharp and bitter. Cold and sad seemed the world that day.

4. *The Prince and the Princess*

GERDA was again obliged to stop and take rest. Suddenly a large raven hopped upon the snow in front of her, saying, "Caw! Caw!—Good-day! Good-day!" He sat for some time on the withered branch of a tree just opposite, eyeing the little maiden, and wagging his head; and he now came forward to make acquaintance, and to ask her whither she was going all alone. That word " alone " Gerda understood right well—she felt how sad a meaning it has.

She told the raven the history of her life and fortunes, and asked if he had seen Kay.

And the raven nodded his head, half doubtfully, and said.

" That is possible—possible."

" Do you think so? " exclaimed Gerda, embracing the raven so fiercely that it is a wonder she did not squeeze him to death.

" More gently—gently! " said the raven. " I think it may be little Kay; but he has certainly forsaken thee for the princess."

" Dwells he with a princess? " asked Gerda.

" Listen to me," said the raven; " but it is difficult to speak your language! Do you understand Ravenish? If so, I can tell you better."

" No! I have never learned Ravenish," said Gerda, " but my grandmother knew it. Oh, how I wish I had learned it! "

" Never mind," said the raven, " I will relate my story in the best manner I can, though bad will be the best; " and he told all he knew.

" In the kingdom in which we are now sitting there dwells a princess—a very clever princess. All the newspapers in the world she has read, and forgotten them again, so clever is she. It is not long since she ascended the throne—which I have heard is not quite so agreeable a situation as one would fancy—and immediately after she began to sing a new song, the theme of which was this, ' Why should I not be wed? ' ' There is some sense in this song! ' said she; and she determined she would marry, but at the same time declared that the man whom she would choose must be able to answer sensibly whenever people spoke to him, and must be good for something else besides merely looking grand and stately.

" The ladies of the court were then all gathered together, in order to be informed of her intentions, at which they were highly delighted, and one exclaimed, ' That is just what I wish; ' and another, that she had lately been thinking of the very same thing. Believe me," continued the raven, " every word I say is true, for I have a tame beloved one who hops at will about the palace, and she has told me all this.

" Proclamations, adorned with borders of hearts, were immediately issued, in which, after giving the rank and titles of the princess, it was set forth that every handsome youth was free to go to the palace and talk with the princess, and that whoever should speak in such a way as showed that he felt himself at home there, would be the one the princess would choose for her husband.

" Yes, indeed," continued the raven, " you may believe me; all this is as true as that I sit here. Young men hastened in droves to the palace; there was a tremendous crowd; but it was all of no use, either the first or the second day. The young men could speak well enough while they were outside the palace gates, but, when they entered, and saw the royal guard in silver uniform, and the lackeys on the staircase in gold, and the spacious salon, they were quite confounded.

" They stood before the throne where the princess sat, and when she spoke to them they could only repeat the last word she had uttered, which, of course, it was not particularly interesting for her to hear over again. It was just as though they had been struck dumb the moment they entered the palace, for as soon as they got out they could talk fast enough. There was a regular procession constantly moving from the gates of the town to the gates of the palace.

" I was there, and saw it with my own eyes," said the raven. " They grew both hungry and thirsty whilst waiting at the palace, but no one could get even so much as a glass of water; to be sure, some of them, wiser than the rest, had brought with them slices of bread-and-butter, but none would give any to his neighbour, for he thought to himself, ' Let him look hungry, and the princess will not choose him '."

" But Kay, little Kay, when did he come ? " asked Gerda. " Was he among the crowd ? "

" Presently, presently; we have just come to him. On the third day arrived a youth with neither horse nor carriage; gaily he marched up to the palace; his eyes sparkled like yours; he had long, beautiful hair, but was very meanly clad."

" That was Kay ! " exclaimed Gerda, " had he a sledge, for he had a sledge with him when he left home ? "

" It is possible," rejoined the raven. " I did not look very closely, but this I heard from my beloved, that when he entered the palace gates and saw the royal guard in silver, and the lackeys in gold upon the staircase, he did not seem in the least confused, but nodded pleasantly and said to them, 'It must be very tedious standing out here, I prefer going in.'

"The halls glistened with light; cabinet councillors and high officers were walking about bare-footed and carrying golden keys. It was just a place to make a man solemn and silent; and the youth's boots creaked horribly, yet he was not at all afraid."

"That most certainly was Kay!" said Gerda. "I know he had new boots; I have heard them creak in my grandmother's room."

"Indeed, they did creak," said the raven; "but he went merrily up to the princess, who was sitting upon a pearl as large as a spinning-wheel, while all the ladies of the court, with the maids-of-honour and their hand-maidens, ranged in order, stood on one side, and all the gentlemen-in-waiting with their gentlemen, and their gentlemen's gentlemen, who also kept pages, stood ranged in order on the other side, and the nearer they were to the door the prouder they looked. The gentlemen's page, who always wears slippers, one dare hardly look at, so proudly does he stand at the door."

"That must be dreadful!" said little Gerda. "And has Kay really won the princess?"

"Had I not been a raven I should have won her myself, notwithstanding my being betrothed. The young man spoke as well as I speak when I converse in Ravenish; that I have heard from my tame beloved. He was handsome and lively. 'I do not come to woo you,' he said, 'I have only come to hear the wisdom of the princess;' and he liked her much, and she liked him in return."

"Yes, to be sure, that was Kay," said Gerda; "he was always so clever. Oh, will you not take me into the palace?"

"Ah! that is easily said," replied the raven, "but how is it to be done? I will talk it over with my tame beloved; she will advise us what to do, for I must tell you that such a little girl as you are will never gain permission to enter publicly."

"Yes, I shall!" cried Gerda. "When Kay knows that I am here, he will immediately come out and fetch me."

"Wait for me at the trellis yonder," said the raven. He wagged his head and away he flew.

The raven did not return till late in the evening.

" Caw, caw," he said. " My tame beloved greets you kindly, and sends you a piece of bread which she took from the kitchen; there is plenty of bread there, and you must certainly be hungry. It is not possible for you to enter the palace, for you have bare feet; the royal guard in silver uniform, and the lackeys in gold, would never permit it: but do not weep, you shall go there. My beloved knows a little back staircase leading to the sleeping apartments, and she knows also where to find the key."

And they went into the garden, down the grand avenue, where the leaves dropped upon them as they passed along, and, when the lights in the palace one by one had all been put out, the raven took Gerda to a back door which stood half open.

Oh, how Gerda's heart beat with fear and expectation! It was just as if she was about to do something wrong, although she only wanted to know whether Kay was really there—yes, it must be he, she remembered so well his bright eyes and long hair. She would see if his smile were the same as it used to be when they sat together under the rose-trees. He would be so glad to see her, to hear how far she had come for his sake. Her heart trembled with fear and joy.

They went up the staircase. A small lamp placed on a cabinet gave a glimmering light. On the floor stood the tame raven, who first turned her head on all sides, and then looked at Gerda, who made her curtsey, as her grandmother had taught her.

" My betrothed has told me much about you," said the tame raven; " your adventures too, are extremely interesting! If you will take the lamp, I will show you the way. We are going straight on, we shall not meet anyone now."

" It seems to me as if some one were behind us," said Gerda; and, in fact, there was a rushing sound as of something passing. Strange-looking shadows flitted rapidly along the wall—horses with long, slender legs and fluttering manes, huntsmen, knights, and ladies.

" These are only dreams ! " said the raven; " they come to amuse the great personages here at night; you will have a better opportunity of looking at them when you are in bed. I hope that, when you arrive at honours and dignities, you will show a grateful heart."

" Do not talk of that! " said the wood-raven.

They now entered the first salon; its walls were covered with rose-coloured satin, embroidered with gold flowers. The Dreams rustled past them, but with such rapidity that Gerda could not see them. The apartments through which they passed vied with each other in splendour; and at last they reached the sleeping-hall.

In the centre of this room stood a pillar of gold resembling the stem of a large palm-tree, whose leaves of costly glass, formed the ceiling; and near the door there hung from the tree two beds in the form of lilies. The one was white, and on it reposed the princess; the other was red, and there must Gerda seek her play-fellow, Kay.

She bent aside one of the red leaves and saw a brown neck. Oh, it must be Kay! She called him aloud by his name; held the lamp close to him. The Dreams again rushed by—he awoke, turned his head, and behold! it was not Kay.

The Prince resembled him only about the throat; he was, however, young and handsome; and the princess looked out from the white lily petals, and asked what was the matter. Then little Gerda wept and told her whole story, and what the ravens had done for her.

"Poor child!" said the prince and princess; and they praised the ravens, and said they were not at all angry with them. Such liberties must never be taken again, but this time they should be rewarded.

"Would you like to fly away free to the woods?" asked the princess, addressing the ravens—"or would you rather be appointed permanent court-ravens with the perquisites belonging to the kitchen, such as crumbs and leavings?"

And both the ravens bowed low and chose the appointment at court, for they thought of old age, and said it would be so comfortable to be well provided for in their declining years. Then the prince arose, and gave Gerda his bed to sleep in; and she folded her little hands, thinking. "How kind both men and animals are to me!"

She closed her eyes and slept soundly and sweetly, and all the Dreams flitted about her: they looked like angels from heaven, and seemed to be drawing a sledge on which Kay sat. He nodded to her, but this was only fancy, for as soon as she awoke all the beautiful visions had vanished.

The next day she was dressed from head to foot in silk and velvet.

She was invited to stay at the palace and enjoy all sorts of pleasures; but she begged only for a little carriage and a horse, and a pair of little boots—all she wished was to go again into the world to seek Kay.

They gave her the boots, and a muff besides, she was dressed so prettily. And as soon as she was ready there drove up to the door a new carriage of pure gold, with the arms of the prince and princess glittering upon it like a star; the coachman, the footman, and outriders, all wearing gold crowns. The prince and princess themselves helped her into the carriage and wished her success.

"Farewell! farewell!" they cried. Little Gerda wept and waved till the palace was out of sight.

5. *The Little Robber-Maiden*

THEY drove through the dark, dark forest; the carriage shone like a torch. Unfortunately its brightness attracted the eyes of the robbers who dwelt in the forest shades.

"That is gold! gold!" they cried. Forward they rushed, seized the horses, stabbed the outriders, coachman, and footmen to death, and dragged Gerda out of the carriage.

" She is plump; she is pretty; she has been fed on nut kernels," said the old robber-wife, who had a long bristly beard, and eyebrows hanging like bushes over her eyes.

" She is like a little fat lamb; and how smartly she is dressed! " and she drew out her bright, glittering dagger. " Oh, oh! " cried the woman; for at the very moment she had lifted her dagger to stab Gerda, her own wild and wilful daughter jumped upon her back and bit her ear violently. "You naughty child! " said the mother.

" She shall play with me," said the little robber-maiden; " she shall give me her muff and her pretty frock, and sleep with me in my bed! " And then she bit her mother again, till the robber-wife sprang up and shrieked with pain, whilst the robbers all laughed, saying, " Look at her playing with her young one! "

" I will get into the carriage;" and so spoiled and wayward was the little robber-maiden that she always had her own way. So she and Gerda sat together in the carriage, and drove over stock and stone farther and farther into the wood.

The little robber-maiden was about as tall as Gerda, but much stronger; she had broad shoulders, and a very dark skin; her eyes were quite black, and had an expression almost melancholy. She put her arm round Gerda's waist, and said, " She shall not kill thee so long as I love thee! Art thou not a princess? "

" No! " said Gerda; and then she told her all that had happened to her, and how much she loved little Kay.

The robber-maiden looked earnestly in her face, shook her head, and said, " She shall not kill thee, even if I do quarrel with thee; then, indeed, I would rather do it myself! " And she dried Gerda's tears, and put both her hands into the pretty muff that was so soft and warm.

The carriage at last stopped in the middle of the courtyard of the robbers' castle. This castle was half ruined. Crows and ravens flew out of the openings, and some fearfully large bull-dogs, looking as if they could devour a man in a moment, jumped round the carriage; they did not bark, for that was forbidden.

The maidens entered a large smoky hall, where a tremendous fire was blazing in the stone floor. The smoke rose up to the ceiling, seeking a way of escape, for there was no chimney. A large cauldron full of soup was boiling over the fire; while hares and rabbits were roasting on the spit.

" Thou shalt sleep with me and my little pets to-night! " said the robber-maiden. Then they had some food, and afterwards went to the corner in which lay straw and a piece of carpet. Nearly a hundred pigeons were perched on staves and laths around them; they seemed to be asleep, but were startled when the little maidens approached.

" These all belong to me," said Gerda's companion; and seizing hold of one of the nearest, she held the poor bird by the feet and swung it. " Kiss it," said she, flapping it into Gerda's face. "The rabble from the wood sit up there," continued she, pointing to a number of laths fastened across a hole in the wall. " Those are wood-pigeons; they would fly away if I did not keep them shut up. And here is my old favourite! "

She pulled forward, by the horn, a reindeer who wore a bright copper ring round his neck, by which he was fastened to a large stone. " We are obliged to chain him up, or he would run away from us: every evening I tickle his neck with my sharp dagger; it makes him fear me so much! " and the robber-maiden drew out a long dagger from a gap in the wall, and passed it over the reindeer's throat. The poor animal struggled and kicked, but the girl laughed, and then she pulled Gerda into bed with her.

" Will you keep the dagger in your hand whilst you sleep? " asked Gerda, looking timidly at the dangerous plaything.

" I always sleep with my dagger by my side," replied the little robber-maiden; " one never knows what may happen. But now tell me all over again what you told me before about Kay, and the reason of your coming into the wide world all by yourself."

And Gerda again related her history and the wood-pigeons imprisoned above listened, but the others were fast asleep. The little robber-maiden threw one arm round Gerda's neck, and, holding the dagger with the other, was also soon asleep. One could hear her heavy breathing, but Gerda could not close her eyes throughout the night; she knew not what would become of her, whether she would even be allowed to live. The robbers sat round the fire drinking and singing. Oh, it was a dreadful night for the poor girl !

Then spoke the wood-pigeons, " Coo, coo, coo! we have seen little Kay. A white fowl carried his sledge; he himself was in the Snow Queen's chariot, which passed through the wood whilst we sat in our nest. She breathed upon us young ones as she passed, and all died of her breath excepting us two—coo, coo, coo! "

" What are you saying? " cried Gerda. " Where was the Snow Queen going? Do you know anything about it? "

" She travels most likely to Lapland, where ice and snow abide all the year round. Ask the reindeer bound to the rope there."

" Yes, ice and snow are there all through the year; it is a glorious land! " said the reindeer! " There, free and happy, one can roam through the wide sparkling valleys! There the Snow Queen has her summer-tent; her strong castle is very far off, near the North Pole, on the island called Spitsbergen."

" Oh, Kay, dear Kay! " sighed Gerda.

" You must lie still," said the robber-maiden, " or I will thrust my dagger into your side."

When morning came Gerda repeated to her what the wood-pigeons had said, and the little robber-maiden looked grave for a moment, then nodded her head, saying, " No matter! No matter! Do you know where Lapland is? " asked she of the reindeer.

" Who should know but me? " returned the animal, his eyes kindling. " There was I born and bred; there have I bounded over the wild icy plains! "

" Listen to me! " said the robber-maiden to Gerda; " you see all our men are gone, my mother is still here and will remain, but towards noon she will drink a little out of the great flask, and after that she will sleep—then I will do something for you!"

And, so saying, she jumped out of bed, sprang upon her mother, pulled her by the beard, and said, "My own dear mam, good-morning!" and the mother caressed her so roughly that she was red and blue all over. However, it was from pure love.

When her mother was fast asleep, the robber-maiden went up to the reindeer and said, "I should have great pleasure in stroking you a few more times with my sharp dagger, for then you look so droll. But never mind; I will unloose your chain and help you escape, on condition that you run as fast as you can to Lapland, and take this little girl to the castle of the Snow Queen, where her play-fellow is. You must have heard her story, for she speaks loud enough, and you know well how to listen."

The reindeer bounded with joy, and the robber-maiden lifted Gerda on to his back, taking first the precaution to bind her on firmly. She also gave her a little cushion to sit on. "And here," said she, "are your fur boots, which you will need in that cold country. The muff I must keep myself, as it is too pretty to part with; but you shall not be frozen. Here are my mother's huge gloves; they reach up to the elbow; put them on—now your hands look as clumsy as my old mother's!"

Gerda shed tears of joy.

"I cannot bear to see you crying!" said the little robber-maiden, "you ought to look glad. See, here are two loaves and a piece of bacon for you, that you may not be hungry on the way." She fastened this provender also on the reindeer's back, opened the door, called away the great dogs, and then, cutting asunder with her dagger the rope which bound the reindeer, shouted to him, "Now then, run! but take good care of the little girl."

And Gerda stretched out her hands to the robber-maiden and bade her farewell; and the reindeer fleeted through the forest, over stock and stone, over desert and heath, over meadow and moor. The wolves howled and the ravens shrieked. "Isch! Isch!" a red light flashed—one might have fancied the sky was sneezing.

"Those are my dear old Northern Lights!" said the reindeer; "look at them, how beautiful they are!" And he ran faster than ever; night and day he ran. The loaves were eaten, and so was the bacon—at last they were in Lapland.

6. *The Lapland Woman and the Finland Woman*

THEY stopped at a little hut, a wretched hut it was; the roof very nearly touched the ground, and the door was so low that whoever wished to go either in or out was obliged to crawl upon hands and knees. No one was at home except an old Lapland woman, who was busy boiling fish over a lamp filled with train oil.

The reindeer related to her Gerda's whole history, not, however, till after he had made her acquainted with his own, which appeared to him of much more importance. Poor Gerda, meanwhile, was so overpowered by the cold that she could not speak.

"Ah, poor things!" said the Lapland woman, "you have still a long way before you! You have a hundred miles to run before you can arrive in Finland: the Snow Queen dwells there, and burns blue lights every evening. I will write for you a few words on a piece of dried stock-fish—paper I have none—and you may take it with you to the wise Finland woman who lives there; she will advise you better than I can."

So when Gerda had warmed herself and taken some food, the Lapland woman wrote on a dried stock-fish, bade Gerda take care of it, and bound her once more firmly on the reindeer's back.

Onwards they sped; the wondrous Northern Lights, now of the loveliest, brightest blue colour, shone all through the night, and amidst these splendid illuminations they arrived in Finland, and knocked at the chimney of the wise woman, for door to her house she had none.

It was very hot within—so much so that the wise woman wore scarcely any clothing; she was low in stature, and very dirty. She immediately loosened little Gerda's dress, took off her fur boots and thick gloves, laid a piece of ice on the reindeer's head, and then read what was written on the stock-fish: she read it three times. After the third reading she knew it by heart, and threw the fish into the porridge-pot, for it might make a very excellent supper, and she never wasted anything.

The reindeer then repeated his own story, and when that was finished he told of little Gerda's adventures; and the wise woman twinkled her wise eyes, but spoke not a word.

"Thou art so powerful," continued the reindeer, "that I know thou canst twist all the winds of the world into a thread, and if the pilot loosen one knot of it he will have a favourable wind; if he loosen the second it will blow sharp, and if he loosen the third, so tremendous a storm will arise that the trees of the forest will be uprooted, and the ship wrecked. Wilt thou not mix for this little maiden that wonderful draught which will give her the strength of twelve men, and thus enable her to overcome the Snow Queen?"

"The strength of twelve men!" repeated the wise woman, "that would be of much use, to be sure!" and she walked away, drew forth a large parchment roll from a shelf and began to read.

But the reindeer pleaded so earnestly for little Gerda, and Gerda's eyes were raised so earnestly and tearfully, that at last the wise woman's eyes began to twinkle again out of sympathy, and she drew the reindeer into a corner, and putting a fresh piece of ice upon his head, whispered thus——

"Little Kay is still with the Snow Queen, he believes it to be the best place in the world. But that is because he has a glass splinter in his heart, and a glass splinter in his eye. Until he has got rid of them he will never feel like a human being, and the Snow Queen will always maintain her influence over him."

"But canst thou not give something to little Gerda whereby she may overcome all these evil influences?"

"I can give her no power so great as that which she already possesses. Seest thou not how strong she is? Seest thou not that both men and animals must serve her—a poor girl wandering barefoot through the world?

"Her power is greater than ours; it proceeds from her heart, from her being a loving and innocent child. If this power which she already possesses cannot give her access to the Snow Queen's palace, and enable her to free Kay's eye and heart from the glass fragments, we can do nothing for her! Two miles hence is the Snow Queen's garden; thither thou canst carry the little maiden. Put her down close by the bush bearing berries and half covered with snow: lose no time and hasten back to this place!"

And the wise woman lifted Gerda on the reindeer's back, and away they went.

"Oh, I have left my boots behind! I have left my gloves behind!" cried little Gerda, when it was too late. The cold was piercing, but the reindeer dared not stop; on he ran until he reached the bush with the red berries. Here he set Gerda down, kissed her, the tears rolling down his cheeks the while, and ran fast back again. And there stood poor Gerda, without shoes, without gloves, alone in that barren region, that ice-cold Finland.

She ran on as fast as she could, and a whole regiment of snow-flakes came to meet her. They did not fall from the sky, they ran straight along the ground, and the farther Gerda advanced the larger they grew. They were living forms; they were, in fact, the Snow Queen's guards. Their shapes were the strangest that could be imagined; some looked like great ugly porcupines, others like snakes rolled into knots, with their heads peering forth, and others like little fat bears with bristling hair. All, however, were alike dazzlingly white—all were living snow-flakes. As she hurried on, Gerda prayed.

The cold was so intense that she could see her own breath, which, as it escaped her mouth, ascended into the air like vapour. The cold grew intense, the vapour more dense, and at length it took forms of little bright angels, which as they touched the earth, became larger and more distinct.

They wore helmets on their heads, and carried shields and spears in their hands; their number increased so rapidly that, by the time Gerda had finished her prayer, a whole legion stood around her. They thrust with their spears against the horrible snow-flakes, which fell into thousands of pieces, and little Gerda walked on unhurt. The angels touched her hands and feet, and then she scarcely felt the cold and boldly approached the Snow Queen's palace.

7. *The Snow Queen's Palace, and what came to pass there*

THE walls of the palace were formed of the driven snow, its doors and windows of the cutting wind. There were above a hundred halls, the largest of them many miles in extent, all illuminated by the Northern Lights, all alike vast, empty, icily cold, and dazzlingly white.

In the midst of the empty, endless snow salon lay a frozen lake; it was broken into a thousand pieces, but these pieces so exactly resembled each other that the breaking of them might well be deemed a work of more than human skill.

The Snow Queen when at home, always sat in the middle of this lake; she used to say that she was then sitting on the Mirror of Reason, and that hers was the best, indeed the only one, in the world.

Here now sat little Kay all alone. He was quite blue with cold. But he did not observe it, for the Snow Queen had kissed away the shrinking feeling he used to experience; and his heart was like a lump of ice. He was busied among the sharp icy fragments, laying and joining them together in every possible way.

Kay could form the most curious and complete figures—that was the ice puzzle of reason. He often formed whole words, but there was one word he could never succeed in forming—it was Eternity. The

Snow Queen had said: "When thou canst put that figure together, thou shalt become thine own master, and I will give thee the whole world, and a new pair of skates besides."

But he could never do it.

Now Kay looked at the fragments, and thought and thought till his head ached.

Cold and cutting blew the winds when little Gerda passed through the palace gates, but she repeated her evening prayer, and they immediately sank to rest. She entered the large, cold, empty hall: she saw Kay, she flew upon his neck, she held him fast, and cried, "Kay! dear, dear Kay! I have found thee at last!"

But he sat still as before, cold, silent, motionless. Hot and bitter were the tears Gerda shed; they fell upon his breast; they reached his heart; they thawed the ice and dissolved the tiny splinter of glass within it. Then Gerda sang her old hymn.

And then Kay burst into tears. He wept till the glass splinter floated in his eye and fell with his tears; he knew his old companion immediately, and exclaimed with joy, "Gerda, my dear little Gerda, where hast thou been all this time? And where have I been?" He looked around him. "How cold it is here! how wide and empty!" and he embraced Gerda, whilst she laughed and wept by turns.

Even the pieces of ice took part in their joy; they danced about

merrily, and when they were wearied and lay down of their own accord they formed the word Eternity.

And Gerda kissed his cheeks, which then became fresh and glowing as ever; she kissed his eyes, his hands, his feet, and he was once more healthy and merry. Kay was free.

They took each other by the hand, and wandered forth out of the palace; and as they walked on, the sun burst forth.

When they arrived at the bush with the red berries, they found the reindeer with another younger reindeer awaiting their arrival.

The reindeers now carried Kay and Gerda on their backs, first to the wise woman of Finland, and afterwards to the abode of the Lapland woman who provided them with a sledge.

On they went till they came to the boundary; but when the green leaves began to sprout, the reindeers took their leave.

Then the first little birds they had seen for many a long day began to chirp and the trees of the forest burst upon them full of rich foliage. Suddenly the green boughs parted and a spirited horse galloped up.

On it sat a young girl. It was the robber-maiden, who, weary of her home in the forest, was going on her travels. She at once recognised Gerda, and most joyful was their greeting.

Then Gerda and Kay told her their story.

" Snip-snap-snurre-basselurre! " said the robber-maiden. She pressed the hands of both, promised that if ever she passed through their town she would pay them a visit, and then bade them farewell.

Kay and Gerda walked on hand in hand, and wherever they went it was spring. They arrived at a large town, the church-bells were ringing merrily, and they immediately recognised the high towers rising into the sky—it was their town. Joyfully they passed through the streets; joyfully they stopped at the door of Gerda's grandmother; they walked up the stairs and entered the well-known room.

Only one alteration could they find, and that was in themselves, for they saw that they were now full-grown persons. The rose-trees on the roof blossomed and beneath them stood the children's seats.

Kay and Gerda went and sat down upon them, still holding each other by the hands. There they sat, grown-up and yet children in heart, while all around them glowed bright glorious summer.

THE EMPEROR'S NEW CLOTHES

MANY years ago there was an Emperor who was so very fond of new clothes that he spent all his money on dress. He did not trouble himself in the least about his soldiers; nor did he care to go either to the theatre or to the chase, except for the opportunities then given him of displaying his new clothes. He had a different suit for each hour of the day; and as one is accustomed to say of any other king or emperor, "He is sitting in council," it was always said of him. "The Emperor is sitting in his wardrobe."

Time passed away merrily in the large town which was his capital; strangers arrived every day at the court. One day two rogues, calling themselves weavers, made their appearance. They said that they knew how to weave stuffs of the most beautiful colours and elaborate patterns; the clothes made from these would have the wonderful property of remaining invisible to everyone who was unfit for the office he held, or who was extraordinarily simple in character.

"These must indeed be splendid clothes!" thought the Emperor. "Had I such a suit, I might, at once, find out what men in my realm are unfit for their office, and also be able to distinguish the wise from the foolish! This stuff must be woven for me immediately." And he caused large sums of money to be given to both the weavers, in order that they might begin their work at once.

So the two supposed weavers set up two looms, and pretended to work busily, though in reality they did nothing at all. They asked for the most delicate silk and the purest gold thread; put both into their own knapsacks and then sat at the empty looms until late at night.

" I should like to know how the weavers are getting on with my cloth," said the Emperor to himself, after some time had passed. He was, however, rather embarrassed when he remembered that a simpleton, or one unfit for his office, would be unable to see the material. " To be sure," he thought, " *I* have nothing to risk; yet, I should prefer sending somebody else."

All the people throughout the city had heard of the wonderful property the cloth was to possess; and all were anxious to learn how wise, or how ignorant, their neighbours might prove to be.

" I will send my faithful old minister to the weavers," said the Emperor at last; " he will be best able to see how the cloth looks; for he is a man of sense, and no one could be more suitable for his office."

So the faithful old minister went into the hall, where the knaves were working at their empty looms. " What can be the meaning of this ? " thought the old man, opening his eyes very wide. " I can see nothing here ! " However, he did not express his thoughts aloud.

The imposters requested him very courteously to come nearer their looms; and then asked him whether the design pleased him, and whether the colours were not very beautiful. The poor old minister looked and looked, he could not discover anything on the looms, for a very good reason—there was nothing there.

" What ! " thought he again, " is it possible that I am a simpleton ? I have never thought so myself; and no one must know of it, if I am so. Can it be that I am unfit for my office ? No, that must not be said either. I will never confess that I could not see the stuff."

" Well, Sir Minister ! " said one of the knaves, still pretending to work, " you do not say whether you like it."

" Oh, it is excellent ! " replied the old minister, looking at the loom through his spectacles. "This pattern and the colours—yes, I will tell the Emperor how very beautiful I think them."

"We shall be much obliged to you," said the imposters and then they named the different colours and described the pattern of the pretended stuff. The old minister listened attentively in order that he might repeat everything to the Emperor. Then the knaves asked for more silk and gold, saying that it was necessary to complete their work. However, they put all that was given them into their knapsacks, and continued to work industriously at their empty looms.

The Emperor now sent another officer of his court to see how the men were getting on. It was just the same with this gentleman as with the minister; he surveyed the looms on all sides, but could see nothing at all but the empty frames.

"Does not the stuff appear as beautiful to you as it did to my lord the minister?" asked the imposters.

"I certainly am not stupid!" thought the messenger. "It must be that I am not fit for my good, profitable office! That is very odd; however, no one shall know anything about it." And accordingly he praised the stuff he could not see, and declared that he was delighted with both colours and patterns.

"Indeed, please your Imperial Majesty," said he to his sovereign, when he returned, "the cloth which the weavers are preparing is extraordinarily magnificent."

The whole city was talking of the splendid cloth which the Emperor had ordered to be woven at his own expense.

And now the Emperor himself wished to see the costly manufacture whilst it was still on the loom. Accompanied by a select number of officers of the court, among whom were the two honest men who had already admired the cloth, he went to the crafty imposters who, as soon as they were aware of the Emperor's approach, went on working more diligently than ever; although they still did not pass a single thread through the looms.

"Is not the work absolutely magnificent?" said the two officers of the crown, already mentioned. "If your Majesty will only be pleased to look at it! What a splendid design! What glorious colours!" and at the same time they pointed to the empty frames; for they imagined that every one else could see this exquisite piece of workmanship.

"How is this?" said the Emperor to himself. "I can see nothing!

this is indeed a terrible affair! Am I a simpleton, or am I unfit to be an Emperor? That would be the worst thing that could happen—Oh! the cloth is charming," said he aloud. And he smiled most graciously, and looked closely at the empty looms; for on no account would he say that he could not see what two of the officers of his court had praised so much.

All his retinue now strained their eyes, hoping to discover something on the looms, but they could see no more than the others. Nevertheless, they all exclaimed, "Oh, how beautiful!" and advised his Majesty to have some new clothes made from this splendid material, for the approaching procession.

"Magnificent! charming! excellent!" resounded on all sides; and every one was uncommonly gay. The Emperor presented the imposters with the riband of an order of knighthood, to be worn in their button-holes, and bestowed on them the title of "Gentlemen Weavers." The rogues sat up the whole of the night before the day of the procession, and had sixteen lights burning, so that everyone might see how anxious they were to finish the Emperor's new suit. They pretended to roll the cloth off the looms; cut the air with their scissors; and sewed with needles without any thread in them. "See!" cried they at last, "the Emperor's new clothes are ready!"

And now the Emperor, with all the grandees of his court, came to the weavers; and the rogues raised their arms, as if holding something up, saying, "Here are your Majesty's trousers! Here is the scarf! Here is the mantle! The whole suit is as light as a cobweb; one might fancy one has nothing at all on, when dressed in it. If your Imperial Majesty will be graciously pleased to take off your clothes, we will fit on the new suit, in front of the looking-glass."

The Emperor was undressed, and the rogues pretended to array him in his new suit, the Emperor turning round, from side to side, before the looking-glass.

"How splendid his Majesty looks in his new clothes; and how well they fit!" everyone cried out. "What a design! What colours! These are indeed royal robes!"

"The canopy which is to be borne over your Majesty in the procession is waiting," announced the chief master of the ceremonies.

" I am quite ready," answered the Emperor. " Do my new clothes fit well ? " asked he, turning himself round again before the looking-glass in order that he might appear to be examining his handsome suit.

The lords of the bedchamber, who were to carry his Majesty's train, felt about on the ground, as if they were lifting up the ends of the mantle, and pretended to be carrying something; for they would by no means betray anything like simplicity or unfitness for their office.

So now the Emperor walked under his high canopy in the midst of the procession, through the streets of his capital; and all the people standing by, and those at the windows, cried out, " Oh, how beautiful are our Emperor's new clothes! What a magnificent train there is to the mantle; and how graceful the scarf hangs."

In short, no one would allow that he could not see these much admired clothes; because, in doing so, he would have declared himself either a simpleton or unfit for his office. Certainly, none of the Emperor's various suits had ever made so great an impression as these invisible ones.

" But the Emperor has nothing on at all! " said a little child.

" Listen to the voice of innocence! " exclaimed his father; and what the child had said was whispered from one to another.

" But he has nothing at all on! " at last cried out all the people. The Emperor was vexed, for he knew that the people were right; but he thought the procession must go on now. And the lords of the bedchamber took greater pains than ever to appear to be holding up a train although, in reality, there was no train to hold.

THE UGLY DUCKLING

IT was beautiful in the country—it was summertime—the wheat was yellow, the oats were green, the hay was stacked up in the green meadows, and the stork paraded about on his long red legs, discoursing in Egyptian, a language he had learned from his mother. The fields and meadows were skirted by thick woods, and a deep lake lay in the midst of the woods.

Yes, it was indeed beautiful in the country! The sunshine fell warm on an old mansion, surrounded by deep canals, and from the walls down to the water's edge there grew large burdock leaves, so high that children could stand upright among them without being seen.

This place was as wild and unfrequented as the thickest part of the wood, and a duck had chosen to make her nest there. She was sitting on her eggs; but the pleasure she had felt at first was now almost gone, because she had been there so long, and had so few visitors, for the other ducks preferred swimming on the canals to sitting among the burdock leaves gossiping with her.

At last the eggs cracked one after another, "Tchick, tchick!" All the eggs were alive, and one little head after another appeared. "Quack, quack," said the duck, and all got up as well as they could. They peeped about from under the green leaves, and as green is good for the eyes their mother let them look as long as they pleased.

"How large the world is!" said the little ones, for they found their present situation very different from the former one, while they were in the eggshells.

"Do you imagine this to be the whole of the world?" said the mother. "It extends far beyond the other side of the garden, to the pastor's field; but I have never been there. Are you all here?" And then she got up. "No, I have not got you all; the largest egg is still here. How long will this last? I am so weary of it!" and then she sat down again.

"Well, and how are you getting on?" asked an old duck, who had come to pay her a visit.

"This one egg keeps me so long," said the mother, "it will not break; but you should see the others! They are the prettiest little ducklings I have seen in all my days; they are all like their father—the good-for-nothing fellow! He has not been to visit me once."

"Let me see the egg that will not break," said the old duck; "depend upon it, it is a turkey's egg. I was cheated in the same way once myself, and I had such trouble with the young ones; for they were afraid of the water, and I could not get them there. I called and scolded, but it was all of no use. But let me see the egg—ah yes! to be sure, that is a turkey's egg. Leave it, and teach the other little ones to swim."

"I will sit on it a little longer," said the duck. "I have been sitting so long, that I may as well spend the harvest here."

"It is no business of mine," said the old duck, and away she waddled.

The great egg burst at last, "Tchick, tchick," said the little one, and out it tumbled—but oh! how large and ugly it was! The duck looked at it. "That is a great, strong creature," said she, "none of the others are at all like it; can it be a young turkey-cock? Well, we shall soon find out; it must go into the water, though I push it in myself."

The next day there was delightful weather, and the sun shone warmly upon all the green leaves when mother-duck with her family went down to the canal; plump she went into the water. "Quack, quack," cried she and one duckling after another jumped in. The water closed over their heads, but all came up again, and swam together in the pleasantest manner;

their legs moved without effort. All were there, even the ugly grey one.

" No! it is not a turkey," said the old duck; " only see how prettily it moves its legs, how upright it holds itself; it is my own child! It is also really very pretty when one looks more closely at it; quack, quack, now come with me; I will take you into the world, introduce you in the duck-yard; but keep close to me, or some one may tread on you, and beware of the cat."

So they came into the duck-yard. There was a horrid noise; two families were quarrelling about the remains of an eel, which in the end was secured by the cat.

"See, my children, such is the way of the world," said the mother-duck, wiping her beak, for she too was fond of roasted eels. " Now, use your legs," said she, " keep together, and bow to the old duck you see yonder. She is the most distinguished of all the fowls present, and is of Spanish blood, which accounts for her dignified appearance and manners. And look, she has a red rag on her leg; that is considered extremely handsome, and is the greatest distinction a duck can have. Don't turn your feet inwards; a well-educated duckling always keeps his legs far apart, like his father and mother, just so—look! Now bow your necks, and say ' Quack '! "

And they did as they were told. But the other ducks who were in the yard looked at them and said aloud, " Only see, now we have another brood, as if there were not enough of us already; and fie! how ugly that one is, we will not endure it; " and immediately one of the ducks flew at him, and bit him in the neck.

" Leave him alone," said the mother, " he is doing no one any harm."

" Yes, but he is so large, and so strange-looking, and therefore he shall be teased."

" Those are fine children that our good mother has," said the old duck with the red rag on her leg. " All are pretty except one, and that has not turned out well; I almost wish it could be hatched over again."

" That cannot be, please your highness," said the mother. " Certainly he is not handsome, but he is a very good child, and swims as well as the others, indeed rather better. I think he will grow like the others all in good time, and perhaps will look smaller. He stayed so long in the egg-shell, that is the cause of the difference;" and she scratched the duckling's neck, and stroked his whole body. "Besides," added she, "he is a drake; I think he will be very strong, therefore it does not matter so much, as he will fight his way through."

"The other ducks are very pretty," said the old duck. "Pray make yourselves at home, and if you find an eel's head you can bring it to me."

And accordingly they made themselves at home.

But the poor little duckling who had come last out of its egg-shell, and who was so ugly, was bitten, pecked, and teased by both ducks and hens. "It is so large," said they all. And the turkey-cock who had come into the world with spurs on, and therefore fancied he was an emperor, puffed himself up like a ship in full sail, and marched up to the duckling quite red with passion. The poor little thing scarcely knew what to do; he was quite distressed, because he was so ugly, and because he was the jest of the poultry-yard.

So passed the first day, and afterwards matters grew worse and worse; the poor duckling was scorned by all. Even his brothers and sisters behaved unkindly, and were constantly saying, "I wish the cat would catch you, you nasty creature!" The mother said, "Ah, if only you were far away!" The ducks bit him, the hens pecked him, and the girl who fed the poultry kicked him.

He ran over to the hedge; the little birds in the bushes were terrified. "That is because I am so ugly," thought the duckling, shutting his eyes, while he ran on. At last he came to a wide moor, where lived some wild ducks; here he lay the whole night, so tired and so comfortless.

In the morning the wild ducks flew up and perceived their new companion. "Pray, who are you?" asked they; and our little duckling turned himself in all direcitons, and greeted them as politely as possible.

"You are really very ugly," said the wild ducks, "however that does not matter to us, provided you do not marry into our families." Poor thing! he had never thought of marrying; he only begged leave to lie among the reeds, and drink the water of the moor.

There he lay for two whole days; on the third day there came two wild geese, or rather ganders, who had not been long out of their egg-shells, which accounts for their impertinence.

"Hark ye," said they, "you are so ugly that we like you very well. Will you come with us, and be a bird of passage? On another moor, not far from this, are some dear, sweet, wild geese, as lovely creatures as have ever said 'hiss, hiss.' You are truly in the way to make your fortune, ugly as you are."

Bang! a gun went off all at once, and both wild geese were stretched dead among the reeds, and the water became red with blood—bang! a gun went off again, whole flocks of wild geese flew up from among the reeds, and another report followed.

There was a grand hunting party; the hunters lay in ambush all around; some were even sitting in the trees, whose huge branches stretched far over the moor. The blue smoke rose through the thick trees like a mist, and was dispersed as it fell over the water; the hounds splashed about in the mud, the reeds and rushes bent in all directions. How frightened the poor little duck was! He turned his head, thinking to hide it under his wings; and in a moment a most formidable-looking dog stood close to him, his tongue hanging out of his mouth, his eyes sparkling fearfully. He opened wide his jaws at the sight of our duckling, showed him his sharp white teeth, and, splash, splash! he was gone—gone without hurting him.

"Well! let me be thankful," sighed he, "I am so ugly that even the dog will not eat me."

And now he lay still, though the shooting continued among the reeds, shot following shot.

The noise did not cease till late in the day, and even then the poor little thing dared not stir; he waited several hours before he looked around him, and then hastened away from the moor as far as he could. He ran over fields and meadows, though the wind was so high that he had some difficulty in proceeding.

Towards evening he reached a wretched little hut—so wretched that it knew not on which side to fall, and therefore remained standing. The wind blew violently, so that our poor little duckling was obliged to support himself on his tail in order to stand against it; but it became worse and worse. He then noticed that the door had lost one of its hinges, and hung so much awry that he could creep through the crevice into the room—which he did.

In this room lived an old woman, with her tom-cat and her hen; and the cat, whom she called her little son knew how to set up his back and purr; indeed he could even emit sparks when stroked the wrong way. The hen had very short legs, and was therefore called "Cuckoo Shortlegs"; she laid very good eggs, and the old woman loved her as her own child.

The next morning the new guest was discovered; the cat began to mew, and the hen to cackle.

"What is the matter?" asked the old woman, looking round; however, her eyes were not good, and so she took the young duckling to be a fat duck who had lost her way. "This is a captial catch," said she.

"I shall now have duck's eggs, if it be not a drake; we must try."

And so the duckling was put to the proof for three weeks, but no eggs appeared.

Now the cat was the master of the house and the hen was the mistress, and they used always to say, " We and the world," for they imagined themselves to be not only the half of the world, but also by far the better half. The duckling thought it was possible to be of a different opinion, but that the hen would not allow.

" Can you lay eggs? " asked she.

" No."

" Well, then, hold your tongue."

And the cat said, " Can you arch your back? Can you purr? "

" No."

" Well, then, you should have no opinion when reasonable persons are speaking."

So the duckling sat alone in a corner, and was in a very bad humour; however, he happened to think of the fresh air and bright sunshine, and these thoughts gave him such a strong desire to swim again that he could not help telling it to the hen.

" What ails you? " said the hen. " You have nothing to do, and therefore brood over these fancies; either lay eggs, or purr, then you will forget them."

" But it is so delicious to swim," said the duckling; " so delicious when the waters close over your head and you plunge to the bottom."

" Well, that is a queer sort of a pleasure," said the hen; " I think you must be crazy. Not to speak of myself, ask the cat—he is the most sensible animal I know—whether he would like to swim or to plunge to the bottom of the water. Ask our mistress, the old woman—there is no one in the world wiser than she—do you think she would take pleasure in swimming and in the waters closing over her head? "

" You do not understand me," said the duckling.

" What! we do not understand you! So you think yourself wiser than the cat and the old woman, not to speak of myself. Do not fancy any such thing, child, but be thankful for all the kindness that has been shown you. Are you not lodged in a warm room, and have you not the advantage of society from which you can learn something? But you are a simpleton, and it is wearisome to have anything to do with

you. Believe me, I wish you well. I tell you unpleasant truths, but it is thus that real friendship is shown. Come, for once give yourself the trouble to learn to purr, or to lay eggs."

"I think I will go out into the wide world again," said the duckling.

"Well, go," answered the hen.

So the duckling went. He swam on the surface of the water, he plunged beneath, but all animals passed him by, on account of his ugliness. And the autumn came, the leaves turned yellow and brown, the wind caught them and danced them about; the air was very cold, the clouds were heavy with hail or snow, and the raven sat on the hedge and croaked. The poor duckling was certainly not very comfortable!

One evening, just as the sun was setting with unusual brilliance, a flock of large beautiful birds rose from out of the brushwood; the duckling had never seen anything so beautiful before; their plumage was of a dazzling white, and they had long slender necks. They were swans; they uttered a peculiar cry, spread out their long, splendid wings and flew away from these cold regions to warmer countries across the open sea. They flew so high, so very high! and the little ugly duckling's feelings were so strange; he turned round and round in the water like a mill-wheel, strained his neck to look after

them, and sent forth such a loud and strange cry that it almost frightened himself.

Ah! he could not forget them, those noble birds! those happy birds! When he could see them no longer, he plunged to the bottom of the water, and when he rose again was almost beside himself. The duckling knew not what the birds were called, knew not whither they were flying, yet he loved them as he had never before loved anything. He envied them not; it would never have occurred to him to wish such beauty for himself; he would have been quite contented if the ducks in the duck-yard had only endured his company and been patient with him. His life would be so different if only he could find friends—the poor ugly animal.

And the winter was so cold, so cold! The duckling was obliged to swim round and round in the water, to keep it from freezing; but every night the opening in which he swam became smaller and smaller. It froze so that the crust of ice crackled; the duckling was obliged to make good use of his legs to prevent the water from freezing entirely; at last, quite wearied out, he lay stiff and cold in the ice.

Early in the morning by great good fortune, there passed by a peasant who saw the little duckling lying there. He broke the ice in pieces with his wooden shoe, and brought him home to his wife's warm kitchen.

He now revived; the children would have played with him, but our duckling thought they wished to tease him, and in his terror jumped into the milk-pail, so that the milk was spilled about the room. The good woman screamed and clapped her hands; he flew then into the pan where the butter was kept, and from there into the meal-barrel, and out again, and then what a strange sight he was!

The woman screamed, and struck at him with the tongs; the children ran races with each other trying to catch him, and laughed and screamed likewise. It was well for him that the door stood open; he jumped out among the bushes into the new-fallen snow, and lay there as in a dream. So dazed and terrified was the little duckling that he wished he were dead.

But it would be too melancholy to relate all the trouble and misery that he was obliged to suffer during the severity of the winter. He was lying on a moor among the reeds, when the sun began to shine warmly again; the larks sang, and beautiful spring had returned at last.

And once more he shook his wings. They were stronger than formerly, and bore him forwards quickly; and before he was well aware of it he was in a large garden where the apple-trees stood in full bloom, where the lilacs sent forth their fragrance and hung their long green branches down into the winding canal! Oh, everything was so lovely, so full of the freshness of spring. And out of the thicket came three beautiful white swans. They displayed their feathers so proudly, and glided over the water so lightly, so lightly! The duckling knew the glorious creatures, and was seized with a strange melancholy.

"I will fly to them, those kingly birds!" said he. "They will kill me, because I, ugly as I am, have dared to approach them; but it matters not, better to be killed by them than to be bitten by the ducks, pecked by the hens, kicked by the girl who feeds the poultry, and to have so much to suffer during the winter!" He flew into the water, and swam towards the beautiful creatures; they saw him and shot forward to meet him.

"Only kill me," said the poor animal, and he bowed his head low, expecting death. But what did he see in the clear water? He saw beneath him his own form, no longer that of a plump, ugly grey bird—it was that of a swan.

It matters not to have been born in a duck-yard if one has been hatched from a swan's egg.

The ugly duckling felt now really proud of all the troubles and adversities he had experienced, now that he had discovered that he was a beautiful swan, it had all been worthwhile. Oh, happy he was as the larger swans swam round him, and stroked him gently with their beaks.

Some little children were running about in the garden; they threw grain and bread into the water, and the youngest exclaimed, "There is a new one!" The others also cried out, "Yes, a new swan has come!" And they clapped their hands and danced around. They ran to their father and mother, bread and cake were thrown into the water, and everyone said, "The new one is the best, so young, and so beautiful and so graceful!" and all the older swans bowed their heads before him.

The young swan felt quite ashamed, and hid his head under his wings; he scarcely knew what to do, he was so very happy and not at all vain or proud.

He remembered how he had been taunted and scorned, and he now heard everyone say he was the most beautiful of all beautiful birds. The lilacs bent down their branches towards him low into the water and the sun shone warmly and brightly. He shook his feathers, stretched his slender neck, and in the joy of his heart said, "How little did I dream of so much happiness when I was the ugly despised duckling!"

THE CONSTANT TIN SOLDIER

THERE were once five-and-twenty tin soldiers, all brothers, for they had all been made out of one old tin spoon. They carried muskets in their arms, and held themselves very upright, and their uniforms were red and blue—very gay indeed.

The first words they heard in this world, when the lid was taken off the box in which they lay, were, " Tin Soldiers!" It was a little boy who made this exclamation, clapping his hands at the same time. They had been given to him because it was his birthday, and he now set them out on the table.

The soldiers resembled each other to a hair—one only was rather different from the rest; he had but one leg, for he had been made last, when there was not quite enough tin left. However, he stood as firmly upon his one leg as the others did upon their two; and this tin soldier it is whose fortunes seem to us worthy of record.

On the table where the tin soldiers were set out were several other playthings, but the most charming of them all was a pretty pasteboard castle. Through its little windows one could look into the rooms. In front of the castle stood some tiny trees, clustering round a little mirror intended to represent a lake, and waxen swans in the lake were reflected on its surface.

All this was very pretty, but prettiest of all was a little damsel standing in the open doorway of the castle; she, too, was cut out of pasteboard, but she had on a frock of the finest muslin, a little sky-blue ribbon was flung across her shoulders like a scarf, and in the midst of this scarf was set a bright gold wing. The little lady stretched out both her arms, for she was a dancer, and raised one of her legs so high in the air that the tin soldier could not find it, and fancied that she had, like him, only one leg.

" That would be just the wife for me," thought he, " but then, she is of rather too high rank; she lives in a castle. I have only a box; and besides, there are all our five-and-twenty men in it; it is no place for her.

" However, there will be no harm in my making acquaintance with her," and so he stationed himself behind a snuff-box that stood on the table; from this place he had a full view of the delicate little lady, who still remained standing on one leg, yet without losing her balance.

When evening came, all the other tin soldiers were put away into the box, and the people of the house went to bed. The playthings now began to play in their turn; they pretended to visit, to fight battles, and give balls. The tin soldiers rattled in the box for they wanted to play too, but the lid would not come off. The nut-crackers cut capers, and the slate-pencil played at commerce on the slate; there was such a racket that the canary bird woke up, and began to talk too, but he always talked in verse.

The only two who did not move from their places were the tin soldier and the little dancer; she constantly remained in her graceful position, standing on the point of her foot, with out-stretched arms; and, as for him, he stood just as firmly on his one leg, never for one moment turning his eyes away from her.

Twelve o'clock struck. Crash! Open sprang the lid of the snuff-box, but there was no snuff inside it; no, out jumped a little black conjurer, in fact it was a Jack-in-the-box. " Tin soldier! " said the conjurer, " wilt thou keep thine eyes to thyself? "

But the tin soldier pretended not to hear.

" Well, only wait till to-morrow! " quoth the conjurer.

When the morrow had come, and the children were out of bed, the tin soldier was placed on the window-ledge, and, whether the conjurer or the wind caused it, all at once the window flew open, and out fell the tin soldier, head foremost from the third story to the ground.

A dreadful fall was that! His one leg turned over and over in the air, and at last he rested, poised on his soldier's cap, with his bayonet between the paving stones.

The maid-servant and the little boy immediately came down to look for him; but, although they very nearly trod on him, they could not see him. If the tin soldier had but called out, " Here I am! " they might easily have found him; but he thought it would not be becoming for him to cry out, as he was in uniform.

It now began to rain; every drop fell heavier than the last; there was a regular shower. When it was over two boys came by. "Look!" said one, "here is a tin soldier; he shall have a sail for once in his life."

So they made a boat out of an old newspaper, put the tin soldier into it, and away he sailed down the gutter, both the boys running along by the side and clapping their hands. The paper boat rocked to and fro, and every now and then veered round so quickly that the tin soldier became quite giddy; still he moved not a muscle, looked straight before him, and held his bayonet tightly clasped.

All at once the boat sailed under a long gutter-board; he found it as dark here as at home in his own box.

"Where shall I get to next?" thought he. "Yes, to be sure, it is all that conjurer's doing! Ah, if only the little maiden were sailing with me in the boat I would not care if it were twice as dark!"

Just then a great water-rat that lived under the gutter-board darted out.

"Have you a passport?" asked the rat. "Where is your passport?"

But the tin soldier was silent, and held his weapon with a still firmer grasp. The boat sailed on, and the rat followed. Oh! how furiously he showed his teeth, and cried out to sticks and straws, "Stop him, stop him! he has not paid the toll; he has not shown his passport!"

But the stream grew stronger and stronger. The tin soldier could already catch a glimpse of the bright daylight before the boat came from under the tunnel, but at the same time he heard a roaring noise, at which the boldest heart might well have trembled.

Only fancy! where the tunnel ended the water of the gutter fell perpendicularly into a great canal; this was as dangerous for the tin soldier as sailing down a mighty waterfall would be for us.

He was now so close that he could no longer stand upright; the boat darted forwards; the poor tin soldier held himself as stiff and immovable as possible; no one could accuse him of having even blinked. The boat spun round and round three, nay, four times, and was filled with water to the brim; it must sink. The tin soldier stood up to his neck in water; deeper and deeper sank the boat, softer and softer grew the paper. The water went over the soldier's head, and he thought of the pretty little dancer whom he should never see again, and these words rang in his ears:

> " Wild adventure, mortal danger
> Be thy portion, valiant stranger! "

The paper now tore asunder, the tin soldier fell through the rent; but, in the same moment, he was swallowed up by a large fish. Oh, how dark it was, worse even than under the gutter-board, and so narrow too! But the tin soldier's resolution was as constant as ever; there he lay, at full length, shouldering his arms.

The fish turned and twisted about, and made the strangest movements. At last he became quite still; a flash of lightning, as it were, darted through him. The daylight shone brightly, and someone exclaimed, " Tin soldier! " The fish had been caught, taken to the market, sold, and brought home into the kitchen, where the servant girl was cutting him up with a large knife.

She seized the tin soldier by the middle with two of her fingers and took him into the parlour, where every one was eager to see the wonderful man who had travelled in the maw of a fish; however, our little warrior was by no means proud. They set him on the table, and there—no, how could anything so extraordinary happen in this world? —the tin soldier was in the very same room in which he had been before.

He saw the same children, the same playthings stood on the table, among them the beautiful castle with the pretty little dancing maiden, who was still standing upon one leg, while she held the other high in the air; she, too, was constant. It quite affected the tin soldier; he could have found it in his heart to weep tin tears, but such weakness would have been unbecoming in a soldier. He looked at her and she looked at him, but neither spoke a word.

And now one of the little boys took the soldier and threw him without ceremony into the stove. He did not give any reason for so doing, but no doubt the conjurer in the snuff-box must have had a hand in it.

The tin soldier now stood in a blaze of red light; he felt extremely

hot. Whether this heat was the result of the actual fire or of the flames of love within him, he knew not. He had entirely lost his colour. Whether this change had happened during his travels, or was the effect of strong emotion, I know not. He looked upon the little damsel, she looked upon him, and he felt that he was melting; but, constant as ever, he still stood shouldering his arms.

A door opened, the wind seized the dancer, and, like a sylph, she flew straightway into the stove to the tin soldier; they both flamed up into a blaze, and were gone. The soldier was melted to a hard lump, and when the maid took out the ashes the next day she found the remains in the shape of a little tin heart; of the dancer there remained only the gold wing, and that was burned black as coal.

From

THE ARABIAN NIGHTS

ALADDIN
and his Wonderful Lamp

MANY, many years ago there dwelt in one of the largest towns of China a humble tailor named Mustafa. Though industrious he was scarcely able to make both ends meet and very often he, his wife and his only son did not have enough to eat.

This son was called Aladdin and regrettably he had grown up to be a ne'er-do-well. His father had had neither the time nor the money to spend on the boy's education and in consequence Aladdin had learned nothing. In addition he developed very bad habits, was wayward and idle and always disobedient. Since childhood he had done nothing but play with other equally lazy boys of his own age in the streets and squares of the city.

Now Aladdin's father wanted his son to learn the tailoring trade. But Aladdin was a most unwilling pupil. No sooner did Mustafa turn his back than the boy fled from the house and was seen no more till nightfall. Punishment and threats were useless—nothing would change the flighty youth. Finally the father had to give up trying to change Aladdin's attitude, and so grieved and disappointed had the old man become in his only son, that he fell seriously ill and after a few months died.

Aladdin's mother saw that it would be quite useless to expect assistance from her son, so she closed her husband's shop and sold the few tools of his trade. On the little money she obtained from this, together with the pittance she might earn by spinning, she hoped that she and Aladdin might live.

Aladdin felt now completely free to follow his inclinations. He did not heed in the least his mother's scolding, and merely shrugged his shoulders at her threats. He continued to play in the streets and public squares with his companions, returning home only when driven by hunger. Thus he spent his days until he was fifteen years old, thinking not at all of what was to become of him when he grew older.

One day Aladdin was as usual playing with several of his friends in the street, when a stranger approached. He stood watching intently the boys' game and seemed to pay especial attention to Aladdin. The stranger was an African magician who could raise mountains and understood well the art of astrology. He had left his home in Africa two days before. For a little longer he watched the boys at play, then he took aside one of Aladdin's companions and pointing to Aladdin asked the boy his name. On being told, he stepped over to Aladdin and said:

"My son, is not your father the tailor Mustafa?"

"Yes sir," replied Aladdin, "but he is long since dead."

On hearing this the stranger straightway fell on the young man's neck, kissing and embracing him again and again, while tears streamed from his eyes.

"Sir, why do you weep?" asked Aladdin, "and how is it that you know my father's name?"

Sadly the African said: "Why should I not weep! Alas, your father was my brother and you are my dear nephew. I have travelled far for many years and now when I hoped once more to see my brother I learn that he is dead. My grief is indeed great but it is at least some consolation to have seen in your features a resemblance to your father."

He then asked Aladdin where his mother lived and pressed into the youth's hand a purseful of coins.

"Go now to your mother," he said finally, "give her greetings and say to her that I shall visit her to-morrow. I should like to see the house where my brother lived and where he also died."

When Aladdin told his mother of his meeting with his uncle, and gave her the purse, she was quite mystified.

"My son, your father had only one brother," she said, "and he died many years ago. This man is an imposter."

Next day, however, the African magician again came to watch the boys at play. After a little, just as on the previous day, he again approached Aladdin and embraced and kissed him affectionately. Then he gave the boy two gold pieces, saying:

"My son, take this immediately to your mother. Tell her that I should like to visit her this evening and that this money is to buy what

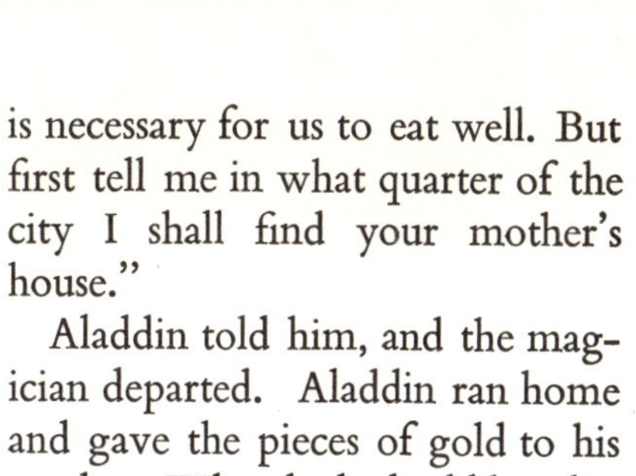

is necessary for us to eat well. But first tell me in what quarter of the city I shall find your mother's house."

Aladdin told him, and the magician departed. Aladdin ran home and gave the pieces of gold to his mother. When he had told her that his supposed uncle intended to sup with them, she went out and bought a plentiful supply of the best food.

In the evening when all was ready Aladdin's mother said, "Now go and look out for your uncle: perhaps he does not know the way." Aladdin was on the point of obeying when there was a knock at the door. Opening it, he at once recognised the stranger. Two servants

followed behind, carrying wine and a variety of luscious and expensive fruits.

The magician paid his respects to Aladdin's mother, and requested her to show him where his brother had sat upon the sofa. When she pointed it out, he knelt down before it and kissed the place, while tears seemed to flow from his eyes.

"My poor brother," he sobbed. "How unfortunate it is that I shall never again see you in this life."

Aladdin's mother still could not quite believe that the stranger was in truth her husband's brother. But then he began to talk.

"Dear sister-in-law, do not think it strange that you have never before met me or heard from me. It is almost forty years since I left this country and I have journeyed round the whole world." And he related how he had travelled through India, Persia, Arabia, Syria, and Egypt; and how at length he had felt a longing for his homeland.

"To the place where a man is born" he concluded, "he should at last return. I said to my self, 'Now I am rich, but my brother perhaps is poor and I might help him!' But the hope of seeing my brother has been shattered: When I saw his son playing in the street, I noticed immediately the resemblance to my brother. And so I spoke to him."

Then turning to the boy, he said: "Well, Aladdin, what work do you do? Do you have a trade?"

At this question Aladdin hung his head, and felt very uncomfortable. But his mother answered for him.

"Aladdin is a very idle boy. All day he does nothing but play in the streets with his friends. His father tried to teach him a trade; he wished to make a useful man out of him, but all in vain. Anxiety over his son brought his father to an early grave. He does not listen to me and sometimes I am tempted to close the door against him forever."

"I am disappointed in you, Aladdin," said the African magician, when he heard the mother's complaints. "A young man should learn to be independent. As I am a rich man, however, I should be glad to buy for you a shop. There you might sell finest materials."

This offer flattered Aladdin's vanity. The prospect of becoming a rich merchant pleased him greatly. He thanked his uncle and said he should all his life be grateful.

"I am glad you will accept," said the magician. "Tomorrow I shall come and take you to town. I shall buy you rich clothes as are proper to be worn by a prosperous merchant."

Aladdin's mother no longer doubted that the magician was in fact the brother of her husband. She brought in supper and as they ate, they discussed the magician's plans for Aladdin. At last the magician rose to take his leave.

He returned the next morning to the widow of Mustafa the tailor, as he had promised and took Aladdin away with him to a merchant's where garments, made of the finest stuffs, were sold.

When Aladdin was clothed from head to toe, he thanked his uncle, and kissing his hand, begged him never to leave home again. The magician promised, then led Aladdin to the street where the richest merchants had their shops.

"Soon you will be a merchant like one of these," he said. "You must come here often and meet them." Then they visited several of the most beautiful mosques in the city and also went to gaze at the Sultan's splendid palace.

At last, after a long walk, they returned to the inn where the magician was staying. There they found a few merchants whom the magician had met since coming to the city. To these men he introduced his nephew and they all dined together.

Later in the evening, the magician accompanied Aladdin back to

his mother's house. Great was the amazement and delight of Aladdin's mother when she beheld her son so richly clothed.

"Dear brother-in-law," said she, "I do not know how to thank you for all your great kindness. My son will be ungrateful indeed if he does not prove himself worthy of your generosity."

To this the magician answered: "Aladdin is a good young man, and comes from excellent stock. We shall make a useful man of him yet. I am only sorry that I was unable to buy a shop for him today; but tomorrow is Friday, and the shops will be shut. The merchants will leave town and rest in their gardens. We must therefore wait until Saturday. But I shall come tomorrow and take Aladdin to see the gardens and squares of the town. There too we shall meet the merchants and their families and I can introduce Aladdin to those he did not see today." And with these words the magician departed.

The next morning Aladdin got up and dressed himself in his new clothes very early. He had been unable to sleep all night for excitement and waited for his uncle with great impatience.

When the magician arrived, he greeted Aladdin affectionately.

"Come, my boy," said he, with a smile, "I will today show you some things which you have never in your life seen before." Together they left the city, admiring as they went the magnificent houses and gardens. At each especially beautiful house or garden, the magician would stop. Each time he would ask Aladdin what he thought of it. And Aladdin, who had never seen anything so magnificent would answer: "Uncle, everything is wonderful."

And so they walked farther and farther away from the city until the African magician, who wanted to carry out a secret plan of his own, suddenly turned into one of the gardens and sat down by a fountain of pure and sparkling water. Feigning tiredness he told Aladdin to rest a while.

The magician then took from a pocket a linen cloth. In this were fruits, cakes and other good things which he shared with Aladdin before resuming their journey.

On past the gardens they walked and into the country till they were quite close to the mountains. Aladdin, who had never in his whole life before taken so long a walk, began to feel very tired.

"Where are we going, my dear uncle?" said he at last. "I can see nothing but hills and mountains before us. And if we go any farther, I know not whether I shall have strength to walk back to the city."

"Be of good cheer," replied his supposed uncle; "we have not much farther to go. I just want to show you yet another garden which is more wonderful by far than any you have seen today. Be patient, Aladdin, I promise we shall soon be there." And he took Aladdin's arm in a friendly fashion and led him on, telling him stories to make the way seem shorter.

They at length came to a narrow valley between two hills. This was the spot to which the magician wanted to bring Aladdin; it was here that the grand plan that was his real reason for coming to China was to be carried out.

"We shall now," said he to Aladdin, "go no farther. Here I shall show you some wondrous sights never before seen by man. They are so marvellous that you will be truly amazed. I am now going to strike a light, and in the meantime I want you to collect all the dry sticks and leaves that you can find lying about so that we may make a fire."

Aladdin soon gathered more than enough for a fire. The magician lighted the match and set them on fire. As soon as they were alight, the African cast over them a secret perfume and pronounced some strange words which Aladdin did not at all understand and a dense smoke immediately arose on all sides. At the same moment, the ground trembled and before their eyes appeared a square stone. It was about a foot and a half across, set horizontally, and in its centre was a heavy brass ring.

At this Aladdin was terrified and made as if to run away. Whereupon the magician flew into a temper, and seizing the unfortunate youth by the arm gave him a resounding blow on the ear and Aladdin fell full length to the ground.

Aladdin began to weep bitterly. " Uncle," he sobbed, " what have I done that you should strike me? I do not understand why you have brought me here, but you frighten me and I want to return immediately to the city."

The magician began to pacify him: " I have brought you here for your own good. You need have no fear. But you must listen to me carefully. Beneath the stone which you see before you lies vast treasure. It is for you alone and will make you richer than the most wealthy monarch. But you and only you are allowed to touch the ring and only you are allowed to raise the stone. Even I am forbidden to touch the stone or enter the treasure vault when it is opened. To make quite sure of success, you must follow exactly the instructions I am about to give you.

Completely bewildered by all that his uncle had told him, but overjoyed at the thought of becoming richer than the richest king, Aladdin with both hands seized the ring which was attached to the stone and heaved mightily. To his surprise, he found that he could raise it without any trouble. He laid it aside.

When the stone was removed, Aladdin could see a small hole about three or four feet deep and at the bottom of this there was a small door with steps leading down still lower.

" You must now, dear nephew," said the African magician to

Aladdin, " listen very carefully to everything I am now about to say and follow my instructions exactly. " Go down these steps until you reach the floor of the cavern. There you will find an open door which leads into a huge vaulted hall divided into three lesser halls. In each of these you will see to the left and right of you four immense bronze vases, filled with gold and silver. But you must take especial care not

to touch these vases or take anything at all from them. Raise the hem of your robe from the ground and wrap it tightly round your body lest it brush against anything; otherwise you will assuredly fall dead on the spot. Walk straight through all three of these halls, remembering always to allow your robe to touch neither floor, walls nor the vases, and in the last hall you will see before you a door. It leads into a large and beautiful garden where grow many trees laden with fruit. Go through this garden by the path which you will see, until you reach the foot of a flight of fifty steps; climb these and at the top you will find yourself on a terrace. There you will look round until you see a niche in which stands a burning lamp. Take up this lamp, extinguish the flame and empty out the oil. Put it then under your robe and bring it to me. You need have no fear that the contents of the lamp will stain your robe—it is not ordinary oil which it burns. On the return journey, if you would like to gather fruit from the garden, you may certainly do so, as much as you want and are able to carry. As long as you have the lamp, all this belongs to you."

At the end of this speech the magician took off and placed on Aladdin's finger, his signet ring, saying: " My son, this ring will protect you from all evil and dangers. Go now, descend these steps, but remember all that I have said to you. When you return I promise that we two shall be the richest people in the world and remain so for the rest of our lives."

With a light heart Aladdin sprang down the steps. He found and walked quickly through the three halls, carefully wrapping his robe tightly round his body just as he had been told to do. He did not want to risk losing his life now. He found the door in the garden and hastened to climb the steps to the terrace. There he saw the lighted lamp standing in its niche. He extinguished the flame and after pouring out the oil, concealed it under his robe.

Aladdin then left the terrace and on the return journey stopped in the garden and stood amazed gazing at the beautiful fruit-laden trees which he had scarcely glanced at before. The fruits which were really precious jewels were of a variety of colours—white, red, green, blue and violet. The white ones were pearls, others which glistened like crystal were diamonds, the dark red fruits were rubies, the paler red a type of ruby called balas, the green were emeralds, the blue, sapphires and turquoises, the violet, amethysts. All of them were very large and quite perfect in shape. No king in the whole world possessed such a wealth of precious stones. Aladdin, however, had no idea at all of the value of these stones; he took them to be but bright glass. He far preferred to these the real grapes, apples and other fruits which grew so plentifully in China. But yet the bright colours and sparkle of these pleased him greatly and he proceeded to gather some, which he put in the pockets and folds of his robe. He then filled two new purses which the magician had given him at the same time as he bought his new clothes. He also concealed some of the jewels in the thickness of his silken girdle. Finally, growing bolder, he even filled the space between his body and his shirt.

Thus, without knowing, Aladdin was laden with untold riches. He then hastened back through the three halls; he did not want to keep his uncle waiting too long. Quickly he climbed the steps which led to the entrance to the cave. There his uncle awaited him with the greatest impatience.

The last step was rather steeper than the others and as soon as Aladdin saw the magician, he called out, "Give me your hand, uncle, to help me up."

"You had better, my dear boy," replied the magician, "first give me the lamp, as that will only hinder you."

"It is not at all in my way," said Aladdin, "and I will give it to you when I am out."

And so they argued, the magician becoming more and more impatient. But Aladdin absolutely refused to hand over the lamp, concealing it instead among the jewels which nestled under his shirt. Then the magician flew into a fearful rage. He thought of course that the young man wanted to keep the lamp for himself. At last he completely lost patience with Aladdin. Murmuring angrily to himself, he suddenly threw something on to the fire which he and Aladdin had earlier lit. Scarcely had he uttered two magic words than the stone which covered the entrance fell into place. He scattered some earth over it and everything appeared as it had done before.

For forty years the magician had studied the arts of magic. Then he discovered that somewhere in the world there was a wonderful lamp which could make its owner the richest and most powerful man in the world. He had also discovered where this lamp was hidden—in an underground place near Aladdin's home town. But he himself did not dare fetch the lamp. Another must descend into the vault and bring it up. For this task he had chosen Aladdin.

But now his wicked plan was foiled. Aladdin had not given up the lamp and fearing that a stranger would discover its secret he had locked

Aladdin up in the earth. The very same day he started back for Africa taking the least frequented roads so as to avoid the city where he had met Aladdin.

But now let us return to Aladdin. What had become of him? Terrified almost to death, he stood alone in the darkness. Loudly he called out to his uncle, begging him to come back and release him and promising to hand over the lamp. Tears coursed down his cheeks, but all his cries and lamentations were in vain. Nothing stirred. No noise could he hear. He groped around, trying to find a doorway, but it was useless. The magician had by his secret words closed even the door which led into the halls. At last, exhausted, the youth sank down on the cold earth. He had no hope that he would ever again see daylight. He was certain that all was lost.

For two days and two nights Aladdin sat in the unfriendly darkness without either food or drink. On the third day, believing that all hope was gone, he clasped his hands together and began to pray to Allah.

" There is no power or strength other than Yours, Almighty God," he began, and without thinking he rubbed the ring which the magician had placed on his finger. All at once a genie of enormous size stood before him. He was so tall that his head touched the roof and he was frightful to behold.

Then the genie spoke. " I am your servant; I am ready to obey the man who wears the ring on his finger—I and all the other servants of the ring."

Aladdin was terrified, but he quickly pulled himself together. Boldly he answered: " Whoever you may be, liberate me from this cavern of the earth."

Scarcely had Aladdin made this request to the genie, than he found himself standing in the open air at the very spot to which the magician had brought him.

The bright light of day shone and almost blinded him. He did not at first recognise the place, but soon he noticed the traces of the bonfire. Behind the gardens through which they had come, lay the city and he recognised the road by which his false uncle had brought him. Thanking God for his miraculous rescue he turned towards home and in the evening, dead tired he arrived at his mother's house.

Overcome by weakness and relief at again seeing his mother, Aladdin fell to the ground in a faint. Thereupon his mother, who had given up all hope of seeing her son again, was filled with both joy and concern. Aladdin, however, soon recovered and his first words were: " Dear Mother, bring me, I beg you, something to eat, for I have not had a morsel of food these last three days." And straightaway his mother brought him all the food she had.

Aladdin then told her everything that had happened.

" Dear Mother," he began, " this stranger was no uncle of mine. He made us great promises and told me that I should become a rich man. But he was a magician, a wicked man and a liar. Finally he even wanted to kill me. I would be dead at this moment if God had not saved me through a miracle." When he had finished his story he brought out the lamp from under his robe and showed it to his mother. He drew out also the glittering stones. His mother, as much as he, was ignorant of their value. She put the precious stones aside and Aladdin put the two full purses behind a cushion on the sofa.

Then he went on with his story and told how he had been buried underground. Tears came into his eyes when he spoke of his despair; only the goodness of God had rescued him when he had turned the ring and been brought once more to daylight.

As Aladdin had not closed his eyes all the time that he was in the underground cavern, it is small wonder that he slept very soundly that night and long into the next day.

When he awoke, his first words were: " Mother, I am hungry."

" Alas, my boy," said his mother, " I have not a crust of bread in the house. What I had, you ate yesterday. You must be patient; I still have a little cotton which I shall go and sell in the town. With the money, I shall buy bread and something for dinner!"

" Dear Mother," replied Aladdin, "keep your cotton. Give me instead the lamp which I brought back from the cave. I think we shall get more money for it—than for your cotton."

Aladdin's mother brought the lamp, saying: " Here it is, but it is very dirty. Let me polish it for you so that it looks like new."

She then brought water and some fine sand and began to rub the lamp. But she had scarcely started when a gigantic genie rose up before her, crying in a voice like thunder: " What do you desire? I am your servant and the servant of anyone who holds this lamp in his hand; I and all the other slaves of the lamp will obey you."

Aladdin's mother was quite unable to answer. So terrified was she by the genie's appearance that she fell fainting to the floor.

Aladdin, however, had already met a similar apparition in the cavern, and without hesitation he seized the lamp and cried boldly: "Servant of the lamp, I am hungry. Bring me something to eat."

The genie at once vanished but reappeared in a moment, bearing a large silver basin in which were twelve covered dishes filled with the most expensive meats and other food. He then placed two bottles of superb wine and two silver cups upon the table, together with six loaves of the finest white bread. Having arranged all this before Aladdin, the genie again disappeared.

Aladdin's mother, meantime, still lay in a faint, but the smell of the costly food made her open her eyes.

" Mother!" cried Aladdin. " Stand up! Look at this rich food! It will surely restore your strength and still my hunger."

When his mother saw the loaded table, she cried out in utter astonishment. " What kind benefactor has done this for us?"

" Dear Mother," her son said, " do not ask questions, but come and eat."

While they ate Aladdin told his mother what had happened when she fainted. His mother, amazed, said, " Why did this fearful spirit speak to me and not to you? It was to you that he appeared in the underground vault."

" Dear Mother," answered her son, " this was a different spirit from the one which I saw in the vault. There was indeed a resemblance to the other, but he was the slave of the ring; the other was the slave of the lamp."

" Then the lamp is the cause of the appearance of this hateful spirit?" cried his mother. " Take it from my sight! Hide it or sell it or throw it away. If this spirit comes again I shall die of shock. I will have nothing more to do with spirits."

" No, Mother," answered Aladdin. " Now I shall not sell the lamp. Can you not understand its value? It has given us food when we were hungry, and it will do so again in the future. Think of the African magician! He made a long and difficult journey solely to acquire this wonderful lamp. He had no interest in the gold underground. He knew that this lamp was worth more than all the silver and gold in the world. Now that we know the secret power of the lamp we must take the greatest care of it.

" Fear not, Mother, I shall keep the lamp from your sight and you will never see the genie. The ring too I can not sell or throw away. It saved my life. Who knows what dangers it may yet save me from!"

" My son, you must do as you please," said his mother, "as long as I never again see the slaves of either the lamp or the ring."

After supper the next evening very little remained of the food which the genie had brought. Aladdin who was unwilling to wait until it was completely gone, decided the following morning to try to sell one of the silver dishes. He left the house very early and happening to meet, on the way to the city, a Jew, he stopped him. Showing him the dish, Aladdin asked if he would like to buy it.

The Jew examined the dish carefully and saw that it was of real silver. Quickly realising that Aladdin had no idea of its value, he took the dish, giving the youth a piece of gold which was but a fiftieth part of its true worth.

As Aladdin turned for home the Jew already regretted giving the ignorant boy even that much and wanted to call him back. But

Aladdin ran so quickly that he was almost immediately out of sight.

On the way home, Aladdin stopped at a baker's shop, changed the gold piece and bought some bread. The change and the bread he gave to his mother and she set off for the market to buy enough food for several days.

And in this way they lived, Aladdin selling dish after dish as the need arose to the Jewish merchant. At last all twelve dishes were sold and Aladdin took up the basin. This vessel was ten times as heavy as the dishes. In fact it was too heavy to carry to the city, so he fetched the dealer to his mother's home. The Jew examined it carefully and counted out ten gold pieces and with this amount Aladdin was overjoyed.

As long as these ten pieces lasted, they were spent on the day to day necessities of the household. Meantime Aladdin remained in idleness, but since his adventure with the magician, he no longer played in the streets with his former companions. He spent his time walking or conversing with people whom he met. Often he was to be found in the shops of the prosperous merchants, listening to their talk and in this way he picked up both some knowledge of business and of the world in general.

At last when the ten gold pieces had all been spent, Aladdin turned again to the lamp and rubbed it at exactly the same spot as his mother had rubbed it. Instantly the same genie which had appeared already, rose up before him. As Aladdin had rubbed the lamp more gently than his mother had done, the genie spoke to him in a much milder tone. " What do you desire of me? I am your servant and the servant of all those who hold the lamp in their hands. I and all the other servants of the lamp are ready to obey you."

" I am hungry," Aladdin cried. " Bring me something to eat."

The genie disappeared but in a moment reappeared with similar silver dishes as before, each filled with the finest of food. Placing his load before Aladdin the genie again disappeared.

Aladdin's mother had had not the least desire to meet the genie again and had immediately left the house when she saw her son take up the lamp. Now she appeared in the doorway and stood staring in the greatest amazement. Once again the table was completely covered with silver dishes full of the most delicious and fragrant food. Then she and her son sat at the table and ate. After they had finished their meal there was still enough food for the following day.

When their supply of food had again been exhausted, Aladdin took one of the silver dishes and set out to find the Jewish merchant. On the way he had to pass the shop of an old and thoroughly honest goldsmith. Looking up and catching sight of Aladdin, the old man called him in. " What have you there, my son ?" he asked. I have seen you often before, carrying similar dishes into the town and always you return with empty hands." Aladdin was quite willing to show the goldsmith his dish and the old man, after carefully examining and weighing it, told the youth that it was worth fifty gold pieces.

" Will you sell it to me ?" he asked the youth. Aladdin then realised how he had been tricked by the Jew. He told the goldsmith about the silver plates which he had already sold, each for one gold piece.

" You have been cheated," cried the goldsmith. " In future come to me. I shall give you the true value of your silver dishes."

And so whenever Aladdin wanted to sell a dish he went with it to the goldsmith; he took also the cups and each time received their full

value in gold pieces. They lived in this manner for some years, with occasionally the assistance of the miraculous lamp.

Aladdin continued to go among the merchants conversing with them about business and materials and from the goldsmith he learned much about precious stones and their value. Thus he realised that the marvellous fruit which he had brought from the underground garden was in fact composed of the most costly jewels. Then he knew that the two purses hidden behind the cushion on the sofa contained untold treasure. But Aladdin was wise enough to tell no one and for keeping silent he was to be indeed thankful in the days to come.

One day on his way to the goldsmith's shop, Aladdin heard an order from the Sultan being proclaimed in the streets. Everyone was to retire indoors immediately—no one, on pain of death must appear in the open. Princess Badroulboudour, the daughter of the Sultan, was going to the bath.

Aladdin had heard that the princess was extremely beautiful and he was seized with curiosity to see her without her veil. He hid therefore behind the door of the bath. No sooner did Aladdin see her lovely face than he fell deeply in love.

When he returned home, Aladdin was quite unable to hide his confusion and distress. Perplexed,

his mother asked finally if something unpleasant had happened to him or whether he felt ill. But Aladdin merely sighed, and for the rest of the day would neither speak nor eat.

Aladdin spent a restless night. Next morning, however, he at last broke his silence and said:

"You may well have thought, Mother, that I was ill," he began. "But I was not ill and am still not ill. I can not express easily how I feel but I shall tell you what happened a few days ago so that you can try to advise me. On the day that it was announced that Princess Badroulboudour would go to the bath, I was lucky to find a narrow slit through which I could see her arrival. This is the reason for my unhappiness. When I saw her beautiful face I fell in love with her instantly. My longing for her grows ever stronger as the days pass and I shall never know peace again until I have made her my wife."

Aladdin's mother listened attentively to all that her son said but when he talked of marrying the Sultan's daughter she had to laugh. "My dear son, are you mad that you should think of such a thing?" she asked him.

" No, Mother," Aladdin answered, " my determination has never been so strong before. You cannot hope to persuade me to put the princess out of my mind. I must win her, no matter how."

" Oh my Son, do not talk such nonsense," said his mother. " How do you propose to approach the Sultan? Who is going to speak for you to him."

" No other than yourself, Mother," was his reply. " I want you to go and tell him of my desire to court his daughter."

" I? " cried his mother. " I should never undertake such a mission. Do you forget that you are only the son of a poor tailor? How can you think of marrying the Sultan's daughter? "

" Dear Mother," replied Aladdin. " I have thought of all this already. I know that you speak good sense. Nevertheless it makes no difference. My mind is made up. You must go to the Sultan if you love me. Such a thing may never happen to me again. If the princess does not become my wife I shall no longer feel like living."

Aladdin's mother laughed again at her son's obstinacy. Certainly she would have liked to see his wish come true, but this plan of his she considered both foolish and impossible. She tried to reason with him.

" My son, I should like to try to help you to fulfil your wish but you must see the difficulties. The first question anyone asks of a suitor is what he possesses in order to maintain a wife and later a family. You have nothing, how then can you even think of the Sultan's daughter? Even if I were not too ashamed to go, how would I obtain an audience with the Sultan. And even if I did see him I should be taken for a fool if I were to make such a request of him. Besides anyone seeking audience of the Sultan must take him a gift. What sort of gift have you to offer, valuable enough to make him give you his daughter as your wife?"

Aladdin listened quietly to his mother's objections.

" Dear Mother, you are right. Thank you for reminding me that the Sultan must have a gift. You need have no fear that it will be a worthy one. I alone have something which will bring any prince or king to his knees. You know, mother, that I brought back with me from the underground garden many coloured stones. We thought these stones were made of glass but in fact they are precious gems of the greatest beauty—there are no others like them in the whole world. In the goldsmith's shop I have seen many gems but none as fine as mine. They would sell for an unbelievably high price. You have a porcelain vase, mother. Give it to me and we shall fill it with jewels. Then you will surely marvel at the glittering splendour. I am quite certain the Sultan will never have seen anything so brilliant."

His mother brought the vase and Aladdin took the stones from the purses and placed them in it. They shone and gleamed in the vase so that both the mother and son were almost blinded by the sight. When first they had looked at them it had been by lamplight but now the bright sunshine struck a million gleaming lights from them.

"Do you believe now, mother," cried Aladdin "that this is a fitting gift for the Sultan? Now you can surely go to his court. With this in your hand you will be bound to be received graciously."

Aladdin's mother was not so overcome by the valuable present as her son. Nevertheless she hoped it would find favour. But when she thought of her son's request she was still far from confident. Aladdin and the Princess!

"Dear son," she said, "this gift is beautiful and of great value. It will be accepted with much graciousness by the Sultan, I am quite sure, but I have not the courage to introduce the question of his daughter. But if I should bring myself to speak to the Sultan of your desire he will still, this great gift notwithstanding, take me for a fool and order me to be thrown out of the palace and perhaps even put to death."

Aladdin's mother brought up more reasons for not going to the Sultan. But Aladdin continued to beg and press his mother until at last she gave in.

It was too late then to go to the Sultan, so the matter was postponed till the next day. Until that time mother and son spoke of nothing but her visit to the court. Aladdin tutored her again and again on what she must do and say.

Although it was very late when they retired, it was not yet day-break when Aladdin wakened his mother. He urged her to dress quickly and hasten to the palace gate.

Aladdin's mother consented. She covered the vase in which the jewels lay, in a very fine cloth. She then covered that with a coarser cloth and fastened it at each corner so that she could carry her burden easily on her head. Finally to Aladdin's great joy, she set off on the road to the Sultan's palace.

The grand vizier together with all the other officers of the court were just entering the palace when she arrived at the gate. A great crowd of petitioners and others who had business at court streamed after them. Aladdin's mother followed the train and found herself in the large and beautiful salon where the Sultan held his audiences. She placed herself directly opposite the Sultan's throne. To the left and right of it stood the greatest and richest in the land. Names were called out from a long list and the Sultan heard their requests in turn and administered justice. Finally the council broke up, the Sultan rose and the grand vizier and other officers also retired.

When Aladdin's mother saw that the Sultan had left the salon, she realised that the audience was over for the day and she too left the palace and made her way homewards.

When Aladdin saw his mother return still carrying the vase, he did not understand what it could mean. He was afraid his gift had been refused.

Impatiently he listened to his mother's explanation, but when she promised to return to the palace on the next day, he was relieved that at least she no longer feared to stand in the presence of the Sultan.

Next morning she again hastened with her gift to the Sultan's palace. But alas the gate was shut and from people passing by she learned that only every second day did the council sit. She had therefore to return home and give her son this information. Once again Aladdin had to contain his impatience.

Six times Aladdin's mother made the journey to the Sultan's palace and each time she placed herself directly opposite the throne; but each time she was equally unsuccessful. Never did she have the courage to step forward or utter a word to him. Probably she might have gone there in vain a hundred times if the Sultan himself had not become aware of her and wondered at her silent persistence.

At the end of the following sitting of the council he turned to his grand vizier and said: " For some time now I have noticed a woman who comes to each sitting of the council. Always she stands directly opposite me and she holds in her hands something which is wrapped in a cloth. From the beginning to the end of the audience she remains standing there, saying nothing. Do you know why she comes and what she wants?"

The grand vizier knew as little about it as the Sultan, but he did not want to have no answer ready. Therefore, he said:

" Sire, women very often come here for the most trivial of reasons. Perhaps this one wants to make a complaint about her husband or a neighbour, or perhaps some shopkeeper has sold her bad meat or vegetables."

The grand vizier's answer, however, did not at all satisfy the Sultan and he ordered him to have the woman summoned at the next sitting of the council. He would, he said, hear her plea.

Thereupon the grand vizier kissed his master's hand, then placed it on his head, as was the usual custom when the Sultan gave an order.

On the next day that the council sat, Aladdin's mother again returned to the audience chamber and as usual she took up her position opposite the Sultan.

The Sultan noticed her immediately and turning impatiently to his grand vizier, he said: " There stands the woman of whom I spoke to you. Have her summoned and we shall hear her request." The grand vizier immediately signed to Aladdin's mother to come forward. Trembling, she approached the foot of the throne and prostrated herself before the Sultan.

Ordering her to rise, the Sultan asked her what business brought her to his court.

" Sire," she mumbled, " I have a request to make which is so unusual that I tremble and am ashamed to speak of it."

So that she might have freedom and privacy the Sultan ordered the court to be cleared. He and the grand vizier alone would hear her request. Turning to Aladdin's mother, he told her to speak without fear.

Hesitantly, she then confessed to the Sultan how her son had seen, fallen in love with and desired the hand of his daughter in marriage.

The Sultan listened with patience and good humour. There was no trace of anger or even scorn in his face. But before he gave her an answer, he asked with a smile what she carried in her bundle. At once Aladdin's mother uncovered the vase and offered it to him.

Astounded and almost blinded, the Sultan looked upon the jewels and at first could not utter a single word. Never before had he seen so many costly gems collected together in one single vase. They were also of such a size that he had never known existed. At last he took the vase from the hands of Aladdin's mother exclaiming: " How truly magnificent!" And one after the other he picked up the jewels to admire their perfection and dazzle. Then turning to show some to his grand vizier, he said: " Look at these jewels! The man who possesses stones of such splendour and colour must indeed be wealthy! He who can send such a valuable gift is indeed worthy of becoming my son-in-law."

On hearing these words, the grand vizier became extremely agitated. He had believed that the Sultan proposed that his daughter should marry his own son. Now he feared, and with reason, that dazzled by the splendour of this gift, the Sultan had other plans.

Coming close to the Sultan, therefore, he whispered that perhaps he might wait three months before making up his mind to present his daughter to an unknown man, however wealthy. He then reminded his sovereign that he had earlier promised that his son should marry the princess. " In three months, Sire," he concluded, " I shall bring to you a gift of equal value." Though the Sultan doubted that this would be possible, he agreed to grant his vizier the three months.

He turned back then to Aladdin's mother and said: "Thank your son for his magnificent gift and tell him that I shall consider carefully his request. He must, however, have patience for three months. There is much to be discussed and that period of time is necessary for all arrangements to be made for the wedding of a princess. You may return here when the three months have elapsed."

Aladdin's mother, full of gratitude, again prostrated herself at the Sultan's feet and humbly thanked him for listening to her request.

Aladdin's mother went home feeling the greatest joy because she, a poor and humble woman had spoken to the Sultan. Her joy was all the stronger now that she could tell Aladdin that she had received a favourable answer when she had expected a rebuke.

Aladdin saw his mother return earlier than usual and this time without the vase on her head. When she entered the room smiling, his spirits rose immediately, He was sure that this time she had good news for him.

" Dear Mother," he asked her, " was the Sultan gracious and has he accepted the present? What did he say to your request? "

His mother took off her veil and sat down beside her son on the sofa. Then she began to speak: " Aladdin, I shall not leave you in suspense. The Sultan has promised that his daughter will become your wife." And she told him how it had all come about.

She told him how she had introduced the subject of the betrothal and repeated word for word what the Sultan had said about their present. But it had not escaped her notice that the grand vizier was not happy about the news. He had apparently wanted to persuade his master to refuse his consent.

Joyfully and full of hope, Aladdin listened to the news his mother had brought. He thought himself richer and more fortunate than any man alive. Three months seemed to him an eternity, but there was nothing for it but to wait its passing patiently. To him the word of the Sultan was binding, but his longing made him count the hours, the days and the weeks.

Two months of this waiting period had already passed when Aladdin's mother, discovering one evening that she had no oil for her lamps, left the house to buy some. To her great surprise on reaching the city, she found that it was ablaze with lights. The townspeople had decked their houses with flowers and decorations, each one vying with the others to be gayer and more splendid. In the streets there were crowds of people dressed as for a festival and every face was alight with happiness. Court officers in ceremonial dress, accompanied by attendants and slaves, rode richly caparisoned horses through the streets and everywhere there was an air of excitement and expectancy.

Making her way through the crowds, Aladdin's mother at last reached the oil merchant. She asked him what the festivities were about.

"Where do you come from, my good woman?" asked the oil merchant. "Don't you know that this evening the Princess Badroulboudour, the daughter of the Sultan, is to marry the son of the grand vizier? Presently she will leave the bath and all these officers on horseback whom you see there, have gathered to escort her in state back to the palace. There the wedding will take place."

Aladdin's mother in dismay waited to hear no more but ran home to tell Aladdin. She met him at the door. He was quite unprepared for her news.

"My son," she called, "all is lost. The Sultan is not going to keep his word."

"Why should he not keep his word?" cried Aladdin. "Who told you this?"

"This very day," replied his mother, "the princess is going to marry the grand vizier's son. The whole town is speaking about it."

And she told him all she had heard. Now no longer could Aladdin be in doubt.

Without saying a word against the Sultan or the grand vizier, Aladdin turned to his mother saying, " Dear mother, I think the grand vizier's son will not be as happy as he hopes. But let us speak no more about it. Prepare supper for us, then I shall go for a little into my room."

Aladdin's mother suspected what her son was about to do—he would use the magic lamp to stop the marriage of the princess. She was quite right.

After supper Aladdin went into his room and locked the door. Then he pulled out the lamp and rubbed it.

Immediately the genie appeared and said: " What do you desire? I am your servant and ready to obey you."

" Listen to me," cried Aladdin, " until now you have brought me rich food and drink when I commanded it; this time I have a very different and much more important commission for you. The Sultan has promised me the hand of his daughter in marriage, but today he is about to break his word. Before the passing of the three months of waiting which he decreed, he is about to give his daughter to the son of the grand vizier. I order you now, as a true slave of this lamp to wait until the two are wed, then bring the bride and bridegroom here immediately."

" Master," replied the genie, " I will obey you. Have you another wish?"

" Not at present," said Aladdin, and the genie vanished.

Aladdin then went back to his mother and spent a peaceful evening. After a time he again went to his room to await the return of the genie and the completion of his orders.

He did not have to wait long. Almost immediately the genie brought the newly-wed couple to him. To their great astonishment he set them down in the middle of Aladdin's room. " Take this bridegroom and shut him in the lumber room," Aladdin commanded. " Tomorrow morning at daybreak come back to me."

Immediately the genie took the grand vizier's son and transported him to the lumber room. Then he breathed upon him so that he

became immediately paralysed and was not able to move a muscle for the entire night.

Aladdin was overjoyed at last to see the princess at close quarters. But he did not try to talk long to her, merely saying: " Do not be afraid, my beautiful princess. You are quite safe here; nothing and no one shall harm you. I have been compelled to take these unusual measures purely out of my deep love for you, and to punish your father for allowing you to marry the son of the grand vizier, thus faithlessly breaking his promise to me."

The princess was so disturbed and alarmed by these unexpected and incomprehensible events that she scarcely heard a single word of Aladdin's speech and consequently the young man could get no reply from her. Indeed so agitated was she that she was not even able to remember his words later.

But Aladdin was content with the progress of events. He went to

bed and was soon sleeping peacefully. Not so the princess. It was the first time in her life that she had been in such a small, dark room and she never spent a worse night than this one. Still worse was the plight of the grand vizier's son who in the dark hole of the lumber room could not even move.

Next morning Aladdin had no need to rub his lamp to summon the genie. Punctually he stood in the room and said:

" My lord and master, I am here! Command and I shall willingly obey."

" Go," answered Aladdin, " and fetch the son of the grand vizier and return him and the princess to the palace."

Immediately the genie went to put an end to the discomfort of the bridegroom and in an instant both he and the princess were in the palace in the same chamber from which they had been taken.

Needless to say, neither time was the genie seen by the princess or the son of the grand vizier. Had they seen his fearful form they would probably have died of fright. Neither did they hear a single word which passed between Aladdin and the genie.

Scarcely had the genie returned the bridal couple to their room than the Sultan entered to wish his daughter good morning and to ask her how she had slept. The grand vizier's son who had lain freezing all night had again to leave his warm bed. Wretched and miserable he threw on some clothes and quickly retired to the adjoining room.

Stepping up to his daughter's bed, the Sultan stooped and kissed her on the brow, as was his custom. But the princess gave her father no answer, and when he looked at her more closely he was immediately struck by the utter desolation of her expression. Sadly she looked up at her father but said nothing. Confounded, the Sultan realised that her silence must have extraordinary cause. He therefore went at once to the room of the Sultana to tell her of the woeful state in which he had found his daughter.

" I will go and see her," said the Sultana; " I am sure she will not receive me in the same manner."

The Sultana went to the princess's room and was amazed to find her morning kiss was not returned. Her daughter looked very depressed. Something unusual must have happened to her, otherwise she would not look so disturbed. But what was it?

" My dear daughter," she began, " why do you speak not to me, tell me what has happened? Do not leave me in this state of uncertainty."

Then the princess raised her head and sighing deeply said, " Dear Mother, do not be angry if I have not received you properly, but last night such strange things happened that I even now cannot understand them. I find it difficult to explain it to you."

The princess related to her mother, in the most lively colours, how she and her husband had been transported to a miserable room and then how she had found herself quite alone and separated from her husband, without knowing at all what had become of him.

" In the room was a strange young man," she went on. " He spoke to me, but in my excitement I did not understand what he said. Then the young man went to bed and fell asleep. I, on the other hand, spent the worst night of my life. This morning I and my husband were brought back to the palace. Scarcely had we arrived, when my father came to my room. But I was not fit to answer his questions. He was angry with me because I did not receive him well. However he will understand my sad plight when he learns of my dreadful night. I hope he will then forgive me."

The Sultana listened to her daughter's story attentively and quite calmly, but she found it hard to believe.

" My dear child," she said to the princess, " you were quite right not to recount this tale to your father. Say nothing of this to anyone at all if you do not wish people to think that you have lost your senses."

" Mother," answered the Princess, " I am not insane, but in full possession of my wits. I have told you the truth as it happened. Ask my husband, he will tell you the same story."

" I will talk with him," answered the Sultana, " But even if he tells me the same story, I shall scarcely believe it. Put this folly out of your head! Listen how the drums and trumpets are sounding. They are calling the whole country to join in the celebration of your marriage. Put on your most beautiful clothes and be happy. Above all, forget this hair-raising tale that you have told me. Perhaps it was only a bad dream."

She went to the Sultan and told him that the princess had spent a bad night and had had fearful dreams, but that she was calmer now. Then she summoned the grand vizier's son and asked him if there was any truth in the story that his young wife had told her. The grand vizier's son was very much afraid that he would lose his bride if he told his story, so he answered that he knew nothing about it. Then the Sultana was convinced that her daughter had dreamt it all.

The festivities continued for the rest of the day with dancing and singing and joyous music, but the princess remained wretched.

The grand vizier's son felt no less miserable after his disturbing night, but he tried hard to hide it. People must think that as the husband of the Princess Badroulboudour he was the happiest of men.

Aladdin had gone into the city to look at the festivities. The people talked everywhere of the good fortune and honour which had fallen on the grand vizier's son by his marriage with the Sultan's daughter. When Aladdin heard this he had to laugh. He thought to himself: if only you knew what a night he spent, you would not think him fortunate. After a time he went home and fetching out the lamp he rubbed it. Immediately the genie appeared and asked him what he desired.

" Go, and as soon as it is evening bring here the princess and her husband as you did yesterday,"said Aladdin.

The genie disappeared once more and the events of the preceding night were repeated. The grand vizier's son was left again in the cold lumber room and the princess again tried in vain to sleep. Next morning, as before, the genie returned and transported them back to the palace.

Impatiently the Sultan waited for the morning. Would his daughter again give him a cold reception? It was very early when he went to her chamber and his son-in-law, his teeth chattering with cold was just climbing into bed. As before, he hastily left the apartment. Approaching the princess's bed, the Sultan wished her good morning. To his horror the princess burst into tears. She then told her father everything that had happened.

After hearing the dreadful story, the Sultan stormed angrily to his apartment and immediately summoned the grand vizier. " Have you spoken to your son?" he demanded, beside himself with rage. " Has he told you how his last two evenings were spent?" And he brandished his sabre in front of the startled counsellor.

When the latter replied that he had not seen his son, the Sultan told him everything he had heard from the Princess Badroulboudour. " I have no doubt that my daughter has told me the truth, but I want to have confirmation from your son. Go to him immediately."

The grand vizier instantly went to his son and told him what the Sultan had said, and commanded him not to disguise the truth, and tell him everything that had happened.

" My father," cried the young man, " I shall hide nothing from you. All that the princess has said is quite true. But she could not tell everything, for she did not know how *I* fared.

" Since my marriage I have lived through two of the most frightful nights imaginable. Words fail me to describe the the horrors I have experienced or the sheer terror that I have felt. Four different times I been taken up from my bed and transported to a strange place, I know not by what means. The place where I found myself was a wretched lumber room, cold, dark and ugly. All night my teeth chattered with cold and I was forced to stand straight up, unable to move a single muscle, although there seemed to be nothing to prevent me. Father, I am quite certain that for the future comfort and happiness of the princess as well as of myself, we must no longer remain husband and wife. I am fully aware of the great honour which has been conferred on me by the Sultan, but I now entreat and implore you to persuade him to declare the marriage null and void. Assuredly I would rather die than spend another such dreadful night."

The angry Sultan, on hearing the grand vizier's plea, had no hesitation in annulling the marriage. He then ordered the festivities to stop instantly in the palace and throughout the city. As for the princess, she remained in her own apartment refusing all company and her father tried in vain to comfort her.

All the people were amazed when the festivities came so suddenly to an end. There were many and very different rumours in the city, but no one knew the truth. They had seen the grand vizier and his son leaving the palace sadly. The only person who knew the secret was Aladdin. But he said nothing and just smiled to himself. Now he had no rival to fear. And he needed no further help from the genie.

The Sultan thought no more of his promise to Aladdin. The grand vizier also had forgotten about the whole affair. It never entered the heads of either of them that Aladdin had played the part of magician.

Aladdin allowed the three months which the Sultan had decreed to pass without a word. He felt quite confident that soon the princess would be his wife. Then when the full time had elapsed, he sent his mother to the palace with instructions to remind the Sultan of his promise. Accordingly, she set off for the palace and took up her old position in the council chamber exactly opposite the Sultan's throne.

It was not long before the Sultan caught sight of her and at once he recalled his promise. Turning to his grand vizier he indicated Aladdin's mother. "That is the woman," he whispered, "who some time ago brought the magnificent gift of jewels. I had quite forgotten until now that I asked her to return here in three months' time. Have her brought before me instantly and let me hear what she has to say. We shall postpone your usual report until later."

The usher led Aladdin's mother before the Sultan and she immediately threw herself at the foot of the throne. She wished the Sultan power, fortune and long life. When she rose, the Sultan asked her what she desired.

"Sire," she answered, "three months have elapsed. After this period you vowed to fulfil your promise. I come now on behalf of my son and ask you to consent to his marriage with your daughter."

The Sultan, after some little reflection turned to the grand vizier and consulted with him in low tones. At last he turned back to Aladdin's mother saying: "Sultans should keep their promises but I must make sure that your son is able to provide for my daughter. Take this message to Aladdin:—I shall keep my word and give him the hand of my daughter if he will send me forty large basins of beaten

gold, filled to the brim with such costly jewels as you have already brought to me. Also I should like them to be carried by forty black slaves; forty well-grown white slaves, handsome and richly dressed, must also accompany them. When your son has fulfilled these conditions I shall be very willing to allow him to wed my daughter."

Aladdin's mother again prostrated herself at the foot of the throne and retired. Hastening home, she told her son in detail what the Sultan had said.

"Now, my son, the Sultan awaits your answer, but I think he will have to wait a long time."

But Aladdin said with a smile, "Not so long as you think, mother. The Sultan is mistaken; his conditions are not so difficult as he thinks. I thought he would have demanded a higher price for the princess. What he is asking is for me a trifle. I would give a thousand times

more in order to call the princess my wife. Go now, order provisions and let me think it over."

As soon as his mother had left the house, Aladdin fetched the lamp and rubbed it. As usual the genie appeared instantly and asked what his master now desired of him.

Aladdin spoke. "The Sultan is ready to give me his daughter in marriage. First, however, he has asked me to send him forty basins of beaten gold, filled to the brim with the same sort of fruit as I gathered in the garden of the cavern. Forty black slaves must carry these basins and the same number of white slaves, young, handsome and dressed in fine clothes must accompany them. Go and carry out my wishes at once. I shall send the slaves with these gifts to the palace before the council rises."

The genie said that his commands should be instantly obeyed and disappeared.

Only a very short time passed before the genie again stood before Aladdin. Forty black slaves accompanied him, each one bearing on his head a heavy basin of beaten gold, filled with diamonds, rubies, emeralds and pearls, all of the same magnificent size and excellence as the ones which Aladdin had already presented to the Sultan. The basins were covered in cloth of gold, richly embroidered. Outside in the courtyard of the little house stood forty well-grown white slaves. All of them were richly clad and waited to accompany the black slaves to the palace.

When Aladdin's mother returned from the market and saw this extraordinary sight, she knew immediately that they had the lamp to thank. She was on the point of taking off her veil when her son stopped her.

" Dear Mother," said he, " we must lose no time. I should like you to accompany these slaves to the Sultan at once. Before the council rises, his demands must be fulfilled. Then will he recognise how important to me it is that I should marry the princess."

Aladdin opened the door that led into the street, and ordered all the slaves to go out one after another. He then placed a white slave before each of the black ones, who carried the gold basins on their heads.

When the eighty slaves reached the Sultan's palace, everyone stopped and stared at the magnificent spectacle, and from all sides people hurried to look. As the first slave arrived at the gate, the

porters took him for a king and tried to kiss the hem of his robe.

"We are only slaves," said this man solemnly. "Our master will appear shortly."

The Sultan who had been informed by attendants of the arrival of the slaves, commanded that the palace gate should be flung open and the procession brought into the council chamber. In perfect order, the eighty slaves stepped through the gateway and into the chamber, forming there a complete half-circle in front of the throne of the Sultan. Then, taking the golden basins from their heads, the black slaves placed them on the floor in front of them and prostrated themselves before the Sultan, their foreheads almost touching the carpet. The white slaves did likewise. In a moment or two, having paid homage to the monarch, they all stood up and as one man, the black slaves pulled the rich coverings from the golden basins to reveal their glittering contents.

Meanwhile Aladdin's mother approached the Sultan's throne and humbly threw herself at his feet with her forehead touching the carpet.

"My Lord," she said, "my son values the princess over everything. He values her much higher than he can show by these gifts. But he hopes that you will accept them graciously and that they will satisfy the conditions that you have laid down."

The Sultan was overwhelmed by the costliness and splendour of the gifts and quite dazzled by the beauty and fire of the gems. He stood astonished before Aladdin's mother. "How could Aladdin have produced such treasure in so short a time?" he wondered. Scarcely an hour had passed since he had issued his demands. He hesitated no longer. He did not even think of asking whether Aladdin possessed any other qualifications that would render him worthy of becoming his son-in law.

"What say you now, vizier?" he asked his adviser. "Is this man not worthy to marry my daughter?"

The grand vizier was still more overcome by the magnificence of the presents than was his master. Envy and jealousy gnawed him to think that a stranger should win the Sultan's daughter and so belittle the rank of his son as to become the son-in-law of the Sultan. He would have preferred that the marriage of the princess with Aladdin should never take place but he dared not express his real thoughts.

" Sire," he answered " there are no precious stones worthy of your daughter. But this man has sent priceless gifts, therefore we must do him the honour of allowing him to become your son-in-law."

The other gentlemen of the court also with loud applause gave their assent to the marriage.

The Sultan hesitated no longer and to Aladdin's mother said: "Go, my good woman, and tell your son that I am waiting with open arms to receive and embrace him."

The Sultan then ordered the council to adjourn. Sending for the princess's servants, he gave orders that they should take the golden vessels to his daughter. Instantly they carried out his order.

The eighty white and black slaves had to go to the inner parts of the castle and take up their places in long rows before the rooms of the princess. The Sultan had already told the princess of the magnificence of the presents. Now she was curious to see them for herself. She was astounded at the brilliance of the stones and at the splendour of the slaves. This pleased her father greatly. At last she was again taking an interest in the world.

" Dear daughter," he cried, " I think that your new husband will please you better than the son of the grand vizier. I pray that you will be happy with him."

When Aladdin's mother arrived home she told her son what the Sultan had said on receiving the presents. Aladdin was so delighted at this news that he hardly answered his mother, but retired to his chamber and summoned the genie to him.

"I have called you to take me immediately to a bath; and when I have finished bathing, I wish you to have in readiness for me a richer, and if possible, more magnificent dress than was ever worn by any monarch."

Scarcely had he spoken these words than Aladdin became invisible and he felt himself being taken up in the genie's arms. In an instant he had been carried to a bath more splendid than was ever seen by a king. It was made of the finest marble of many colours and paintings of great value adorned the walls. In an adjoining salon studded with precious stones, Aladdin was undressed. He was then led to the bath itself and bathed in warm water scented with fragrant essences. At no time did he see who it was who attended him. After bathing, Aladdin felt a completely different man. His complexion was rosy and his skin fresh and white; he was alive and active in body and mind. In the salon were waiting not the clothes which he had just taken off, but the most costly robes imaginable. Aladdin had never seen raiment so magnificent. The genie helped him to dress and Aladdin could not help exclaiming aloud with joy as he put on each garment.

When he was ready, the genie carried him back to his own room. There he asked Aladdin if there was anything else that he desired.

"Yes," replied Aladdin. "I want now a horse whose beauty and fleetness must surpass any horse possessed by the Sultan; its saddle and trapping must be worth ten thousand pieces of gold.

"Provide me also," Aladdin continued, "with twenty slaves as a retinue. They should be as richly clad as the forty whom I sent to the Sultan. A further twenty shall walk before me in two ranks. Also my mother will need six female slaves to attend her and they must be at least as finely dressed as those of the princess. Each of these slaves should bring a costly robe as beautiful as those worn by the Sultana herself. Finally bring me ten purses, each containing a thousand gold coins. For the present that is all that I require. Go quickly."

The genie disappeared but in a very short time had returned leading a fine arab steed richly caparisoned. Following behind came the forty slaves, each fourth man bearing a purse full of gold coins. The six female slaves each carried a beautiful dress—they were all for Aladdin's mother, and were magnificent enough to grace a queen.

Of the ten purses of gold, Aladdin left only six with the slaves; the other four he gave to his mother. He then instructed the slaves to scatter among the people the gold pieces in the six purses, three pursefuls to the right and three to the left, as they made their way to the palace. The six female slaves he presented to his mother. Aladdin finally sent off a slave as courier to the palace to ask if the Sultan would now receive him. The slave set off at top speed and soon returned with the message that the Sultan awaited Aladdin's arrival.

Aladdin then mounted his horse and the procession started for the palace. A wonderful spectacle it presented, and soon the streets were thronged with astonished citizens. Their astonishment changed to joyful cries when the gold coins began to rain among them. And so Aladdin, looking like a king, rode with his train to the palace where the Sultan had given orders for his immediate admission.

When the Sultan saw Aladdin he was astounded at the handsome appearance, stately bearing and magnificent dress of the young man who desired to marry his daughter. The poor clothing of his mother had led him to expect something quite different. Recovering in a moment from his astonishment, however, he rose and stepping quickly down from the throne went forward to meet Aladdin. He had no wish that so majestic a figure as Aladdin should throw himself on the floor at his feet. Instead the Sultan embraced him most warmly and led him up the steps of the throne. There, Aladdin tried to kneel, but the Sultan, taking him by the hand, insisted that he should sit between himself and his grand vizier.

"Honourable Sire," Aladdin began when he was seated, "you have given me the hand of your daughter, and yet I am one of the humblest of your servants. Forgive me for daring to raise my eyes to the princess but my love for her was too powerful. I would have died if she had refused me."

"My son," answered the Sultan, "I promised that you should marry her and I do not regret that I have kept my word."

So saying, the Sultan made a sign and immediately the air was filled with music; then rising, he led the way into a magnificent salon. There a rich repast awaited them. The Sultan ate alone with Aladdin and they were waited on by the dignitaries of the court. During the meal they talked and Aladdin showed so much understanding of various topics that the Sultan grew more and more impressed by the young man. His appearance too so pleased the Sultan that his eyes never left Aladdin's face.

After the meal the Sultan gave orders to the grand judge of the city to draw up immediately a contract of marriage between his daughter, the Princess Badroulboudour and Aladdin.

When this had been done, Aladdin asked permission to leave the palace, but the Sultan wanted him to remain so that the marriage could be celebrated that same day.

" Sire," replied Aladdin, " my longing for the princess is great; in spite of this, I beg that a short interval may elapse in order that I may build a palace worthy of my bride."

" My son," said the Sultan, " you may choose any site which pleases you. The wide space opposite my own palace would, I consider, be ideal for your plan. But make haste with your preparations; I am most anxious to see you wed to the princess as quickly as possible."

So saying, he embraced Aladdin, who then took his leave of the Sultan and mounting his horse rode home through crowds of rejoicing citizens. Alighting from his horse, he went immediately to his room, and taking up the lamp, summoned the genie. He appeared at once and asked what his master desired.

"Genie," said Aladdin, "up until now I have been well pleased with you; you have carried out my wishes promptly and exactly. But today I ask of you a very special service, which must be executed with all care and speed. I order you to build for me a palace in the empty space opposite the Sultan's palace. It should be a worthy home for the Princess Badroulboudour who is about to become my bride. The choice of building materials and the design I leave to you; but I must have at the top of my palace a vast domed salon, the walls of which are to be inlaid with gold and silver. On each of the four walls I must have six windows, the lattices of which should be richly adorned with diamonds, rubies and emeralds and these stones must be of the highest excellence. This is to be the most beautiful room in the world. One window, however, you will leave without ornament. Also I wish that the palace should have a courtyard before and behind as well as a fine garden. Above all there must be a treasure chamber containing a goodly supply of gold, silver and precious stones. Dining rooms, kitchens, reception rooms with rich furnishings should also not be forgotten. Also I want stables full of fine horses and several grooms to attend to them. Let there also be servants for the kitchen and female slaves to attend the princess. I am sure I may rely on you to carry out my wishes," Aladdin said at last. "Go now and return to me when all is ready."

It was already evening when Aladdin dismissed the genie. But his love for the princess allowed him no sleep and it was very early when he arose. He had scarcely finished dressing, however, when the genie appeared before him.

"Sire," said the genie, "your palace is ready. I should like you to come with me and see if all is as you desire." And he took up Aladdin and bore him to the newly built palace. Aladdin found the palace everything he had hoped for and was overjoyed at the noble building. The genie led him from room to room and everywhere Aladdin saw riches, beauty and splendour. Servants and slaves he saw all richly clad and when the genie showed him the treasure room filled with gold, silver and precious stones, his heart leapt with joy. Cooks were busily at work in the kitchens, cupboards were filled with costly robes and the stables were full of beautiful horses. Of all the splendid

rooms, the most magnificent in the palace was the salon with the cupola, where the lattices enclosing twenty-three of the twenty-four windows blazed with jewels.

Aladdin made a complete tour of the palace admiring and wondering at all the genie had accomplished. Everything was even more marvellous than he had imagined. Finally he turned to the genie saying: " Only one thing is missing; it is something which I myself forgot."

" Command me, master," replied the genie, " and it shall be done."

" It is this," said Aladdin. " I want a broad carpet made of the finest velvet embroidered with gold to stretch from the gate of the Sultan's palace to the door of the apartment which will belong to the princess. On it my bride will walk when she leaves her father's palace."

The genie disappeared, returning again in an instant. " Your wish has been fulfilled, master," he announced. Aladdin gazed in wonder at the sumptuous carpet which stretched between the two palaces.

" I am satisfied," cried Aladdin. " Now take me home before the Sultan and his household awake."

Dawn was breaking and the gate of the Sultan's palace was as usual thrown open by the porters. On looking up, they could scarcely believe their eyes. Where yesterday there was an open space a magnificent new palace now towered. And from it to the gate where they stood, a marvellous carpet stretched. Like wild fire the news of this miraculous appearance spread throughout the Sultan's palace.

The Sultan was standing at his window lost in admiration of the palace which had so suddenly appeared, when the grand vizier announced himself. "This is the work of a magician," he cried: "for no man in the world could build such a palace in a single night."

"Vizier," said the Sultan, "why do you speak of sorcery? You

know that the future husband of my daughter wished to build a palace here. He is so rich it seems to me not unlikely. With money man can work wonders. I think that you are envious and so you speak ill of him."

When Aladdin arrived home he was pleased to see that his mother had put on one of her beautiful new dresses. He bade her then go, accompanied by her slaves, to the Sultan's palace. Aladdin requested her to ask permission of the Sultan to escort the Princess Badroulboudour to her son's palace that same evening. His mother promised to do so and left the house looking like a Sultana attended by her slaves. The people in the street stood still in admiration as she passed by. This time, however, the crowds were smaller as the women were veiled and scattered no gold.

A little later, Aladdin left his mother's house, never again to return. He did not forget, however, to take with him his wonderful lamp. He had asked the genie for ten thousand pieces of gold and these his slaves scattered to a joyful crowd on the way to the palace.

Aladdin's mother was received with all honour by the Sultan who led her immediately to the princess's apartment. The princess embraced her warmly and plied her with rich food while she herself was dressed by her attendants. Then she was adorned with some of the jewels which Aladdin had presented to the Sultan. Presently the Sultan entered; he wished to be with his daughter just once more before she left his palace.

In the evening the princess with tears in her eyes took leave of her father. Again and again they embraced one another until at last the Sultan gave orders that an escort should assemble to accompany his daughter to Aladdin's palace. Immediately dignitaries of the city mounted their horses and formed two ranks one on either side of the princess. Musicians headed the procession playing gay airs, then followed soldiers, servants, slaves and four hundred pages, bearing torches to light the way, walked on both sides.

And so the princess, accompanied by Aladdin's mother, stepped on to the carpet which led to her new home.

Aladdin welcomed the princess with the utmost delight. "Dearest Princess," said Aladdin, and bowed low, "I hope you will pardon me for insisting that you should be my wife. But your beauty so bewitched me that without you I could no longer have gone on living."

"My Prince," answered the princess. "I obeyed the wish of my father. But now that I know you, I shall very willingly be your wife."

Aladdin took her hand and kissed it tenderly. Then he led the princess into a brightly lit room where supper awaited them and Aladdin, his mother and the princess sat down to a magnificent banquet. They ate from gold plate and drank from gold cups and the whole room glittered magnificently.

The next morning servants brought Aladdin a complete new wardrobe and helped him to dress. Then he called for his horse and rode to the Sultan's palace. When he reached the throne room the Sultan hastened to meet him and embraced and kissed him warmly. Then he bade Aladdin sit with him and together they had breakfast.

At last Aladdin turned to the Sultan.

" Sire," he said, " I have a favour to ask of you. Will you do me the honour of coming with your grand vizier and others of your court to sup in the palace with me and your daughter, the princess."

" With all my heart," replied the Sultan and followed by the gentlemen of his court, accompanied Aladdin to his palace.

When the Sultan stepped into the palace he was quite overwhelmed by its magnificence and as he passed from one splendid room to another, his admiration grew and grew. At last in the great domed salon with the twenty-four windows he could no longer conceal his amazement. Never in his life had he seen anything to compare with the beauty of the ruby, diamond and emerald studded lattices. He stood looking at them speechless with wonder.

Suddenly he was surprised to see that one of the windows was unfinished.

" Vizier," said the Sultan turning to his first minister, " do you know why this window is unfinished? " " Sire," said the vizier, " certainly the time was too short for Aladdin to complete it. No doubt he will work on it further. He has jewels in abundance."

" My son," said the Sultan to Aladdin, " this palace with its handsome rooms is truly wonderful. But tell me one thing. Why is there one window here which is not completed? "

" Sire," answered Aladdin. " This window was intentionally left unfinished. It was fitting for your reputation that this window be completed by you. And I ask you to fulfil this wish."

" I will certainly complete the window," said the Sultan. " I shall issue orders immediately." And he called for jewellers and goldsmiths.

Meantime Aladdin conducted the Sultan to the room where he had entertained the Princess Badroulboudour on the evening of their wedding, where a rich repast now awaited them. The repast highly pleased the Sultan's tastes, and he confessed that he had never eaten anything more excellent.

When the meal was over the jewellers and goldsmiths were gathered together and the Sultan called them into the room with the dome. Then he pointed to the unfinished window.

" I have called you here," he said, " to complete this work for me. Do your best to produce work equally fine. But lose no time! "

The jewellers and goldsmiths looked carefully at the workmanship and ornamentation of the twenty-four windows. They discussed the materials which were at their disposal and finally came to the conclusion that they were quite unable to undertake the work. Such magnificent stones they had never possessed and together they went to the Sultan to announce their decision.

" Sire," said one jeweller, " despite all our art, we are quite unable to complete the work. Never have we seen such fine gems as these and so we cannot unfortunately fulfil your wish."

" Then come with me to my palace," replied the Sultan. " Look there among my gems and take what you need."

So the jewellers went to the palace, and there chose the biggest and most beautiful stones. They took all the jewels which Aladdin had presented to the Sultan, but still there were not enough. A month passed, only half of the window was finished and the beauty of the work remained far inferior to the splendour of the other windows.

One day Aladdin went into the room with the cupola and he saw that much still had to be done to the window. Then Aladdin told the jewellers to stop work and dismantle all that they had already done. The jewels he ordered to be taken back to the Sultan. Retiring to his room he rubbed the lamp and immediately the genie appeared.

" Ask what you will," said he, " and I shall obey."

" Genie," said Aladdin, " complete now the window in the great salon which you left unfinished."

When after a time Aladdin climbed again to the room of the cupola he found the window completed. It was just as beautiful as the others.

Meantime the jewellers had gone to the Sultan to give back to him his jewels and to tell him that they had at Aladdin's command destroyed their work.

Then the Sultan had his horse saddled and accompanied by only a few of his courtiers, rode to Aladdin's palace.

Dismounting, he hastened to Aladdin.

" My son," he cried, " I have come myself to ask why you have ordered the craftsmen to destroy their work."

" Sire," he answered, " you have seen this room unfinished. But look now and tell me if it lacks anything."

The Sultan went straight to the window which he had seen uncompleted. Now, he saw that it was the same as all the others. He looked at Aladdin.

" My dear son," said he shaking his head," what sort of man are you! What others failed to complete after months, you have completed in one night! "

Aladdin listened to the Sultan's praise with all humility and assured him that all he wanted was to serve his king.

When the Sultan told his grand vizier what he had just seen, this man was more certain than ever that Aladdin's palace was the work of sorcery. But the Sultan did not allow him to speak.

" Vizier," he said, " you are envious of Aladdin."

The grand vizier then saw that he could not raise this matter with his master, but that he must keep silent.

Aladdin meanwhile did not shut himself up forever in his palace. Each day he rode through the town and his slaves threw among the crowd gold pieces and everyone praised him for his generosity.

Many years passed, and the wicked magician, who had returned to Africa frequently thought of Aladdin.

Although quite certain that Aladdin had died a miserable death in the subterranean cavern where he had left him, he nevertheless thought he might as well make certain. As he had a complete knowledge of the science of sorcery he took out of a drawer a sort of square, covered box, such as he used when he made observations in this science. He then sat down on the sofa, and placed the square instrument before him. He uncovered it, and carefully made the sand with which it was filled quite smooth and even. Then he arranged the points, drew the figures, and made a horoscope, When he examined it, instead of finding Aladdin dead in the cave, he discovered to his extreme dismay, that he had escaped, and that he now lived in the greatest splendour.

" I have taken so much trouble and pains to acquire that lamp," he said to himself, " but it has all been in vain. And this good-for-nothing takes it without even trying. Certainly he has now recognised the magical power of the lamp and has thus become a rich man."

The magician wasted no time. Very early next morning he mounted

a Barbary horse and started out on his journey. He travelled over land and sea, from city to city, never sparing himself and stopping only long enough to allow his horse to rest. And so at last he arrived in China and made his way immediately to the Sultan's capital. Alighting from his horse outside an inn, he hired a room. Here he would recover from the hardships of his journey.

Next morning the African magician arose quite early and went into the city. He wanted to listen to what people said of Aladdin and heard how he was regarded.

Everywhere he heard of Aladdin's wonderful palace and turning to one man the magician asked, " Who is this man, Aladdin?"

"Where have you come from?" said the man. "It must be from a great distance, otherwise you would know about Prince Aladdin and have already seen his palace." For since Aladdin married the Princess Badroulboudour he had become a prince. "His castle," continued the man, "is more than a wonder of the world. It is *the* most wonderful building in the world. Go and see it for yourself."

"Pardon my ignorance," said the African magician, "but I only arrived here yesterday from distant Africa. Meanwhile I have lost no time in listening to people talk, but I have not really learned anything about this whole affair. I will go immediately to see this palace. If you want to do me a favour, you will conduct me there."

The man led him willingly to Aladdin's palace. When the magician saw the building he was then sure that Aladdin could only have achieved it with the help of the lamp. Angrily he muttered:

"This rascal. I shall dig him a grave! He was not even able to learn the art of tailoring. And now he lives in a palace. I will kill him! And his mother will return to her spinning as she did before." Grumbling and furious about the good fortune of Aladdin he returned to his inn.

To find out the exact location of the wonderful lamp was the African magician's one thought. Did Aladdin carry it about with him, or was it hidden in his palace? By means of his magic arts he would know. Taking out his square box and his magic sand, he drew some figures and in a few moments he knew exactly where the lamp was concealed. The magician's joy knew no bounds. Rubbing his hands in glee, he at once began to scheme and plan how he would retrieve the lamp and so bring about Aladdin's downfall.

It so happened that Aladdin himself was just then not in the city. He had gone on a long hunting expedition and was not expected to return for several days. This information the magician had learned from the inn-keeper.

He needed to know no more. "This is exactly the time to strike," he said to himself. "I must not waste a single moment before putting my plan into action." And he smiled evilly to himself.

Leaving the inn he went straight to a shop where lamps were made and sold. "My friend," he greeted the shopkeeper. "I need a dozen copper lamps: can you sell them to me now?"

The man regretted that he did not have so many lamps in his shop, but promised that he would have them ready without fail on the following day. The magician agreed to return, and telling him to have the lamps well polished, he left promising to pay him well.

The next morning the magician went to fetch the lamps. Some of them he tied to his girdle, the others he put in a basket and at once set off for Aladdin's palace, crying loudly as he went, "Who will change old lamps for new?"

"This man is mad," said the people in the streets to one another. "How can he afford to exchange new lamps for old?" And the children at play left their games, and screaming with laughter, ran

after him crying " Fool, fool!" But the magician ignored them and continued his cry. " New lamps for old! New lamps for old!"

Soon he had reached the palace and his cry was heard by Princess Badroulboudour, who was sitting with her female slaves in the room with the twenty-four windows. The shrieks of the children, however, made it difficult for her to hear his words. She therefore sent down one of her slaves to discover what he was crying.

The slave returned almost immediately, laughing so heartily that, looking at her, Princess Badroulboudour had to laugh too.

At last the princess said with a smile, " Come now, tell me what causes this merriment. I am most curious to hear."

" Princess," said the slave, " it would make anyone laugh! Down there a man carrying beautiful new lamps in a basket is calling, ' who will exchange old lamps for new?' It is small wonder that the children shout after and mock him."

Unfortunately, Aladdin after last using the wonderful lamp had forgotten to return it to its place in the treasure room, but had left it out in full view in his own apartment. One of the slaves had noticed it, and now approached the princess. " Madam," she said, " in your husband's room I have seen an old lamp. Let us prove if this man is indeed mad enough to give us a new one in its place."

The princess knew nothing of the value of Aladdin's lamp and had no idea that the palace and all the treasure it contained had appeared through its magic powers. She therefore readily agreed to this request and a slave was sent down with the lamp to make the exchange. Approaching the magician he held out Aladdin's lamp, saying:

" Here is an old lamp. Give me one in exchange."

The magician had no doubt that this was the lamp he was seeking, because he thought there would not of course be any other such lamp in Aladdin's palace, where everything that could be was made of gold and silver. Eagerly he took the lamp from the slave, and after having thrust it as far as he could under his robe he presented his basket and told the slave to take the lamp which he liked best.

The children shouted and romped round the magician and laughed even louder at this exchange. But he let them jeer. His remaining lamps he handed to those people who wanted to exchange their old ones.

Putting down the empty basket in a convenient corner the magician quickly hurried away unobserved. He hastened through one of the city gates and finally reached open country where he sat down and waited for nightfall. Towards midnight he took the lamp from under his robe and rubbed it. Immediately the genie appeared.

" What do you wish ? " he cried. " I am ready to obey you as your slave, and the slave of those who have the lamp in their hands, both I and the other slaves of the lamp."

" I command you," replied the African magician, " instantly to take the palace which you and the other slaves of the lamp have erected and transport it, with me at the same time, into the farthest part of Africa."

Without making any answer, the genie, assisted by the other slaves of the lamp, took both him and the whole palace, and transported it to the farthest part of Africa.

But let us leave the magician and the palace together with its inmates in Africa, and return to the Sultan and Aladdin.

Each morning the Sultan went to the window in an alcove of his room in order to look at and admire Aladdin's palace and to think lovingly of his daughter and her happiness.

But this morning when he looked across as usual, he saw nothing but an empty space. He rubbed his eyes, believing that he was dreaming, but nothing changed. There was indeed no palace opposite—not a trace remained. The Sultan was so astounded that he remained rooted to the spot. Then he thought of his daughter and tears began to course down his cheeks. Would he ever see her again?

The Sultan, filled with grief, summoned the grand vizier to his presence. The grand vizier came in great haste and for that reason failed to see that Aladdin's palace had vanished. When he came before the Sultan he saw at once that something was wrong.

"Forgive me, Sire," he said, "why are you in such distress? Has something extraordinary happened?"

"Yes," answered the Sultan, "tell me, where is Aladdin's palace?"

"Aladdin's palace!" asked the grand vizier astounded. "I have just come past it. It was in its place."

"Then go into the neighbouring room," answered the Sultan; look out of the window, and tell me what you see!"

Shaking his head in perplexity, the grand vizier went to the alcove. From there he looked over towards Aladdin's palace but there was nothing to see. Amazed he returned to the Sultan.

"Now," asked the latter, "did you see Aladdin's palace?"

"Sire," answered the grand vizier, "you did not believe me before! I told you already that the palace was the work of sorcery. But you would not listen to me!"

This the Sultan could not deny. But just for that reason he became very angry.

"Where is Aladdin, this cheat and scoundrel?" he called. "I shall have his head cut off instantly."

"Sire," answered the grand vizier, "some days ago he was given leave to go hunting. When he comes back, we shall ask him: he will, I suppose, know where the palace is."

"That is showing him too much leniency," answered the Sultan. "Give orders immediately that thirty soldiers shall go and find him! When you have him, arrest and bring him to me in chains."

The grand vizier instantly gave the orders, and instructed the officer of the Sultan's guard how to prevent Aladdin's escape. They set out and about five or six leagues from the city, met Aladdin returning from the chase.

Aladdin having naturally no inkling of the real reason for the appearance of the Sultan's guards, greeted their leader in a friendly fashion and continued to hunt on the homeward journey. About half an hour's distance from the city, however, the guards suddenly surrounded him.

" Prince Aladdin," said their officer, " do not be angry with us. The Sultan has ordered that we arrest and lead you before him, bound like a criminal. We ask you humbly to pardon us. We only do our duty in obeying the commands of our sovereign."

This speech astonished Aladdin greatly. But he answered:

" Here I am. Do with me whatever the Sultan has ordered. I am innocent I swear of any crime against thc state, but the commands of my lord I must always obey."

The soldiers immediately took a long stout chain, threw it about Aladdin's neck and wound it round his body so that his arms were tied fast to his sides. One of the soldiers then seized the end of the chain and mounting his horse rode with it in his hand while Aladdin on foot had to run behind. In this way was he conducted through the streets of the city to the Sultan's palace.

The people in the suburbs when they saw Aladdin being led along bound like a state criminal, did not doubt that he was about to lose his head. But Aladdin, thanks to his friendliness and generosity towards the people remained popular with them. Now many among the crowds who saw him go by seized sabres and stones, and with threatening gestures at the guards, cried out that Aladdin should be instantly set free. The soldiers at the rear turned and tried to disperse the crowds, but this served only to increase the people's wrath. There was nothing else that the soldiers could do but occupy the entire breadth of the streets which they passed along. In this way the people were pressed against the walls of the houses.

A large crowd, however, followed behind, their angry cries becoming ever louder and more menacing. The guards were glad indeed when at last they reached unscathed the gate of the palace. There the soldiers formed one line to keep the crowd at bay, while the officer loosened Aladdin's chain and escorted him into the palace. The gate was shut with all speed behind them to prevent anyone from following.

Aladdin was brought before the Sultan, who, with the grand vizier, awaited him on a balcony. The Sultan no sooner saw Aladdin than he commanded the executioner, who was already present by his orders, to strike off his head. He wished to hear not a word of explanation.

The executioner approached Aladdin and seized him in a firm grasp. Then removing the chain, which still hung loosely round Aladdin's neck and body, proceeded to bind a cloth over his eyes. He then ordered Aladdin to kneel down. Drawing his sword he walked three times round Aladdin, brandishing his weapon in the air. He awaited only a signal from the Sultan before dealing the deadly stroke which would sever Aladdin's head from his body.

But the people at the gate had witnessed the entire scene on the balcony. They saw that Aladdin was in the greatest danger and immediately a furious roar went up. With angry shouts they threatened to storm the palace and bring it to the ground if Aladdin suffered the slightest injury.

The grand vizier heard the noise.

" Sire," he turned in agitation to the Sultan. " The people are threatening to overthrow the palace. We are in the greatest danger if you execute their hero, Aladdin. I beseech you, therefore, to spare his life. The people love him more than they do you, their sovereign."

The Sultan's mind had been too occupied with hatred of Aladdin and the desire to avenge himself for the loss of his daughter, to hear the angry tumult of the crowd. But at the grand vizier's words, he started in terror. Looking out towards the gate he saw the multitude, many of whom had already climbed into the palace courtyard.

Pale, and trembling with fear, the Sultan gave orders that Aladdin should be immediately released. A herald was then commanded to announce to the angry people that Aladdin had been pardoned and that they might all now return peacefully to their homes.

Aladdin was free again. Raising his head he looked towards the balcony on which stood the Sultan.

" Sire," he cried, " I thank you for your gracious pardon. But I beg of you to grant me one further favour. Tell me, I entreat you, how I have displeased you."

" I cannot believe that you do not know the nature of your crime," the Sultan answered angrily. " Come, villain, I will show it to you."

Aladdin arose. " Follow me," commanded the Sultan, and went over to the window. Gesturing with his arm, he said: " Now look at your palace. You ought to know what has become of it."

Aladdin, naturally, could see no sign of his palace. Aghast he stared out of the window and could think of no explanation.

" It does not distress me in the least that your palace has vanished," the Sultan continued. " A thousand times more valuable to me, however, is my daughter. Where is she? Return her to me instantly or I shall have you beheaded."

" Sire," answered Aladdin, at last finding his voice, " I do not know what has become of my palace or of your daughter. Believe me, it is none of my doing. I can only beg you to grant me fourteen days in which to search for the princess whom I too love dearly. If I have not returned your daughter to you at the end of that time, I shall willingly lay my head at your feet."

" I shall grant your request," replied the Sultan. " Fourteen days you may have, but do not think that you can abuse this favour. Do not try to escape my wrath. I shall know how to find you even if you are in hiding at the farthest corner of the earth."

Deeply distressed, Aladdin left the Sultan's palace. For three days, he went from house to house, asking in vain if anyone had seen his palace. So changed in appearance did he become in this short time that many did not recognise him and thought him a madman or a fool. Without the lamp he had no money and had to subsist on the little food he was able to beg.

At last he left the city and not heeding in which direction he walked, so great was his misery, he found himself towards nightfall on the bank of a wide river. In his despair he resolved to throw himself into the water, but as a pious man he would first offer up a prayer. Before doing so, he knelt down on the bank and leant over to scoop up a little water to wash his face and hands. But at this point the bank was steep. Aladdin's foot slipped and he would have fallen into the river had his hand not touched and grasped a jagged rock which jutted above the surface near the shore.

In coming against the piece of rock, he had rubbed the magician's ring, which he had forgotten he still wore, so hard that the genie, whom he had last seen in the underground cave, instantly appeared.

"What do you wish?" cried the genie. "I am ready to obey you as your slave."

Aladdin was most agreeably surprised and replied instantly, "Save my life, genie, a second time by telling me where the palace is which I have built. If you can, let it be brought back to the place where it formerly stood."

" What you demand," the genie replied, "is impossible. Only the slave of the lamp can do this; I am only the slave of the ring."

" Then take me at least," Aladdin urged, " to the place where my palace now stands, no matter how far distant, and put me down under the window of the princess's apartment."

He had scarcely said this before he found himself in a meadow near a large city. Here the palace stood, and looking up, Aladdin saw that he had been set down directly under the princess's window.

As it was now night, the whole palace was at rest. So Aladdin stepped under a tree and sat down on the grass. And because he had not slept for six days he was almost immediately asleep.

At daybreak the song of the birds in the palace garden wakened him. His glance fell at once on his magnificent palace, and hope rose in him that soon he would once again see his princess. This thought made him feel light and gay. For a little he walked to and fro under her window, hoping that she might look out and see him.

That morning Princess Badroulboudour rose earlier than she usually did since being carried off by the magician's art. Miserably unhappy, the princess was forced to see the magician every day, but always she remained coldly aloof. She had passed a sleepless night thinking of the unhappy fate which had befallen her and it was scarcely dawn when she summoned her slaves to help her dress. One of the slaves looking through the lattice suddenly caught sight of Aladdin, and with a happy cry, beckoned to her mistress to come quickly. The princess could scarcely believe her eyes when she saw Aladdin standing there. Just then he raised his head and, seeing her, greeted her joyfully.

" Come quickly," cried the princess; " my slaves have gone to open the secret door." She then shut the lattice.

In a moment the secret door was opened by a slave and Aladdin quickly entered the palace. Throwing themselves into each other's arms the princess and Aladdin laughed and wept for joy at being once again reunited with each other.

The princess then told Aladdin everything that had happened. She told him how the lamp had been exchanged for a new one, which she showed him, and how next morning she had found herself in a strange land. " This country is Africa," she continued. " The magician who has betrayed us informed me, and with the help of the lamp, he has set down the palace here."

"O Princess," replied Aladdin, interrupting her, "if this is Africa, I know the villain who has caused our misery. He is the most wicked of men. But this is neither the time nor the place to tell you of all his crimes. I entreat you only to tell me what he has done with the lamp and where he has put it."

"He carries it always with him inside his robe," answered the princess, with a sigh. "I know this with certainty, because he has taken it out in my presence to tease me and gloat over me in my misery."

"What is this misery you speak of?" asked Aladdin in alarm. "What has this man said? I beg you, tell me everything!"

"Since I have been here," answered the princess "he comes to me

once a day. He insists that I forget you and become his wife. He assured me that you were dead, that the Sultan had beheaded you. He says too that you were only a poor son of the people and you owed all your wealth to him. With soft words he has tried to win me, but without success. I have given him not one friendly word. Perhaps he will not come so often now that you are here. Nevertheless I am afraid that he may bring disaster in the end."

"Do not give up hope," Aladdin interrupted. "I have a plan which will rescue us both from our enemy. But first I must go into the town; I will return about noon, and tell you everything, for you yourself must help me. Do not be astonished if you see me return in a different dress; and be sure you give orders so that I do not have to wait at the private door, but am admitted the instant I knock."

The princess promised to follow Aladdin's instructions exactly and assured him that the door would be opened immediately.

Aladdin then left the palace by the secret door and walked on until he came to a meadow which lay not far from the palace. There he saw a peasant at work. Approaching him, Aladdin proposed that they should exchange clothes. At first the man refused, but Aladdin persisted and seeing that Aladdin's garments were of fine stuff, the peasant at last agreed. Behind a nearby bush they exchanged clothes and Aladdin then took the road to the city.

After asking for directions from many of the townspeople, Aladdin reached the busiest part of the city and came at length to the quarter in which each street was devoted to a specific trade. One of these was the street of druggists and this was Aladdin's goal. Walking its length he examined each shop carefully. Finally he stopped before the largest, and entering, asked the shopkeeper if he stocked a certain powder.

The merchant, seeing the poverty of Aladdin's clothing, thought that he would not have enough money to pay for it. He therefore answered that he did have the powder but that it was very expensive. But Aladdin, thanks to his magic ring had with him a purseful of gold pieces. Taking out one coin, he asked for half a dram of the powder. The shopkeeper's attitude changed at once; hastily he weighed out the required quantity, wrapped it and handed it to Aladdin who immediately gave the man his gold piece and left the shop. He did not spend more time in the city, but quickly made his way back to the palace. He was admitted at once and hastened to the apartment of the Princess Badroulboudour.

"Now," said Aladdin, "listen to me carefully, my princess. I know that you have suffered greatly and that what I am about to ask of you will be distasteful. But it is not difficult and highly necessary. You must, therefore, force yourself to obey me. When it is over you will, I promise, see your homeland again and be once more reunited with your father. Here then are my instructions:—Put on one of your finest dresses and adorn yourself with diamonds and pearls. When the magician arrives, treat him with politeness and frankness as if nothing had happened. Invite him to have supper with you—he will be delighted to accept—and tell him that you would like to taste the best wine of the country. He will then undoubtedly fetch some. At the meal see that his cup remains full and after a time, when you notice his attention to be wandering, put this powder into your own cup. Fill it up with wine and offer then to exchange cups with him. He will be so overjoyed at your graciousness that he will agree and empty his cup at one draught. When he has drunk the doctored wine, he will sink down as if dead to the floor. Do not be afraid; the effect of the powder is very rapid. The magician will have no time to harm you."

"I am ready to do what you ask," replied the princess. "It will cost me a great effort to act in a friendly fashion to the African magician, but I shall willingly force myself to do it."

Aladdin then sat down to eat with his wife, after which he took his leave, promising to return at sunset to the secret door.

At the usual hour the African magician presented himself to the princess where she awaited him in the salon with the cupola. In the full glory of her beauty and splendid raiment, she greeted her hated captor with a smile and invited him to take a seat near her. Such a reception from the princess was unexpected and the magician was so overwhelmed and blinded by her magnificent appearance that he did not dare to sit down. But the princess indicated the place on her right hand and he at last obeyed.

"I apologise," began the princess, "for having never until now received you graciously. But now I realise your true worth as a man. I am quite persuaded that my husband no longer loves me and I have lost all hope of seeing him again. My father the Sultan has had him executed and my tears will not bring him back to life. Therefore to-day I invite you to have supper with me. I should like too to taste some of the wine of your country to see how it compares with that of my own."

Delighted by her change of attitude towards him, the magician leapt to his feet. "Princess," he cried, "let me fetch two bottles from my own cellar."

"Send a servant," she answered. "I should be sorry to give you the trouble."

"Princess," said the magician, "I myself must go. No one else knows where my cellar is and I alone possess the key."

The magician, overjoyed by the graciousness of the princess, ran as fast as he could to his cellar and in a very short time returned. Thereupon they sat down at the table and ate together in the happiest of spirits. A slave saw to it that the magician's goblet was always full. The princess drank the health of the magician and he in turn wished her a joyful and long life. And so the magician emptied many goblets.

Unnoticed by the magician, the princess, his hostess, drank little. So completely fascinated was he by her kindness and affable manners that he had no doubt that her friendliness towards him was sincere.

His thoughts were gradually becoming confused, however, and the princess noticed that the wine was going to the magician's head.

" In our country it is the custom," she said to him, " for two good friends to drink from each other's glass. Is this not done in Africa?"

Without waiting for his answer, she seized his glass and passed him hers into which she had already tipped the powder when the magician's eyes were not upon her.

The African magician was delighted with this idea.

" Princess," he exclaimed before he drank, and holding the goblet in his hand, " you will never know what an honour you do me. Never shall I forget that I was allowed to drink from your glass. Your former treatment of me is forgotten. Now you have made me the happiest of men."

The princess, bored with the magician's empty talk, at last interrupted him saying: " Now shall we drink together." Immediately she put her own glass to her lips and pretended to drink. The magician did likewise and in one draught emptied his glass. Almost at the same moment his eyes closed, the glass fell from his hand and he sank back dead in his chair. How overjoyed the princess was! And all her slaves rejoiced too and hurried to open the secret door and let Aladdin into the palace.

Quickly Aladdin came up to the room where the Princess had dined. There he saw the magician who had now slid to the floor. With open arms the Princess came to meet Aladdin, but he turned aside and said urgently.

" Princess, it is not time to rejoice yet. I beg of you, go with your slaves to your room and take care that I am not disturbed."

The princess obeyed immediately, and with her slaves retired. Aladdin shut the door behind them, then quickly stepped over to the lifeless magician. Opening his robe, he removed the wonderful lamp. At last it was in his possession once more. Aladdin stood for a moment gazing at it. Finally he rubbed it and immediately the genie appeared.

" Master," said he, " I am here. What do you desire?"

" Genie," answered Aladdin, " I command you to take up this palace and transport it back to my homeland, to the exact spot where it stood before, opposite the palace of the Sultan."

Aladdin then went to join the princess in her apartment where they embraced

joyfully, so thankful were they to be rid of the wicked magician.

Meanwhile the genie took up the palace and set it down in the place where it had formerly stood. Only two slight tremors were felt, one when it was raised, and one when it was put down again.

Then did Aladdin and his princess rejoice, and for Aladdin who had eaten nothing, a rich meal was immediately prepared. Together he and his princess sat down at the table, ate the costly dishes and drank the magician's wine. Happy talk and laughter made the time pass quickly. Before they realised it, morning light was stealing across the sky.

Let us now return to the Sultan:—Since the disappearance of the princess, his daughter, he had suffered deeply and in his grief was inconsolable. He spent sleepless nights and for days on end would speak to no one. Almost hourly he went to the window to gaze at the spot where the palace had stood. Constantly he thought of his daughter whom he was sure he would never see again and he wept for his loss until he was almost blinded by tears.

On the day that Aladdin's palace had been brought back by the genie, the Sultan, as usual, had risen early and gone to the window which looked out on the empty space. The morning was misty and at first the Sultan saw nothing. Gradually, however, the mist was dispersed by the rays of the sun and no longer did the Sultan gaze upon an empty space.

At first he thought he must be dreaming; he rubbed his eyes and looked again. It was no dream. Aladdin's palace stood there and joy surged up in the Sultan's heart. Grief and pain forgotten, the Sultan hurried to his own apartment and ordered his horse to be saddled immediately. He could not wait to see his daughter again.

Aladdin had expected this visit from his father-in-law and had already put on his finest robe. His wife, the princess had also been dressed and adorned with jewels by her hand-maidens in readiness to meet her father. So excited was she at the thought that her eyes rivalled her jewels in sparkle.

Aladdin from a window saw the Sultan arrive and hastened to him.

" Aladdin," the Sultan greeted him, " where is my daughter? I must first see and embrace her before I can speak with you."

Already the princess was hurrying down the steps. Reaching her father, she threw herself into his arms and they embraced each other, while tears of joy glistened on both their cheeks. At last all three climbed the staircase to the princess's own apartment.

Then the princess told her father all that had happened since the exchange of the lamp. She described the magician and how miserable he had made her. Then she told of Aladdin's arrival and how he had regained possession of the lamp.

" The worst thing of all about the whole affair," she continued, " was being separated from my dear husband and from you. You would scarcely have recognised me, dear father had you seen me then. But the arrival of my husband yesterday has given me new life and happiness. And now when I see you again my joy is complete."

Aladdin had a little to add to her tale. " When I saw the magician lying there," he said, " I sent your daughter and slaves into a neighbouring room. Then I took out the lamp from under the robe of the dead magician. Through the wonderful power of the lamp I was then able to have the palace transported here. And your daughter, honoured Sire, I return to you unharmed. That I am reunited with her makes me the happiest man in the world. The truth of all this you may verify for yourself if you will step into the adjoining room. There lies the body of the wicked magician."

The Sultan rose and with Aladdin went into the next room. There lay the dead magician and the Sultan ordered it to be carried off and burned, the ashes to be scattered to the four winds. He embraced Aladdin in a fatherly way saying:

" My son, my love for my daughter made me order your death. I believed I had lost my child. Pardon me now for the sake of the wife you love."

Aladdin answered, " Sire, I have no reason to complain. What you did was understandable. But none of it was my fault. All our misfortune has been due to this villainous magician. But now he has got his deserts."

The Sultan then announced ten days' feasting in the city. The return of his daughter and her husband was to be celebrated properly.

Aladdin had now narrowly escaped death twice: but it was not to be

the last time: another danger no less frightful awaited him. Of this we shall now hear.

The African magician had a younger brother. This man also understood the arts of sorcery and resembled closely his brother in wickedness and cunning. He lived far away from his brother but from time to time made it his business to have news of him.

Shortly after the magician had been put to death by Aladdin, his brother took up his box of magic sand. He drew with his wand figures in the sand to find out by this means how his brother fared, and so discovered that he was no longer alive. Now he wanted to know where and under what circumstances his brother had died. Through his magic instruments he discovered that a young man named Aladdin had poisoned him in his palace and had thus been responsible for his death. This young man he learned was the husband of the Sultan's daughter.

The magician lost no time in fruitless mourning, but vowed to avenge his brother's death. He immediately set out on his journey and after a month's journey over hills and through valleys, suffering unbelievable discomfort and misery, he at length arrived in the Sultan's city. By his magic art he knew he was in the right place and he took lodgings in an inn in the city.

The day after his arrival the magician walked through the streets. He had to find ways and means of bringing about his revenge. He visited the most frequented places in the city and soon was entering into conversation with the people. Finally he came to a coffee house in the market place. There he was told of the wonderful deeds of a woman named Fatima. Hidden from the world she lived in a little cell outside the town. The magician thought this woman might help him with his plans and therefore asked someone for more information about her.

" Why, have you never seen her ? " asked this man. " You have never before heard of the wonders she can perform ? Only on Mondays and Fridays does she leave her cell; on these days she comes into the city and performs good deeds. She can heal headaches by laying her hands on one's head. We all love and honour her."

The magician explained his ignorance by telling the man that he had only arrived in the city the day before.

When the hermit appeared in the city on the next day, the magician followed her closely and watched where she went when she left the city in the evening. Then he went into an inn and drank a glass of wine. Afterwards in the dark he walked out to the pious woman's cell.

He pushed open the door a little; it was unlocked. Inside he saw the old woman lying asleep on a mat. He sprang to her bed and pricked her with a dagger. She awoke immediately and was terrified to see a stranger standing over her with dagger raised.

" If you cry out," he warned her, " you will die. Stand up and do what I say and no harm will befall you."

Shivering with fright, Fatima obeyed.

" Fear not," said the magician. " Give me your clothes and take mine."

She gave him her dress, cloak and scarf and took the magician's clothes from him.

" Now dye my face," he continued. " I want to impersonate you and my complexion must be changed."

Fatima went into an inner room and returned with an ointment. This she rubbed over his face and soon assured him that now he resembled her quite closely. Then she arranged the cloak round his head and gave him her veil and her staff. Finally, she showed him how he must walk to look like her. After that she held a mirror before his face.

"Look here," she asked. "You will see now no difference between us."

Satisfied with his appearance, the cowardly villain now broke his promise. Springing at the old woman, he strangled her and quickly buried her in the earth outside her cell. Then without a qualm, he lay down and fell promptly asleep.

In the morning, dressed as Fatima, he left the cell and made his way to Aladdin's palace. On the way he was greeted as Fatima by everyone he met and as he passed through the streets the magician murmured blessings and laid his hands on many who begged him to help their suffering. No one doubted that this was indeed Fatima. At last he arrived at the palace where the crowd around him became even greater and there was a loud noise of weeping and crying everywhere.

The sound reached the Princess Badroulboudour. One of her slaves recognised the old woman from the window and the princess, who had heard of the wonders performed by Fatima, decided now that she would meet her.

"Go," cried the princess to the slave, "and fetch the old woman here. I shall speak with her and ask her blessing."

And so did the magician achieve his aim of entering the palace.

He was led before the princess who waited in the room of the twenty-four windows. Bowing his head he murmured a long prayer followed by a speech which overflowed with blessings and desires that good fortune would attend her always. And no one doubted at all that the holy Fatima herself stood there.

After the prayer the princess approached the false creature, saying: "Good mother, thank you for your beautiful prayer and for your good wishes. I in turn hope that all will go well with you. You will always be an example to me in holiness. I should like it if you would remain here always in the palace. Come nearer and sit by me."

Then with hypocritical modesty and eyes lowered, the magician sat down saying:

" Princess, I am but a poor, humble woman who lives far from the dwellings of men, existing only to serve my God. How could I live a truly pious life amidst the splendour of this palace ? "

" That need not trouble you," answered the Princess. " Here in the palace there are several rooms which are never used. In one of these you can attend to your devotions undisturbed. You can live just as you do in your cell."

The magician raised no further objections. This invitation was just what he had hoped for. From the palace it would not be difficult to carry out his wicked plan. In a few gracious words he accepted the princess's offer.

The princess was delighted and taking the false Fatima by the hand led her through the many rooms of the palace asking her to choose the one she desired. She chose the least magnificent but exclaiming at the same time that it was still much too splendid for her.

The princess now asked her to return to the room of the cupola and to sup with her, but the false Fatima refused, saying that she ate only bread and dried fruit and asked that this might be brought to her in her own room. It was a rule of the holy order to which she belonged, she said, to eat alone. In fact the magician was afraid to raise the veil for fear that his hair and beard should be recognised as belonging to a man. The princess willingly granted her request.

" My good mother," she said, " here you shall live exactly as if you were still in your own cell. But do not fail to return to me after you have eaten."

The Princess supped at mid-day while the magician ate alone in his room. Afterwards he went to the princess in the room with the twenty-four windows.

" Good mother," said the Sultan's daughter, " I am so glad that you will remain in the palace. Do you find it pleasant here and tell me, what do you think of this room?"

The false Fatima till then had kept her eyes lowered, but now lifted her head and examined the room from end to end.

"The room is a wonderful work of art and splendour," she then said. "Probably there is no other in the whole world like it. I am a hermit and I live far from the world, but yet I think that the room lacks something."

"What is that, my good mother?" asked the princess. "Tell me instantly! I myself think the room is quite perfect. But if there is something missing, I should like to put it right."

"My lady," answered the magician, "for this room to be quite perfect, a roc's egg should hang from the dome."

"What kind of bird is the roc?" asked the princess. "Where would one find such a bird, my mother?"

"The roc is a large and powerful bird," said the magician. "He lives in the highest peaks of the Caucasus mountains. The architect of this palace should bring you an egg from this bird."

The princess thanked him for his advice. Then she talked a little longer with the magician. When it was time again to dine, she accompanied the pious woman back to her room. But the princess did not forget about the roc's egg. She wanted to speak of it to Aladdin when he returned from the hunt. He had been absent now for several days and the magician had made good use of this event.

In the evening Aladdin returned. He greeted his wife warmly but soon noticed that she seemed a little abstracted. Her smile was not quite so frank and free as usual.

"What is the matter, dear Princess?" he asked. "Why does this shadow cross your brow? Has something happened in my absence? Tell me, I beg you!"

"It is only a very little thing," answered the princess. "I did not think anyone would notice; but since you ask, I shall tell you. Up till now I thought that our palace was complete and perfect. But I have examined closely the room with the twenty-four windows, and it seems to me that something is missing. I feel that a roc's egg should hang from the cupola."

" Princess," answered Aladdin, " I shall repair this fault immediately. And if you had had a desire a hundred times greater you would only have to name it and I should go to the farthest corner of the earth to satisfy it."

He left the room and immediately went to his room. There he took out his lamp and rubbed it. In an instant the genie appeared.

" What do you desire ? " he said.

" Genie," answered Aladdin. " The room of the cupola lacks the egg of a roc. I wish that one should hang from the cupola."

Scarcely had Aladdin spoken when the genie uttered a fearful shriek. The room rocked and Aladdin was knocked violently to one side.

" Miserable creature," cried the genie in an angry voice, " is it not enough that I satisfy your every wish ? Ungrateful one do you know what you are asking ? Do you want me to hang my master and his wife from the cupola ? But fortunately I know that I have to thank the wicked magician for this wish, he who has murdered the holy Fatima. Disguised as the pious woman he is at present in this palace. He has persuaded your wife to make this wish. You should know that he is the brother of the African magician and that he wants to be avenged for his death. Therefore be on your guard before him ! " After this warning the genie disappeared.

Aladdin was astonished at this news. Of the holy Fatima and her piety he had heard. Now he returned quickly to the princess. Sitting down near her he put his head in his hands, and said that he had suddenly a severe headache. The Princess immediately ordered that Fatima should be brought before them. Meanwhile she told her husband how the holy woman had come to the palace.

When the false Fatima appeared, Aladdin pretended that he knew nothing of the true identity of the supposed hermit. He

rose and kissed the hem of her robe.

"Holy Mother Fatima," he said, "I am glad to see you here and I should be indeed grateful if you could cure this headache. It has come to my ears that you can take away pain by laying your hands on the aching part. I ask you now to heal me."

So saying, Aladdin bent his head so that the magician could touch it. The latter stepped forward and laid one hand on Aladdin's head. With the other he took hold of a dagger concealed beneath his robe, but before the weapon could strike him, Aladdin gripped his hand, and turning the dagger towards the magician stabbed him in the heart so that he fell dead instantly.

Amazed, the princess looked on. "My dear husband," she cried "what have you done? How could you kill this holy woman?"

"No, dearest wife," answered Aladdin softly, "I have not killed the holy woman. I have got rid of the villain who murdered her. Look closely at this face," and Aladdin held back the veil. "This is not Fatima but none other than the brother of the African magician. He came here to murder me in revenge for his brother's death. Had I not been warned, he might have attained his object."

Aladdin had the corpse removed, then he examined the princess closely to discover how the magician had gone about his plans.

"My dear husband," answered the princess when she had told him her story, "can you ever forgive me? I have now twice through thoughtlessness endangered your life."

"Have no fear," answered Aladdin, "for you I will always risk my life."

And thanks to this latest danger their love for each other became even stronger.

Some years later the Sultan died and Aladdin succeeded to the throne. He ruled his subjects justly and well and everyone loved and honoured him. From then on he and his beautiful wife lived an uneventful life. No further perils were ever again to threaten their happiness.

A story by

LUDWIG BECHSTEIN

THE BRAVE LITTLE TAILOR

THERE was once a little tailor who lived in the town of Romadia. While he worked an apple always lay near him and on to it the flies would settle. The tailor was most irritated about this and so, one day, he took a napkin, brought it down on the apple and found when he lifted it away again that seven flies lay dead. " Ah," thought the tailor to himself, " you are a hero! " And abandoning needle, thread and iron, he bought a suit of bright armour and on the breast plate wrote in golden letters ' Seven at one Blow.'

Donning the armour, he set off into the streets and everyone who saw him believed him to be a hero who had killed seven men at one blow, and were afraid of him.

Now there reigned in the land a King whose praise resounded far and wide and to this King went the bold little tailor. Into the courtyard of the royal castle he stepped, lay down on the grass and fell fast asleep.

The servants of the court as they passed in and out saw the tailor lying there resplendent in his new armour, read the inscription written in letters of gold on his breastplate and wondered greatly what such a warlike man did at the King's court in peacetime. They did not in the least doubt that he must be a very important man. The King's counsellors who had also seen the sleeping tailor announced to his gracious majesty with all respect that this might be a very useful man who would render good service to the whole country should any quarrel or war break out. This speech pleased the King and he immediately sent for the little tailor and asked him if he would accept a position as a knight of the court. The tailor answered instantly that he would be most happy to serve his gracious majesty. So the King promised that he should have a position at court with appropriate salary and accommodation so that the tailor could live happily and comfortably when there was no work for him to do.

But it was not long before the King's knights who earned less than the tailor became envious of the little hero and wished him at the bottom of the sea. They were afraid, however, that they would all be killed if they challenged him to fight as he was a hero who had felled seven at a blow. But they would willingly have done something to injure his reputation.

Daily and almost hourly they racked their brains to think of some way of getting rid of the conceited warrior. But try how they might they could think of no trick which would expel the hero from the court. At last the knights decided to go in a body before the King.

When the good King heard that all his loyal servants felt so strongly about the dismissal of one single knight, he was more unhappy than he had ever been in his life and wished that he had never set eyes on the hero. But he hesitated to send him away because he feared that he and all his court might be killed and that finally his kingdom would be ruled by this warrior. So he thought long and deeply about what to do and how to send him away without offence.

At last he thought of a ruse which would free him of the warrior whom no one took for a tailor. The King had the hero summoned and gave him the following message.

" I well know," began the King, "that there is no more powerful or mighty warrior on this earth than you. But in the nearby woods there live two giants whose crimes include robbery, murder and fire-raising. No one by any means can approach them with weapons as they simply strike them dead. I have now made up my mind that these giants must be slain and for this deed I have chosen you. Should you succeed in ridding the land of these giants your reward will be the hand of my daughter in marriage together with half of my kingdom" In addition the King promised to give the tailor a hundred knights to assist him in his task.

Having heard the King's offer the little tailor puffed with pride; already he thought of himself as the King's son-in-law and in possession of half the kingdom. He announced, therefore, briefly and to the point that he would willingly serve his gracious majesty by killing the giants, but that he would not need the help of the hundred knights.

A few hours later he found himself in a dense wood. The hundred knights, who at the command of the King followed the little tailor to the edge of the wood, stopped there to wait for him. The hero himself walked on into the dense trees to spy out the land and see if he could find any trace of the giants. After a lengthy search he finally caught sight of them lying under a tree. They were asleep and snoring so loudly that the ground shook and the boughs of the tree bent over as in a storm.

The little tailor had a plan. With all speed he filled his pockets with stones, climbed into the tree under which the giants lay and began with skilful aim to throw down stones on to one of the giants. Soon he awoke and angrily turning to his fellow giant asked him why he threw stones at him as he slept. The second giant, of course, denied all knowledge of it.

When after a long and angry argument the giants again closed their eyes, the little tailor once more began to throw down stones, this time on to the other giant. The latter jumped up in a great passion and began to rain blows on his companion. This was altogether too much for the first giant who sprang up and both of them proceeded to tear out trees by the roots—but fortunately for our tailor, not the one among whose branches he sat—and using them as weapons, struck at each other so furiously that at last both of them fell dead, side by side.

When the tailor saw what had happened from his perch in the tree, he was even more pleased with himself than he had been before. Joyfully he climbed down, dealt a wound with his sword to each of the dead giants and left the wood to rejoin the hundred knights.

Naturally they asked at once if he had seen the giants.

"Yes," answered the tailor. "I have both seen and slain them. They are lying dead under a tree in the wood."

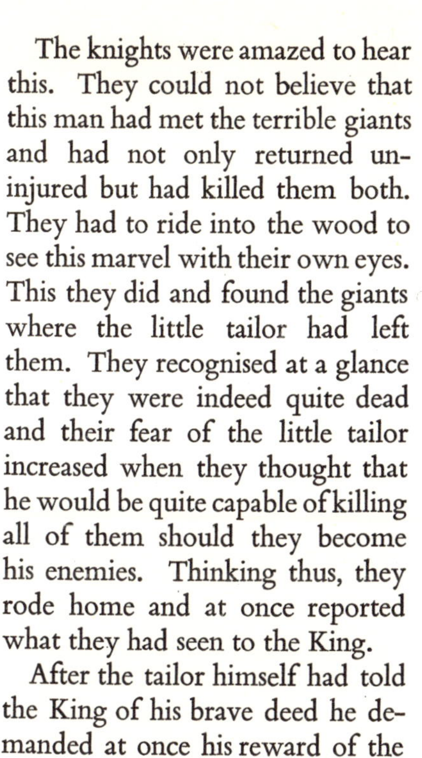

The knights were amazed to hear this. They could not believe that this man had met the terrible giants and had not only returned uninjured but had killed them both. They had to ride into the wood to see this marvel with their own eyes. This they did and found the giants where the little tailor had left them. They recognised at a glance that they were indeed quite dead and their fear of the little tailor increased when they thought that he would be quite capable of killing all of them should they become his enemies. Thinking thus, they rode home and at once reported what they had seen to the King.

After the tailor himself had told the King of his brave deed he demanded at once his reward of the King's daughter in marriage together with half of his kingdom. The King then deeply regretted the promise he had given to his unknown warrior. The giants were dead and would commit no further crimes. What could the King do now to get rid of the hero? As he had no intention of allowing him to marry his daughter, he told the little tailor that in another wood there lived a unicorn who injured both men and animals and that before the little tailor could wed his daughter he must catch this beast.

The good little tailor agreed to undertake this new task, took up a rope and went off to the wood where the wild unicorn lived. He ordered his companion knights to wait for him at the edge of the wood just as he had done before his contest with the giants.

The tailor had been hunting through the wood for some time, when he suddenly spied the unicorn rushing towards him; its deadly horn pointing straight at him. The tailor was not at all put out; he waited until the unicorn was quite close then nimbly sprang behind the nearest tree. The unicorn, approaching at full gallop and quite unable to stop, ran full tilt into the tree, its horn piercing the bark so deeply that it stuck fast. Thereupon the tailor stepped from his hiding place behind the tree and seeing the unicorn's horn wedged there, he quickly tied the rope which he had brought with him round the unicorn's neck and bound it to the tree. Returning to the knights who were waiting at the edge of the wood, he told them of his victory. At their exclamations of astonishment, he smiled proudly and without another word he mounted his horse and rode back to the king, humbly announcing to him the success of his mission. Once again he reminded the King of his promise.

The King did not know what to do for he did not want to give away his daughter as a prize to the little tailor. For some time he racked his brains; then an idea struck him and turning to the hero, he said,

"In yet another wood in my kingdom there lives a fearsome wild boar who is causing terrible destruction. If you succeed in catching this animal, then certainly you shall have the princess as your wife."

The little tailor who was not very pleased about this third order of the King's, assembled a band of hunters and left the town. When he had reached the forest he again ordered them to wait outside. Then the huntsmen rejoiced greatly, for the wild boar had already caught so many of them that they never wanted to see it again. They therefore thanked the little tailor with all sincerity for going alone into the wood and leaving them behind in safety.

The tailor had been but a short time in the wood when the wild boar came in sight. Spying the tailor, it came rushing at him with foaming jaws and pointed tusks as if it would hurl him to the ground. The little tailor's heart thumped as he quickly looked round for a safe place to hide.

As luck would have it, there stood in a nearby clearing a little chapel which had been empty for years. The tailor with a mighty leap jumped into the chapel and with another mighty leap jumped out again through a window in which there was no glass. The wild boar followed the tailor. It too leapt into the chapel and ran round inside roaring angrily. The tailor ran quickly round the outside of the chapel and slammed the door shut before the wild beast had noticed him. Then he ran back to the hunters who were waiting outside the wood and told them what he had done. Amazed they galloped to the chapel to find that what the little tailor had said was quite true. Lost in wonder at this heroic deed, they all rode home to tell the King.

The King did not know whether to be glad or sad at the news. In any case he was now forced to give his daughter to the little tailor, for if he did not do so, he was afraid that the tailor might direct his heroism, of which he had been given ample proof, against himself. It goes without saying that had the King realised that the hero was only a little tailor, he would have given him a rope to hang himself rather than his daughter for a wife.

But whether the King gave his daughter willingly or unwillingly to a man like him, without forebears or noble birth, was not a question which the little tailor thought of asking. He was proud and happy to be allowed to become the King's son-in-law. But on the King's side the marriage was not celebrated with great joy.

After some time had passed the young princess one night heard her lord and husband talking in his sleep. She heard the words quite clearly, " Servants, make ready my garments; mend my trousers; hurry or I shall bring my yardstick about your ears."

It came as a great shock to the princess to discover that her husband was a tailor and she hurried to tell her father what she had discovered, entreating him tearfully to help her to get rid of this man with whom she could not live.

The fact that he had given his only daughter to a tailor made the King shudder. He comforted his daughter and bade her the next night to leave open the bedroom door. Outside the door servants would wait and listen, and if they heard such words again from her husband in his sleep they would rush in and kill him.

The young woman approved of this proposal and promised to do what her father advised. But the King had at his court a knight who had made friends with the tailor. When this man learned of the King's plan he ran quickly to the young prince and told him what he had just heard. Urgently he begged him to take care.

The tailor-prince thanked the knight warmly for his warning and explained that already he knew how he would deal with this affair.

When night fell, the young prince retired to rest and very soon appeared to be fast asleep. Cautiously his wife arose, opened the door of their bedroom, then lay down again. After some time the young prince began to talk in his sleep, but in a louder voice than formerly, so that the listeners outside could hear him quite clearly.

" Servants, make ready my garments—mend my trousers—hurry or I shall bring my yardstick round your ears! I have killed seven at a blow, two giants have I slain, the unicorn will die, the wild boar have I captured—why should I fear those men who are listening outside my door? "

When the King's servants heard these words they fled instantly, for no one dared to face the bold tailor.

And so the brave and wise little tailor remained a prince to the end of his life.

From

THE ARABIAN NIGHTS

ALI BABA
and the Forty Thieves

IN olden times there lived two brothers in a Persian town. One was called Kasim, the other Ali Baba. Their father had died young and had left them but a small inheritance. The brothers had divided it into two portions from which people were to believe that their means were about equal. But fate was to decide otherwise.

Kasim married the daughter of a rich merchant who, on the death of her father, inherited a well-stocked shop and great possessions, so that Kasim became a well-to-do man reputed to be one of the richest in the town. Also through astuteness in business his fortune was always growing.

Ali Baba on the other hand married a poor man's daughter who brought him nothing on their marriage so that his scanty inheritance was soon used up. He and his wife lived in a poor little cottage and he had to sell wood to make a living. For this purpose he had to take to the hills where he cut down trees. He then used three asses to bring the wood into the town where he sold it.

One day when Ali Baba was in the wood and had cut just as much as his asses could carry, he saw in the distance a great cloud of dust which came always nearer. As the cloud grew clearer he made out a troop of horses which approached in good order. He saw also the sparkling of breastplates and the glitter of weapons, whereupon a great fear overtook him. Although no one had ever heard of robbers in this neighbourhood, the thought came nevertheless to Ali Baba that they might indeed be robbers. He therefore cast around for a safe place to conceal himself, and leaving the poor asses to their fate, he quickly climbed a tree and hid among the thick branches. In this way he could see everything without himself being seen. This tree grew at the foot of a steep cliff which offered no possibility of climbing.

The riders, young and strapping men, dismounted at the foot of the cliff and Ali Baba counted forty of them. Having studied their faces and their whole behaviour, he was left in no doubt that these were indeed robbers before him.

Each one unbridled his horse, tied it to a tree and threw a bag containing oats over its head. Then slinging their saddlebags over their shoulders, the men marched after their leader to the cliff. Above them Ali Baba sat shivering with fear on his bough as the captain

stopped in front of a little door, so covered with thorns and briars that Ali Baba would never have discovered it, and uttered these strange words.

"Open Sesame!"

Scarcely had he pronounced them than the door opened and all the robbers disappeared into the cliff, their captain coming last. Noiselessly the door shut behind him.

For a long time the robbers remained inside the cliff and Ali Baba had to wait patiently upon his tree. He was afraid that they would surprise him if he climbed down.

At last the door opened and the robber captain appeared, letting out the other members of his band one by one. As each man passed beneath him Ali Baba noticed that the saddle-bags were now quite empty. When the last robber had come out, he heard the words:

"Shut Sesame!"

And the door in the cliff closed of its own accord. Each man stepped over to his horse and saddled it, then heaving their bags over the saddles they mounted and rode off the way they had come.

Ali Baba followed them with his eyes until they disappeared from view. But he did not immediately climb down from the tree. He was afraid that one of them might have forgotten something and return to the cliff. But when everything remained quiet he climbed down, and pushing through the briars, he approached the little door. Hesitating for only a moment, his curiosity won and he repeated the words which the robber chief had uttered.

"Open Sesame."

Immediately the door sprang open and Ali Baba stepped inside. Behind him the door closed fast.

Ali Baba had expected to find a dark, narrow hole. On the contrary he found a wide, brightly lit vault which had been built by man and adorned with marble slabs and high pillars. Light streamed from holes in the ceiling. Here was amassed all that the heart could desire—carpets of great richness, bales of costly brocades and rich garments. But Ali Baba preferred the masses of gold and silver before all else.

The coins filled bins and chests, they lay in heaps like sand on the floor and overflowing sacks were arranged side by side against the wall. Countless pearls and precious stones gleamed with all the colours of the rainbow round the cave, like pebbles in a brook. It struck Ali Baba that the robbers' vault had served as a hiding place for centuries.

He did not spend long in thought—the carpets and silver coins interested him little. He went immediately to the sacks of gold and dragged out as many as he thought his asses could carry. Each time he wanted to leave or enter the cave he cried:

"Open Sesame!"

and the door opened instantly. When he had gathered enough, he loaded the sacks on to his beasts and covered them with the wood he had felled, so that no one should see his treasure.

Slowly Ali Baba drove his asses home through the town. Having arrived at his cottage he hurried into the yard, shutting and locking fast the door behind him. No one must take him by surprise. The wood he stacked in the usual place, but the sacks of gold he carried into the house to his wife. One after the other he dragged them before her. His wife watched him with growing amazement. Finally she lifted one of the sacks and felt it. When she found that it was full of gold, she immediately suspected that her husband had stolen all this money.

"Husband," she scolded, "How could you have been so dishonest?"

Ali Baba retorted with these words. "Silence woman, I am no thief! I have not stolen it. This money I have taken from a band of robbers. Rejoice with me over our good fortune."

And he proceeded to empty the sack on to the floor. It made a great heap of gold and Ali Baba's wife was quite dazzled by the brilliance. Her husband then told her all that happened from beginning to end, finally cautioning her to say nothing to anyone else.

Then the wife's horror turned to joy. Immediately she wanted to count the gold piece by piece, but Ali Baba refused impatiently, saying:

"Do not trouble yourself; you are neither clever nor quick enough. How long do you think it would take to count all this? I would rather dig a hole at once and bury the gold. But we must work quickly; no one must discover our secret."

"I should very much like to know approximately how much is there," announced his wife. "I shall just borrow a measure from your brother Kasim and weigh the gold while you dig a hole."

Kasim was not at home. But her sister-in-law was there and she

asked whether Ali Baba's wife wanted a big or a little measure. On being told a little measure, she replied immediately:

"Of course! Wait a moment. I shall bring it right away."

But Kasim's wife was curious and thought to herself: "These people own nothing at all; I wonder what they have to weigh." And before handing over the measure she slyly put a little piece of suet at the bottom where it would not be noticed.

Suspecting nothing, Ali Baba's wife thanked her sister-in-law and quickly ran home. There she set the measure by the heap of gold.

Again and again she filled it with gold and again and again she emptied it until all the gold had been weighed. She was overjoyed at the amount and hastened to tell her husband how much the sacks contained.

Meantime Ali Baba had dug a hole and together they buried the gold. Then Ali Baba filled in the hole and spread earth on top so that no one would notice anything.

Ali Baba's wife then took back the measure to Kasim's wife, but neither she nor Ali Baba realised that one piece of gold had stuck to the piece of suet at the bottom of the measure.

" Sister-in-law," said she, " here is your measure. You see I have not kept it very long. Many thanks for lending it to me." And happily Ali Baba's wife returned home.

No sooner had Ali Baba's wife left her than Kasim's wife turned the

measure over and saw to her great astonishment that a gold piece was sticking to it. She could scarcely believe her eyes.

" How is it possible ? " she cried. " Since when has Ali Baba had so much money ? He must already have weighed it. Where, I wonder, does he keep his treasure ?" And the devil of envy crept into her heart.

Kasim, her husband, was still not at home. He was busy in his shop and would not return till evening. His wife could scarcely wait to tell him her story. She burned with impatience to share her news with him. At last she heard him at the door.

" Kasim," she called, " do you consider yourself a rich man ? If so, you are quite wrong. Your brother Ali Baba is a thousand times richer than you. He does not count his gold; he weighs it with scales."

Astonished, Kasim asked his wife what she meant. Then she told him of her discovery and showed him the gold coin which had stuck to the measure. It was very old. The name of the Shah and the inscription on the coin were quite unknown to them. Now Kasim was convinced that his brother must indeed be rich. But he was not

glad about it. Bitter envy seized him and his jealousy did not let him sleep all night. And so on the following day before sunrise he went to Ali Baba's house.

" Ali Baba," he began, " you pretend to be poor and needy and you dress like a beggar. How then is it that you have so much gold that you have to weigh it in a measure ? "

" Dear brother," answered Ali Baba, amazed that his brother knew of his fortune, " explain yourself: What do you mean ? "

" Do not try to deceive me," answered Kasim and brought out the gold coin. " Do you see this gold piece! Yesterday my wife found it at the bottom of the measure which she lent to your wife! How much more gold do you possess ? "

Realising that his brother and sister-in-law knew everything, and that his secret was indeed discovered, Ali Baba shrugged his shoulders and told Kasim how by accident he had found the robbers' hiding place, described the rich hoard in the depths of the rock and proposed that they should share the treasure between them.

" What you have told me is not enough," answered Kasim stiffly. " I want to know everything. How does one get in to this cave? If there is a password I demand to know it. If you refuse to tell me I shall take you to the sheriff and denounce you as a thief."

Ali Baba was not afraid of his brother's threats, but he was a good-natured man and so he told Kasim everything. As soon as he had learned the magic formula which opened the secret door, Kasim waited to hear no more, but rose immediately and hastened home. He wanted to cheat his brother and collect all the treasure for himself. At once he got out ten mules. On to each he loaded two large chests which he planned to fill with treasure and set off on the road described to him by Ali Baba. Reaching the rock, he recognised the tree in which his brother had hidden and pushing through the briars he soon came upon the door in the rock.

In a loud voice he spoke the magic words:

" Open Sesame."

Immediately the door swung open and Kasim entered. Behind him the door shut fast.

With growing astonishment Kasim surveyed the treasure. There was more here than he had ever dreamt of and speechlessly he wandered to and fro gazing and wondering at its magnificence. He looked at and felt the rich materials, the gold and the jewels. He would have liked to stay the whole day amongst the splendour and glitter of gold. But he remembered his mules which were tethered just outside the door to the cave and he began to drag sacks of gold to the entrance ready to load them on to the animals.

But suddenly he realised that he could no longer remember the magic password. So excited had he become at the prospect of this vast wealth, that it had vanished completely from his mind. Frantically he tried all sorts of words, but the door remained shut.

Kasim was not at all prepared for such a misfortune. Perplexed he pushed aside the sacks and sat down. He was at a loss. Vainly he racked his brains to recall the magic password; but it was no use—the words were completely forgotten. Not knowing what to do he stood up and began to run up and down the cave. The treasure now interested him not at all. In a frenzy, he tore at his hair and beard and black despair flooded his heart.

And so we shall leave Kasim for the present bemoaning his fate. He is not worthy of sympathy.

We must return now to the robbers. They had just plundered a caravan and were returning heavily laden with treasure to the cave in the rock.

As they approached the cave, they saw standing outside, the chest-laden mules. With wild and angry cries they charged at them and the

terrified animals galloped in all directions into the wood. Now the robbers had to find out who owned the mules. They crept round the rock, pushed through the bushes and examined all the trees for traces of strangers.

The robber chief meantime with a few others of his band approached the door of the cave and in a loud voice, uttered the magic words.

Inside the cave the terrified Kasim had heard the jingling of the horses' bridles and knew that the robbers had returned. In a vain attempt to escape, he placed himself directly in front of the door—as soon as it opened he would rush out. Then he heard the word " Sesame " being spoken and instantly the door swung open before him. Kasim hurled himself with such force into the open that he knocked the robber chief to the ground. He even passed the second robber in his flight but there were too many of them for him to evade. One thrust of a sabre in his breast and Kasim fell to the ground dead.

The robbers now poured into the cave, anxious to discover if there were any others hidden there. The sacks piled up at the entrance they put back in their places but the fact that other sacks of gold were missing they failed to notice. They wondered how Kasim had got into the cave. The secret word which opened the door they thought they alone held, but plainly someone had discovered or overheard it. But how! The openings in the roof of the cave were much too small and too high and the rock itself was smooth and quite unscalable.

Bewildered, they now set about securing their treasure against future theft. They decided to hack Kasim's body into four and having done this they hung two pieces on the right and two pieces on the left of the door. By this bloodthirsty act they hoped to frighten off anyone from finding the entrance to the cave. These precautions having been completed, the robbers left the cave and mounting their horses rode off to take up again their thieving trade on the busy caravan routes.

Meantime Kasim's wife was growing anxious. She had placed herself at the window to watch for her husband, but as time passed and there was still no sign of his return she ran at last in her anxiety to Ali Baba.

" Dear brother-in-law," she said, " you must know that your brother went today into the wood, but he has still not returned. I am growing most anxious and fear that some misfortune may have befallen him."

Ali Baba had been quite sure that his brother would that day go to the cave. For that reason and in order to avoid strife he had decided

not to go into the wood as usual. Now, on hearing that Kasim had not returned he too thought that some misfortune must surely have overtaken him. But outwardly he remained calm and reassuring. He told his sister-in-law that Kasim would certainly return from the wood during the night, and he counselled her to keep the whole affair strictly secret.

Reassured, Kasim's wife went home. Patiently she waited until midnight, but as her husband still failed to return she again became anxious. Unable to sleep, her worry had increased even more by morning. But she did not dare to weep aloud, otherwise the neighbours would notice her distress. By daybreak she had hastened again to Ali Baba. Sobbing she told him that her husband still had not arrived home.

Now Ali Baba with his three asses set off through the wood to the rock in search of Kasim. On the way he saw no sign of his brother but by the entrance to the cave he immediately spied traces of blood. Then did he fear the worst. Approaching the door he spoke the magic words:

"Open Sesame."

The door opened and aghast he saw hanging to the left and right of the door the pieces of his brother's body. He had to stop himself from crying aloud with horror and pain. Despite his brother's unbrotherly conduct Ali Baba felt he had to pay his last respects to him. In the cave he found amongst the treasure several valuable garments and in these he wrapped the pieces of the body and put the load on one of his asses. He covered it with twigs and sticks so that no one would be suspicious.

The other two asses he loaded quickly with sacks of gold and covered them also with sticks, after which he commanded the door of the cave to shut.

Ali Baba then set off towards the town. At the edge of the wood he halted; he did not want to reach the town before nightfall. At last when darkness had fallen, he led the laden asses through the deserted streets to his house and ordered his wife to unload the gold and bury it with all possible speed. In a few words he told her of Kasim's fate, after which he led the third ass which bore the remains of his brother to the house of his sister-in-law.

Cautiously Ali Baba knocked on her door. Kasim's slave, Morgiana, opened it quietly. She was a wise and capable maiden and when Ali Baba had unloaded the wood and the bundle which was Kasim's body, he took Morgiana aside.

"Listen closely, Morgiana," he whispered, "to what I am about to tell you and you must repeat it to no one. In this bundle is the body of your master. We must bury him with all customary rites and it must appear that he has died a natural death. Take me now to your mistress and I shall tell her everything. Pay close attention to what I have just said."

Morgiana announced the arrival of Ali Baba to her mistress and ushered him in. Kasim's wife was waiting for him with the greatest impatience.

"What sort of news do you bring me?" she cried immediately.

" Your expression bodes no good." Thereupon the poor woman began to weep noisily.

" Sister-in-law," answered Ali Baba, " you must listen to me calmly from beginning to end; no word of what I tell you must you repeat to anyone. Promise me that. It is most important for both of us that no one should ever learn about the events of this day." Kasim's wife promised and with ever mounting grief she heard the news of her husband's murder.

" It is truly a great misfortune which has befallen you," Ali Baba continued. " But it can not be helped. What Allah has willed we must accept. To comfort you I have a proposal to make. When you have mourned your husband long enough, I should like to marry you. Then can we unite our fortunes. My wife will not complain or be jealous; she is good and pious. We shall raise a family and with our fortune we shall live well. But first we must make Kasim's death appear to have been a natural one. Trust in Morgiana's ability. I have given her certain orders and instructions and she will find ways and means to arrange everything."

Kasim's widow did not take long to consider her brother-in-law's proposal and did not think of refusing Ali Baba's offer. She saw clearly the great benefits that would follow upon a marriage with her husband's brother. Ali Baba knowing now that she would accept his offer, left the widow's house. Before he went he stressed to Morgiana the importance of the part she had to play.

Morgiana left the house immediately after Ali Baba, and going directly to a druggist's shop she asked for a drug which was used only for a serious illness. The druggist gave her what she requested, and asked who was ill in her master's house.

" Oh," said she, " it is my master himself. He is critically ill."

And taking the medicine, which of course would no longer be of any use to Kasim, she hurried home.

On the next day Morgiana went to the druggist again. With tears in her eyes she asked for a strong dose of a drug which was given to patients only when very near death. Handing it to her, the druggist asked sympathetically if there was then no improvement in her master's health.

" Alas, even this medicine will not help my poor master," she sobbed. " What a good master he was and now I am about to lose him."

The people of the neighbourhood noticed that all that day Ali Baba and his wife went hurrying back and forward to Kasim's house with sad expressions. And so the rumour of Kasim's illness spread throughout the town. No one was surprised when Kasim's wife and Morgiana began to raise loud wailings which announced to all that Kasim had died.

Early the next morning Morgiana went to an old shoe-maker in the market place. This man always opened his shop long before the other shopkeepers. She greeted him with special politeness and at the same time pushed a gold coin into his hand.

The shoe-maker, a jolly mischievous man was known to the whole town by the name of Baba Mustafa. As it was not yet light he peered closely at the coin from all sides. When he saw that it was indeed a genuine gold coin, he was delighted.

" A fine tip! " he cried, " What can I do for you—anything you want I shall do? "

" Baba Mustafa," said Morgiana to the old man. " Bring your needle and your awl and come with me immediately. I shall guide you to your destination. But you must first allow yourself to be blindfolded."

" No, no," Baba Mustafa waved the proposal aside. " You are asking something from me which must be against honour and conscience."

" God forbid," said Morgiana and pressed another gold piece into his hand. " I ask nothing wicked of you. Come now and have no fear I shall lead you to the appointed place and afterwards I shall guide you safely home again."

Baba Mustafa resisted no longer. A short distance from Kasim's house, Morgiana bound a cloth over his eyes and led him into her master's room. There the body lay arranged in four pieces. Faced with this terrible sight, the shoemaker turned pale and fright made his legs tremble.

" My good old man, do not be afraid," said Morgiana gently. " He

feels no pain. All you have to do is sew together the four pieces of the corpse. Hurry with your work and when you have finished, I shall give you another gold piece." And certain that the gold would be sufficient inducement, Morgiana left him.

When Baba Mustafa had finished his work, Morgiana gave him the promised gold piece. She then bound his eyes again and led him home. On the way she urged him to keep the secret well and at the same spot where she had bound his eyes she took off the cloth. She herself remained there until the old man was out of sight.

On her return to her master's house, Morgiana ordered hot water to be brought so that Ali Baba could bathe Kasim's body and get him ready for burial. With the usual ceremony Ali Baba covered it in a shroud, and placed it in a coffin. After the lid of the coffin had been nailed down, Morgiana went to the morgue to announce that all was ready.

With all speed the Imam arrived with others of the mosque officials. Four neighbours bore the coffin on their shoulders and Ali Baba and many citizens of the town walked behind the Imam who murmured prayers till the burial place was reached. Kasim's wife remained at home. She had raised loud and mournful wailings and the wives of the neighbourhood raised their voices with her so that the whole district for the duration of the burial, resounded with their laments. And so in this way did Kasim's sad fate remain hidden from everyone. No one except his widow, Ali Baba, his wife and Morgiana knew the truth of what had happened.

A short time after this, Ali Baba brought his entire property including his gold to the widow's house. There from now on he meant to live, together with his first wife. No one thought it odd when a little later he took Kasim's widow as his second wife. Such marriages were not at all unusual.

Ali Baba's son meantime took over Kasim's business. He had just finished his apprenticeship as a merchant, and had been given the best of testimonials. Once in charge of the business, his father hoped that he would make a good marriage.

Let us now leave Ali Baba to his newly found good fortune and return to the forty thieves.

After some time the robbers returned to their hiding place in the wood and were astonished to find that the pieces of Kasim's body no longer hung where they had left them. Their astonishment turned to anger when they discovered that a number of sacks of gold were also missing. They were agreed that the dead man must have had companions who also must know their secret. This thought both infuriated and depressed them.

"We are sold and deceived," said the captain. "We must as soon as possible take measures against our enemies, otherwise the treasure which our fathers began to collect, will be lost in a very short time. Most certainly the thief knew the magic password. But another must also know it. He is the one who has removed the corpse and the sacks of gold. We must also kill this second man, and it must be done quickly."

Their chief's proposal appealed to the whole band and they greeted it with loud cries of approval.

"I expected your agreement. We now need a bold and clever man from our band," went on the robber chief. "Dressed as a merchant he will go into the neighbouring town and there he will find out whether people are talking of the death of one of their citizens. Then he must find out where this citizen lived and what business he pursued. It would seem certain that this will be our enemy. But our man must be cunning and clever. Above all he must be very careful not to betray our refuge and if he should bring us false news, death shall be his punishment."

Immediately one of the robbers stepped forward saying, "Let me go into the town! I promise on my honour to risk my life for it. If my mission fails, I will suffer my punishment gladly."

The chief and all his comrades praised him highly and wished him the best of fortune. He dressed so skilfully that no one would have taken him for a robber, and by daybreak he had reached the town. He went straight to the market place, where at that time only a single shop was open. It was that of the shoe-maker, Baba Mustafa.

Already Baba Mustafa was seated on his working stool, awl and

cobbler's needle in his hands. He was just on the point of beginning his day's work, when the robber stepped into his shop. Bidding the old man a friendly good morning, he immediately began to speak.

"Tell me, old man," he began, "are you quite happy with your work? In this half light any man would find difficulty in seeing. As for you, your eyes are already dim and I doubt if you can see to thread your needle."

"You are a stranger in this town," answered the shoe-maker. "You should know that despite my age I have still very sharp eye-sight; for this reason my work is much sought after by both young and old. Just recently I had to sew up a dead body which lay in a room much darker than it is here. In spite of this I gave the utmost satisfaction to my client."

The robber listened intently. Plainly, he had come to just the right man. Now he wanted to hear more.

"A dead man?" he asked. "How is this possible? Who would ask you to sew a corpse together? You surely mean it was the shroud that you sewed."

"No, no," said the cobbler, "I have told you the truth. I know that you want to hear more, but you have come to the wrong person. You will get no more information from me."

"I shall never give away your secret," he said. "I am to be trusted absolutely. Perhaps the dead man was related to me or to an acquaintance of mine. Then it would be my duty to express my sympathy to those who are left behind. I beg you to show me the house where the man died." And he pressed a gold coin into Baba Mustafa's hand.

"Good Sir," he said with a shrug, "even if I wanted, I could not comply with your wish. A slave came to fetch me and at a certain spot on the road, my eyes were bound and she led me thus to the room where the dead man lay. There I carried out my task, and afterwards she led me back still blindfolded to the same place. From there I came home alone. Now do you understand that I can not help you further. I do not know the way to this house."

But the robber began again. "You can remember at least a little of the way. I beg you to come with me. Take me to the place where your eyes were bound. There I will blindfold you just as the slave did; then I will lead you in all directions and perhaps in this way we shall find the house to which you were taken. Come and let us try our luck!" And he gave the old man a second gold coin.

The shoe-maker took the second gold coin, and after examining it carefully, decided to accept it. Smirking a little he rose.

"We shall do as you say," he turned to the robber. "But naturally I cannot promise that I shall find the house."

They set off on their way to the place where Morgiana had bound the old man's eyes.

"Here I was blindfolded," said Baba Mustafa. "I know this is the exact spot."

The robber then tied a cloth over his eyes and taking the old man by the hand let him lead the way. Baba Mustafa first went straight ahead, then he turned to the left and again to the right. At last he stopped in a little street in front of a small house.

"I did not come farther than this," said Baba Mustafa. "At least I do not think so."

In fact he was standing directly in front of Kasim's house. Only now Ali Baba lived there. Before removing the cloth from the old man's eyes, the robber quickly made a mark on the door. Then he asked the old man if he knew to whom the house belonged.

"No," answered the shoe-maker. "This house is too far away from my shop. I do not know the people in this part of the town."

The robber was convinced that the old man could help him no more, so he let him go home to his shop. He himself quickly made his way back to his companions in the wood.

Soon after the robber and Baba Mustafa had gone, Morgiana left the house to visit the market. On her return she noticed the cross which the robber had drawn on the door. Mystified, she stood there gazing at it; then wonder turned to anxiety. "What can this cross mean?" she thought to herself. "It is of course possible that it was scrawled by children at play. But what if it should have been put here by an enemy of my new master who may wish him ill. It is better to be on the safe side."

With that she drew similar crosses on the doors of the neighbouring houses. She then returned to her work, saying nothing to her master or mistress.

The robber had meantime arrived at the wood. Gaily he approached his comrades and told the robber chief of the happy result of his journey to the town. All the robbers were delighted at his news and the leader praised his intelligence and his zeal.

"Comrades," he said turning to his band, "well-armed, you shall go at once into the town. But be very careful that no one sees your weapons. It would be better if you went singly and meet later in the market place. I shall go with our spy to the marked house and take action. I shall give further orders in the market place."

Soon the band were ready to start for the town in twos and threes, their weapons well hidden beneath their clothing so that no one in the town would detect them.

The robber chief and the spy were last to leave. They made their way at once to the little street in which Ali Baba's house stood.

When the man saw on the first door Morgiana's sign, he took it to be the right house. His chief walked farther on so that it might not look suspicious, but seeing the same sign on the next house, he turned back to his companion to ask which house was the right one. The robber, completely perplexed, did not know how to answer his chief.

Going farther he saw to his astonishment that other houses also bore the same sign.

Now the captain was really angry.

" You fool," he said, " you have marked every door in the street."

The robber was certain that he had marked only one door. Who had marked the rest, he did not know. Clearly it was quite impossible in this confusion to pick out the right door. The houses looked all alike, and in the morning he had not looked very closely at the one which he had marked.

The captain realising that somehow their plan had been foiled, turned angrily towards the market place followed by his companion. There the others eagerly awaited them and were surprised when their captain ordered them to return separately to the wood. They knew then that this time their journey to the town had been in vain. The captain himself left the town first, the others following later in ones and twos. They all met in front of the cave in the rock. Then where no one could overhear, the captain explained what had happened. They held judgment at once on the unfortunate spy and with one voice sentenced him to immediate death. While one robber held his head, the spy was at once executed.

Now they discussed among themselves who was to be the new spy, and the chosen man immediately set off towards the town. As his predecessor had done, he went first to Baba Mustafa and in the same way arrived at Ali Baba's house.

The second robber marked the door with red chalk in a less obvious place and in this way he made sure that he could pick it out easily from the doors marked with white crosses. But once again Morgiana noticed the sign when she left the house, and she too drew red crosses on the neighbouring doors.

The robber, full of confidence returned to his companions in the wood. He boasted that he had marked the door unerringly with a sign;

this time the plan could not fail. As before, they all returned to the town and gathered in the market place. The captain and the second spy went at once to the street where Ali Baba lived. There they discovered with horror that this time many doors bore red crosses. Once again it was impossible to recognise the right house.

The captain flew into a temper, but had to control himself in order not to arouse curiosity in the neighbourhood. He explained to his men

why the plan had misfired this time. Again he sent them back to the wood and the boastful spy suffered the same fate as the first.

The captain had thus lost two bold men of his company and had made not the slightest progress. Now, he thought: I shall only lose more of my men if I trust them with this job. They are bold and daring in a fight; they are most useful for plunder and in the spilling of blood, but against cunning and treachery they can not win as they do with weapons.

So he decided to undertake this difficult business himself. As the others had done, he went to Baba Mustafa and had him lead him to Ali

Baba's house. But the captain made no mark on the door. Instead he studied the house very closely, walking past it several times so as to stamp its appearance on his memory.

Returning to the wood, he called together his band.

" Comrades," he said, " now nothing shall deprive us of revenge. I know the villain who has robbed us. On the way here I have been thinking out the best way of tackling this affair. Now, listen to my plan. If any of you can think of a better, let him tell me of it.

" Go into the outlying villages and markets. Buy nineteen asses and thirty-eight large leather bottles for holding oil. Fill one bottle full of oil, the others leave empty. I want each man then to hide in a bottle, and to take his weapons with him. I shall then convey you, unnoticed into town. Leave the rest to me."

In a few days everything was ready. The empty bottles were at first too narrow at the neck for comfort but the leader of the band cut slits in each; these served as air holes. Every man then armed himself and crawled into the bottles and the captain loaded two bottles on to each of the asses.

It was towards evening when the captain of the robbers dressed as a merchant set off for the town, leading his nineteen mules. About an hour after sunset he had arrived and turned towards Ali Baba's house. There his plan was to ask for a night's shelter for himself and his beasts.

On arriving he did not need to knock. Ali Baba was sitting comfortably before the door of his house enjoying the coolness of the evening. The leader of the robbers halted his beasts and gave Ali Baba a courteous greeting.

" Sir," he said, " I have brought my oil a long way. To-morrow I hope to sell it in the market. But I do not know where to find shelter for my beasts at this late hour. Could you perhaps put them up for just one night? I should be most grateful and will pay well."

Now Ali Baba had of course seen the robber chief in the wood and had also heard his voice. But in the guise of an oil merchant it was impossible to recognise him.

" Welcome," said Ali Baba. " You may certainly spend the night at my house." And so saying he made room for him. The beasts were driven into the courtyard where Ali Baba ordered his slave to unload, tether and feed them. He himself went into the kitchen where he gave Morgiana instructions to prepare a good dinner for his guest; also to prepare a bed for him. Ali Baba watched the stranger help his slave to unload the asses, then taking him by the hand invited him into his reception room. The captain at first refused, saying that he did not want to be any longer a burden to his host. In actual fact he wanted to stay near his men. But Ali Baba begged him so insistently and politely that he could at last no longer refuse. The captain then enjoyed a well-cooked meal and the master of the house remained with him for company.

When his guest had finished eating, Ali Baba rose.

" I shall leave you alone now," he said. " If you should want anything, you need only call! Everything in my house is at your service." And Ali Baba went off to the kitchen to talk to Morgiana.

Meantime his guest went down to the courtyard to see that his mules had been stabled.

Ali Baba told his slave to give every attention to his guest. He must want for nothing.

" By the way," he went on. " I intend to-morrow morning to go to the bath. Lay out the bath towels ready, and give them to the slave Abdallah. Do not forget to make some soup. I shall take it after my bath! "

And so saying he went to his room and lay down to sleep.

The robber captain meantime had left the stable. He now gave orders to his men as to what they must do and to this end he walked slowly past the leather bottles.

" If you hear pebbles dropping in the courtyard," he said softly, " cut the bottles with your daggers, then creep out at once and wait for me! I shall be here immediately."

Thereupon he returned to the house. Morgiana led him to a splendid room and asked him if there was anything he wanted. The false merchant thanked her with a shake of the head. Left alone, he put out the light and fully dressed, lay down on the bed, to wait.

Morgiana did not forget her master's commands. She got towels ready and handed them over to Abdallah. Then she went to the kitchen to prepare the soup and kindle the fire. While she worked, the light from the lamp became more and more feeble. Finally it went out altogether. There was no more oil in the lamp and when she got out the oil bottle to refill it, she found it was also empty. There were no candles in the house and she did not know what do to. She needed light to work by, so she asked Abdallah's advice.

" Do not worry," he said. " There is enough oil here for many lamps. Go down to the courtyard. There you will find the oil bottles of the strange merchant. Take as much oil as you want. He will not mind, I am sure. And to-morrow we shall give him the price of the oil."

Morgiana thanked Abdallah for his advice. While he went to bed, she took the oil can to the courtyard and approached the first bottle. The robber inside heard her steps and thought that the captain had arrived at last. He was growing impatient to get out of the bottle. In this uncomfortable position his limbs were aching. " Is it time ? " he asked softly.

Any other woman would have been frightened to death. But Morgiana was not at all put out to find in the bottle, not oil, but a man. In the twinkling of an eye she took hold of herself. Without a sign of panic she assumed the deep voice of the captain.

" Not yet, but soon ! " she said.

Then she turned to the next bottle. The same question followed and she gave the same answer. So it went on right to the last bottle. This one really did contain oil and from it she filled her oil can. Then quickly she hastened back to the kitchen where she filled and trimmed the lamp.

While the lamp grew brighter, she thought quickly. Her master's guest was no oil merchant, but almost certainly a thief. The thirty-seven men in the bottles were evidently awaiting orders from their leader, to commit a horrible crime. She must therefore do something about it. So she took a large kettle into the courtyard and filled it with oil from the last bottle and carrying the full kettle back to the kitchen she set it down over the fire. With several logs of wood, she coaxed the fire into bright flames, and she began to heat the oil until it boiled. Morgiana carried the boiling oil down to the courtyard; then into each bottle she poured enough to kill the robber inside.

Without a sound, she went back to the kitchen and damped down the fire so that it was just bright enough for her to make the soup for her master. She then put out the light, barred the door and silently took a seat by the window. From there she could observe all that happened.

For a quarter of an hour she sat waiting at the window. But no one appeared. The robber captain had waited until all the inmates of the house were asleep. Now he crossed to the window and looked down into the dark courtyard. Nothing stirred. Not a glimmer of light was to be seen. Then he threw down as the pre-arranged signal, a handful of pebbles. Some of the pebbles struck the bottles. But no one stirred. This made the captain angry. He threw down a second and a third handful of pebbles, but all was still. In a passion he hurried silently down to the courtyard. At the first bottle he noticed the smell of hot oil. Everywhere there was silence. He went to the second bottle. Then he knew that his plan had failed. His intention to destroy and plunder Ali Baba's house had come to nothing. He saw that all his men had perished in the same way. In the last bottle he found the large quantity of oil which his men had brought with them. At a loss he saw all his hopes die. Realising that he must save his own life as quickly as possible, he leapt over the wall into the garden of the neighbouring house. From there he fled over fence and hedge, not once stopping for breath until he had reached the shelter of the wood.

Next morning Ali Baba arose early and accompanied by his servant he went to the bath. Of the doings of the night he had no knowledge as Morgiana had told Abdallah not to disturb him.

When Ali Baba left the bath to return to the house the sun was already high in the sky. Amazed, he noticed that the bottles of oil still stood in the courtyard. He had imagined that the strange merchant would have long since left for the market. He asked Morgiana why the merchant was still in the house.

" My master," said Morgiana, " last night Allah saved you from death. Come now and see with your own eyes what you demand to know."

Ali Baba followed the maid as she led him to the first bottle.

" Observe! " she cried, " what sort of oil it contains! " Ali Baba bent over to look into the bottle. When he saw inside a man armed with a dagger, he sprang back with a cry of fright.

" Fear not," said Morgiana, " the man will never do harm again, for he is dead."

Then Ali Baba went along the row, looking into each bottle. And in each he saw a dead and scalded man with a dagger in his hand. In all there were thirty-seven men. In the last bottle there was only oil.

" But what does this mean and what has become of the strange merchant? " he cried.

" The merchant," answered Morgiana, " is as much a merchant as you or I. But I will gladly tell you everything in your room. There you can sit down comfortably and have some strong soup."

Ali Baba went to his room, and Morgiana brought him the soup to drink.

"Now begin!" he cried impatiently. "Tell me this strange story with all speed! I can wait no longer."

Morgiana complied with the wish of her master and gave him an account of the dreadful events of the evening.

She concluded her story by telling Ali Baba of the two crosses which she had discovered chalked on the door.

"I believe now," she said, "that this too must have been the work of the forty robbers in the wood. But why there were only thirty-eight here is not clear to me. At any rate I know that the robbers seek your death, but at most there are now only three of them left. So please take care! As long as there is one of them left, your life is in danger. I myself shall surely do my utmost to guard your life."

Ali Baba realised what a great service Morgiana had rendered him.

"You have saved my life," he said gratefully. "Therefore as a reward I grant you your freedom. One day I hope I shall be able to repay you properly for your loyalty to me. But I am amazed that it was the forty robbers who came here. I tremble to think what might have happened, but for you. But now we must immediately throw the bodies of these villains into a grave. We shall do it with all secrecy. No one shall know if it. Abdallah will help me."

Ali Baba's garden was very long. At the back it was sheltered by high old trees. Ali Baba with the help of his slave dug here a long and deep grave. The earth was loose, so the work was quickly done. They dragged the dead men out of the bottles and threw them one after the other into the grave. Afterwards they threw the earth on top of them and stamped it down. Lastly they scattered loose earth on top of that. Now the ground looked just as it had done before. The oil bottles Ali Baba hid in the house and later he led the asses to the market and sold them. All this Ali Baba did to conceal the secret of his great wealth.

Meantime the robber captain had arrived again at the cave in the rock. Pain and rage filled his heart. Inside the cave he sat down and bemoaned the fate of his band of men. They had come to a frightful end, and never again would he gather together such bold companions! He made a resolution there and then to avenge the loss of

his comrades. Also he vowed that the thief should never have his treasure.

Next morning he donned a rich robe and turning towards the town approached an inn. He believed that the events at Ali Baba's house must by now have become known in the town. So he asked the inn-keeper if there were any outstanding news. The man told him all sorts of unimportant little items of news, but nothing at all of what he had expected to hear. Then he saw that Ali Baba had done his work with great foresight and secrecy. Obviously he did not want to broadcast the news of his wealth. The robber therefore resolved secretly to remove him forever from his path. He bought himself a horse and rode several times back and forward through the wood to the hiding place. Each time he brought with him bales of the finest cloth, rich robes, carpets and precious stones. In the town he rented a shop in which he locked up his possessions. Finally he was ready to open up a lively business, under the name of Kogia Husain. His shop stood directly opposite Kasim's business, which was now being run by Ali Baba's young son.

When the new shopkeeper had established himself, his neighbours called upon him and treated him with all possible courtesy. His pleasantness and dignified appearance soon brought him attention and respect. Ali Baba's son sought his acquaintance and the two were soon good friends. Many a time Ali Baba visited his son and the false merchant recognised him as the owner of the house in which his comrades had lost their lives. When he discovered that the young man was Ali Baba's son he doubled his friendliness towards him, gave him little gifts and invited him often to dine with him.

The young man wished to return so much civility and hospitality. But it was not possible to invite his friend home, for his house was cramped and uncomfortable. One day he spoke to his father. Ali Baba at once told him that he would be very pleased to act as host.

"My son," he said, "to-morrow is Friday. On that day all respectable merchants shut their shops. Take a walk with your neighbour in the town and on your way back come past my house. Morgiana will prepare for you a good supper."

On Friday afternoon Ali Baba's son and Kogia Husain took a walk together. On the way back, as if by chance, they came along the street in which Ali Baba lived. When they reached Ali Baba's door the young man stopped.

"Look, this is our house," he said. "Come in and do me the honour of eating with my father." But Kogia Husain declined the invitation. He put forward many excuses, but the young man pressed him to allow him to return a little of his kindness. Of course the robber chief's one aim was to gain entrance to Ali Baba's house, but for a long time he pretended to be unwilling.

Finally the slave opened the door and the young man gripping his friend by the hand led him into the house.

Ali Baba received Kogia Husain with great friendliness, thanked him for honouring them with a visit and wished him good fortune and happiness.

"I am indeed grateful to you," he added. "You are a man of experience and you do not find it beneath your dignity to befriend my son."

Husain answered suitably and after a short conversation, wished to depart. But Ali Baba held him back and asked that he should do him the honour of taking supper with them.

" Sir," said Husain, " I thank you for your kind invitation. Please do not take it amiss however, if I take my leave. Consider it neither pride nor impoliteness. I have a special reason which you would approve of if you knew it."

" May I hear your reason ? " asked Ali Baba.

The merchant answered. " I shall tell you. I can eat neither meat nor any dish which contains salt. Therefore I should be a poor guest at your table and that I should like to avoid."

In the East when one man eats salt with another, this man becomes his friend and brother; he then can do him no evil. It is important to know this.

" This reason should not rob me of the pleasure of your company," answered Ali Baba. " In my bread you will find no salt. And as for the other dishes which will be served to you, there will be no salt present in them. Stay then ! I shall give orders to the kitchen."

So Ali Baba told Morgiana and ordered her to put no salt in the meat, but to prepare many saltless dishes. Morgiana had been in the midst of preparing the food and she was unwilling to comply with Ali Baba's commands.

" Who is this strange man ? " she asked. " Why will he not eat salt ? If I now prepare different food it will not taste so well."

" Do not be wicked, Morgiana," said Ali Baba. " This man is our guest. Do as I say ! "

Morgiana did so with great reluctance. She was curious to know who this man was and when Abdallah had laid the table she helped to carry in the food. In spite of his disguise she recognised immediately the guest as the robber chief. She noticed too that he carried a dagger in his clothing.

" Aha," she thought, " now I know why this villain will eat no salt with my master. He wants to kill him. But I know how to prevent him."

In the kitchen Morgiana thought how she could best carry out her plan. While the guest ate with her master, she made her preparations. She was just ready when Abdallah asked her for the fruit course.

She carried in the fruit herself and placed it on a little table near Ali Baba. At the door she pulled Abdallah out with her, telling him that their master wanted to be left undisturbed with his guest.

Now the robber chief thought the right moment had come to kill Ali Baba.

" I shall make good use of this favourable moment," he said to himself. " I shall make both father and son drunk, then I shall plunge my dagger into the old one's heart; the son shall live if he does not hinder me, and as before I shall escape over the garden wall. But I must wait a little until the slave and the cook are having supper."

Morgiana had, however, guessed the robber's vile plan and she left him no time to carry it out. Instead of eating, she put on a fine dancing dress, adorned herself with a silver head-dress and fastened on a glittering belt round her waist. On to this belt she hung a dagger set with precious stones. When she was ready she turned to Abdallah.

"Abdallah," she said. "Take your tabor! We shall go into our master and entertain him and his guest."

The slave fetched his drum, and beating it, he preceded Morgiana into the room. Morgiana curtsied deeply with a natural grace and asked permission to show off her dancing skill.

"Brava, Morgiana," cried Ali Baba. "Our guest shall judge your skill." And turning to Kogia Husain, he said, "You see in my house I have everything. I need not hire strange dancing girls; I am entertained well by my slave and my cook. I hope you will enjoy their performance."

Kogia Husain was furious at this turn of events and secretly cursed the two dancers. Now the favourable moment for his crime had passed. But he could not very well refuse to be entertained, so he pretended delight at this unexpected pleasure.

Abdallah at once began to beat his tabor. Then he sang a dance tune and Morgiana danced, her face showing nothing of her feelings. Only the false merchant had no eyes for the graceful movements of the maiden. Deep in thought he looked straight ahead. But Ali Baba and his son were not lacking in their applause.

One dance followed another. The steps became ever faster. Finally Morgiana drew her dagger. With the gleaming weapon in her hand she whirled about the room. Sometimes she held the dagger above her head, sometimes at her side, sometimes she pointed it at Ali Baba, his son or the merchant. At last she appeared to become breathless with the dance. She tore the tabor from the slave's hand. In her right hand she still held her dagger, but now she stretched the hollow side of the tabor towards Ali Baba as if she were asking for coins to be thrown into it.

Ali Baba threw a gold coin into the drum; his son followed his example. Kogia Husain also had reached for his purse. But just as he put his hand in to take out a coin, Morgiana stabbed him with all force in the breast and the merchant sank back lifeless.

Ali Baba and his son at the same time uttered cries of horror.

"Miserable girl," cried Ali Baba. "What have you done? Will you ruin me and my family?"

"No master," answered Morgiana quietly, "I did this to save you. Look, what I am about to show to you."

With these words, she opened the robe of the false merchant and showing her master the dagger concealed below, said:

"Mark well the cruel enemy you were entertaining in your house. Look more closely and you will recognise the disguised oil merchant who in reality was the captain of the forty thieves. He has always sought your death. Now you will understand why he would not eat salt with you. Now do you need greater proof of his intentions? I suspected him and my fears were not groundless. Are you not now convinced?"

Deeply moved, Ali Baba embraced the maiden. She had again a second time saved his life.

"Morgiana," he said, "I have already given you your freedom. I promised too that I should give you further proof of my gratitude. The time has now come for me to keep my vow. Do you know how I shall reward your faithfulness? I shall present to you my son as a husband."

Then turning to his son, he said:

"Dear son, you hear what I have said. I hope that you honour your father enough to be willing to carry out his behest. Perhaps your obligation to Morgiana is no less than mine. Husain sought your friendship only to kill me. Perhaps you too would have been a sacrifice to his revenge. Morgiana will always be an adornment to our family; but to you she will be a support to the end of your days! And so I present her to you!"

The young man was not in the least unwilling. In fact marriage with Morgiana pleased him greatly.

Thereupon they quickly and silently buried the robber chief in the garden near his companions.

The whole affair was known to no one until many years had passed. But by that time no one concerned was still alive.

A few days later the wedding of Morgiana with Ali Baba's son was celebrated. It was a glittering occasion accompanied by song and dance and greatly enjoyed by all. Ali Baba especially was full of happiness because all his guests praised the beauty of the bride although not one knew the reason for the marriage.

Ali Baba had not returned to the cave in the rock since the time when he had found his brother's body. He hesitated for a long time before going again, especially as he knew for certain that only thirty-eight of the robbers were dead. What had become of the remaining two he did not know. He feared that they still lurked in the cave.

A year passed and all remained peaceful, but one morning Ali Baba was seized with curiosity and mounting his horse he rode to the wood. At the rock he looked carefully round. But there was no trace of man or horse. The bushes before the door to the cave had grown almost impenetrable. From this Ali Baba concluded that for a very long time no one had been to the cave, and tying his horse to a tree he crawled through the bushes to the door and spoke the magic words.

"Open sesame!"

Immediately the door opened and entering, he saw that the treasure remained undisturbed. Since Kogia Husain's last visit no one had been to the cave. And so Ali Baba realised that not one of the forty robbers was alive. He alone now knew the secret of the cave and its treasure. He was owner of untold wealth. He filled, however, only one sack with gold, just enough for his horse to carry comfortably. Then he returned joyfully to the town.

From this time Ali Baba lived a happy life. Highly respected by all citizens of the town, he enjoyed his wealth in peace and comfort. The secret of the cave and the magic password he later shared with his son, who in turn entrusted it to his children. They used their riches with prudence and generosity, so that they were beloved by rich and poor alike, and their lives were henceforth spent in good fortune and joy.